Headquarters and Subsidiaries in Multinational Corporations

Headquarters and Subsidiaries in Multinational Corporations

Strategies, Tasks and Coordination

Stewart Johnston

First published 2005 by
PALGRAVE MACMILLAN
Houndmills, Basingstoke, Hampshire RG21 6XS and
175 Fifth Avenue, New York, N.Y. 10010
Companies and representatives throughout the world

PALGRAVE MACMILLAN is the global academic imprint of the Palgrave Macmillan division of St. Martin's Press, LLC and of Palgrave Macmillan Ltd. Macmillan® is a registered trademark in the United States, United Kingdom and other countries. Palgrave is a registered trademark in the European Union and other countries.

ISBN-13: 978–1–4039–3624–0   hardback
ISBN-10: 1–4039–3624–2   hardback

This book is printed on paper suitable for recycling and made from fully managed and sustained forest sources.

A catalogue record for this book is available from the British Library.

Library of Congress Cataloging-in-Publication Data
Johnston, Stewart, 1944–
    Headquarters and subsidiaries in multinational corporations : strategies, tasks and coordination / Stewart Johnston.
        p. cm.
    Based on the author's doctoral dissertation.
    Includes bibliographical references and index.
    ISBN 1–4039–3624–2
        1. International business enterprises–Management. 2. Foreign subsidiaries–Management. 3. Strategic alliances (Business)
    4. International business enterprises–Australia–Management.
    5. Foreign subsidiaries–Australia–Management. 6. Strategic alliances (Business)–Australia. I. Title.

HD62.4.J64 2005
658'.049–dc22   2005042904

10   9   8   7   6   5   4   3   2   1
14   13   12   11   10   09   08   07   06   05

Printed and bound in Great Britain by
Antony Rowe Ltd, Chippenham and Eastbourne

Contents

List of Tables

List of Figures

Preface

This book is a development of my doctoral dissertation. Parts of the material here have appeared in various locations but I have decided to present the results of the research in a classic monograph form in order to facilitate their further dissemination. There are three major reasons for this decision. First, the book presents a more general conceptualization of the headquarters-subsidiary relationship in multinational corporations than any previous model. Second, it adds considerably to the empirical literatures on subsidiary autonomy, control mechanisms and knowledge management and innovation in multinational corporations. Third, from a more parochial perspective, there is a paucity of recent research on multinational corporations in Australia and this book offers, I hope, a baseline and guide for future firm level studies of this topic. The work should be of interest to scholars, practitioners and students alike.

To complete a task of this order required advice, assistance and encouragement and many people made contributions both great and small to this venture. Tim Bartram, Simon Bell, Michelle Brown, Richard Hoffman, Rick Iverson, Angie Knox, Carol Kulik, Ros Makris, Lynn McAlevey, David Merrett and Lea Waters came to my aid in moments of need. Tatiana Zalan and Shey Newitt kindly read and commented upon earlier versions. I owe particular gratitude for the huge contributions of Bulent Menguc to Chapter 8 and Angela Paladino to Chapter 10. Overall, however, the two crutches that I leaned upon most heavily were Christina Cregan and my doctoral supervisor Stephen Nicholas. My grateful thanks to you both.

From Palgrave Macmillan my thanks go to Jacky Kippenberger and, as an ex-subeditor myself, I greatly appreciate the excellent work put in by Shirley Tan at EXPO Holdings.

In addition, I wish to acknowledge the early career researcher and faculty grants I received from the Faculty of Economics and Commerce at Melbourne University and the facilities provided during study leave at the Department of Finance and Quantitative Studies, Otago University, Dunedin, New Zealand and the School of Business, University of Northumbria, Newcastle upon Tyne, UK.

Finally, and of utmost importance, I wish to express my gratitude to the 313 executives whose contributions made the research possible.

Part I

Conceptual Background and Model

1
Introduction

This research is concerned with the relationship between headquarters (HQ) and subsidiaries in multinational corporations (MNCs). This will always be an important theme because the HQ-subsidiary connection is the primary conduit through which HQ is able to manage the corporation. The relationship enables the transfer of the MNC's ownership advantage and the design and implementation of more efficacious and suitable corporate and subsidiary structures, control mechanisms, and knowledge and innovation coordination systems. All of these facilitate inter-unit product, personnel, factor and knowledge flows of every kind.

There has been a tendency in much of the recent literature to eschew what might be perceived as more mundane topics, such as the HQ-subsidiary relationship, in favor of alliances, unit interdependence, knowledge clusters, trust networks and other more academically fashionable concerns in the network capitalism domain. Nevertheless, interest does remains in the HQ-subsidiary relationship and the subsidiary task (see for example Roth and Nigh, 1992; Nohria and Ghoshal, 1994; Gupta, Govindarajan and Malhotra, 1999; Peterson, Napier and Shul-Shim, 2000; Asakawa, 2001a; Shaw, 2001; Kim, 2002; Benito, Grogaard and Narula, 2003; Hewett, Roth and Roth, 2003). The array of more novel alternative topics notwithstanding, in most MNCs the HQ-subsidiary relationship and the consequent tasks performed by the subsidiary remain central to our understanding of MNC functioning.

While Birkinshaw and Hood (1998) suggested that the traditional HQ-subsidiary relationship research stream had come to an end in the mid-1980s, they were circumspect enough to warn against throwing the baby out with the bathwater, 'the subsidiary's most critical relationship was, and still is, with its corporate headquarters' (Birkinshaw and Hood, 1998: 6). The available statistics tend to support Birkinshaw and Hood's prudence. An Organisation for Economic Co-operation and Development (OECD) report (OECD, 2002) indicated that over 79,000 strategic alliances, JVs, R&D and sales/marketing agreements and other forms of international partnerships typical of network capitalism were instituted between 1990 and 2000. This is approaching a mean of 8000 such ventures per year and the database probably underestimates the number. It is an impressive figure and justifies the interest in these phenomena. It must, however, be seen in the context of a global economy containing perhaps 63,000 MNCs with some 700,000 subsidiaries (United Nations Conference on Trade and Development, UNCTAD, 2000).

Despite its obvious importance, only limited progress has been made in understanding the HQ-subsidiary link. The current and previous literatures have begun the process of mapping the detailed inner workings of MNCs but, with only very few exceptions, the HQ-subsidiary link still remains a 'black box'. Consequently, a major aim of this research is to make a contribution to 'mapping' and understanding this important but relatively neglected area.

To facilitate this end, the book develops a new, integrated model of the HQ-subsidiary relationship in the MNC. The model draws on established theories and themes in the International Management (IM) and International Business (IB) literatures and upon recent developments in the knowledge-based perspective on the theory of the firm. The model hypothesizes the existence of six different subsidiary tasks. It is then tested and validated using a large sample of Australian subsidiaries of foreign-owned MNCs. The nature of the HQ-subsidiary relationship associated with five of the six subsidiary tasks is then examined empirically by testing a series of hypotheses concerning several key issues in the HQ-subsidiary relationship: namely subsidiary autonomy, control mechanisms, the use of knowledge management techniques and the embeddedness of the subsidiary in the innovation networks of the MNC. Thus, this book performs three important research tasks. First, a new theory of the HQ-subsidiary relationship is developed and validated empirically. Second, previously presented and accepted theory is examined and extended. Third, new areas of research in the HQ-subsidiary relationship are explored and mapped using a range of investigative methodologies and hypothesis testing techniques.

The central argument is that the corporate and business level strategies instigated by the MNC to gain sustained competitive advantage lead to associated subsidiary tasks that can be statistically identified from the sample of Australian subsidiaries. The relationship of each subsidiary task with its HQ is analyzed within a setting of knowledge asymmetries and the differential policies and initiatives elaborated by HQ to control and coordinate knowledge flows within the MNC and between the MNC and its environment.

The research focuses upon the Australian subsidiaries of US, European and Japanese MNCs. An additional aim of the work is thus to study, for the first time, MNC strategy and structure in the Australian context. In the process of the research, the first large-scale, broadly-based, inquiry into the internal operation of the subsidiaries of foreign-owned MNCs operating in Australia is conducted. As such, it presents the baseline data and understanding for future studies of this topic and a starting point for similar studies in other host countries. Despite its relatively small population of 20 millions, Australia is, in Gross Domestic Product (GDP) terms, the 11th largest economy in the world and the third largest, after Japan and China, in the Asian region. Australia's GDP is larger than the combined GDPs of Indonesia, Singapore, Malaysia and the Philippines. Its political stability, Asian location and favorable business climate have made it a location of choice for many MNCs for manufacturing, distribution or regional services (Anon, 2001). The result of these influences is an unusually strong foreign presence in the Australian economy. Foreign-controlled companies operating in Australia account for 17.9 per cent of the national revenue, a percentage only exceeded by Canada among the major economies. These figures notwithstanding, a Department of Industry, Science and Tourism report stated 'Despite a relatively long history of foreign investment, there are limited detailed data available on the nature and extent of foreign investment ... in Australia' (DIST, 1998: 7). Over the last 30 years, the majority of the Australian literature on MNCs has taken a skeptical and sometimes hostile stance as to the outcomes that MNCs might bring. A more detailed analysis of the place of the present study in the Australian literature on MNCs is presented later in this chapter.

In the canonical text for the study of HQ-subsidiary relationships in MNCs, Otterbeck (1981: 1) asked: 'How are multinationals actually managed? What goes on inside the corporation between the home country firm (parent company or headquarters) and the local firm (subsidiary or affiliated company)? What autonomy does Siemens, IBM, or Ericsson leave its subsidiaries?' These were important questions both theoretically and practically and, despite the efforts of leading scholars, they have not been fully answered. Indeed, since those questions were asked, the context and consequently the answers have probably changed substantially.

In line with the query above, this book addresses the question 'How and why do MNCs manage their Australian subsidiaries in the manner they do?' This is a very broad question and might be interpreted in many ways. To understand why particular topics were chosen as the subjects of this study, it is necessary to first ask the question 'What is meant by management?' There are many definitions of the managerial task but they all converge, explicitly or implicitly, around the means by which firms achieve, sustain and renew competitive advantage. Traditionally management has focused upon creating and sustaining competitive advantage by (1) designing an effective strategy and (2) implementing that strategy efficiently via the control and coordination of the firm's human, financial and knowledge resources. The tenor of the management literature of the last two decades has been to suggest that these two steps are no longer enough to ensure survival and growth. Increasingly, any competitive advantage gained is ephemeral and must be constantly renewed. Continuing corporate success requires innovation and the primary source of successful innovation lies in learning new capabilities and the development of the firm's knowledge resources. The three central tasks of management are now conceived as (1) strategy, (2) administrative control and coordination and (3) knowledge management. These three tasks are interwoven into all of the investigations of the HQ-subsidiary relationship in this research. They are, to some extent, examined separately although, as will be demonstrated, they are theoretically and empirically intermingled. Understanding each issue separately contributes to understanding of the vital and central task of managing HQ-subsidiary relations in the MNC.

In some measure, the MNC is like any other business organization and progress in organization and management research has served to illuminate the MNC as well as domestic firms. There are, however, unique quandaries for the MNC that the domestic firm does not face. The most important of these is that the HQ-subsidiary relationship in the MNC exists between units in different countries. Headquarters and subsidiary are often embedded in dissimilar political, legal, institutional, economic, social and cultural settings. The domestic firm in a large country may face regional differences between HQ and subsidiary to some degree but for the MNC these differences are of a quite different order of magnitude. Between country differences are frequently the major factors in the answers to the questions posed by Otterbeck above.

In this study, Otterbeck's questions are addressed again. All research designs are constrained in some way and while the Australian perspective here may be considered a constraint in that it encroaches upon the universality of the results, the single host country design has a major advantage. It creates a consistent baseline against which to measure effects. With a single host country it becomes easier to make valid comparisons between MNCs from differing home countries, industries and utilizing different strategies and structures.

Outline of the book

The text is divided into two distinct parts – conceptual and empirical. The next three chapters examine the literatures both practical and conceptual that have informed MNC strategy, the HQ-subsidiary relationship and subsidiary tasks. These analyses conclude with a fourth chapter that develops a new model of the relationship and a series of research propositions derived from it. The following five chapters describe the series of empirical studies conducted to investigate this relationship.

A number of streams of research can usefully be applied to the HQ-subsidiary relationship. First, many of the seminal studies in IM focus upon the genesis and growth of the MNC and these have important implications for the nature of the relationship. Second, there is a body of work focusing upon classifications of subsidiaries, based upon their task within the overall corporation. Third, there is a considerable amount of literature concerned with control and coordination of subsidiaries within MNCs. Fourth, the focus in this book on knowledge and innovation requires consideration of recent work in the field of the knowledge management and organizational learning.

Several theoretical perspectives shed light upon the HQ-subsidiary relationship in the MNC but the literatures above indicate that three are of particular value. First, it is evident that, until recently, the strategic contingency approach has been the basis of much of the IM literature. In stressing the importance of the fit between context, strategy and structure, this perspective provides an analytical tool to connect overall MNC strategy to the structure of the MNC and to the HQ-subsidiary link. In many ways the strategic contingency approach acts as a foundation for all theoretical paradigms in IM and IB since the achievement of 'fit' is the ultimate aim of all approaches. The second important theoretical approach is the market imperfections paradigm, in the form of internalization theory and its underpinnings in transaction costs and agency. In the context of this research, multinationality is essentially the existence of overseas subsidiaries and the market imperfections paradigm provides the most widely accepted explanation of foreign direct investment (FDI) and its corollary the MNC. Most importantly it also provides a framework within which to analyze information and knowledge asymmetries and subsequent autonomy and control issues between HQ and subsidiaries. Third, the knowledge-based view of the firm acts as a lens with which to illuminate the increasingly important knowledge management and innovation processes, especially as they are related to HQ-subsidiary relations.

The conceptual origins of the study lie in Chandler's (1962, 1977, 1990) historical analysis of the development of the modern multiivisional organization. In large firms, growth and diversification eventually led to the ascendancy of the multidivisional structure (M-form) over the functional structure (U-form). When the growth and diversification was overseas, this led to the development of MNCs that were, initially, either U-form or M-form. Theoretically and empirically two key issues were generated by this sequence of events. First, diversification could be related or unrelated and subsequent geographic and product line diversification led, in both cases, to a series of potential strategies that the MNC could pursue. Each of these corporate level MNC strategies gave rise to a distinct and compatible subsidiary task. Second, the development of multinationalism, via internalization of the firm's particular specific advantage, led to agency problems especially related to information and knowledge asymmetries between HQ and subsidiaries. These asymmetries have major implications for issues of level of subsidiary autonomy and control and coordination mechanisms and some of these implications are investigated in this study.

The purpose of the following two chapters is to analyze and integrate the literatures that have sought to explain the strategies and structures of the MNC both theoretically and practically. Strategies and structures have been devised and implemented in order to bring about competitive advantage to the MNC. As will be demonstrated in the theoretical model in Chapter 5, they have, in the process, had a determining effect upon the subsidiary task and thus illuminate the character of HQ-subsidiary relationships. There is no existing comprehensive review that has examined the topic from this perspective. The analysis that follows has been shaped by the pattern of evolution of the academic literature and that literature developed to reflect the historical evolution of the MNC as it has adapted to changing environments. These chapters, therefore, examine the studies that analyze the emerging competitive strategies that arose in order to deal with the evolving business environment.

Chapter 2 deals with the strategies that brought about the MNC as an organizational form. In the first section, the highly influential works of Chandler (1962, 1977, 1990) are examined. Chandler expounded the fundamental argument that designing an effective strategy is based upon the attainment of a fit with a given business context and technological imperative. That strategy then triggers the need for a particular corporate structure. The firm is thus conceived as an open system responding to its environment. The environment-strategy-structure theme provides the foundation for the IM approach to the MNC, especially the many studies that came out of the Harvard Business School of researchers. While Chandler's work is the wellspring of the strategic contingency perspective (Donaldson, 1995) and that view can be usefully brought to bear upon every phase of MNC development, the move overseas and the need to protect the firm's ownership advantage have major implications for the HQ-subsidiary relationship and present an additional theoretical problem. Internalization theory is the basic theory of FDI and the MNC. This theory portrays the MNC as a nexus of contracts (Aoki, Gustafsson and Williamson, 1990) that are made immensely more complicated by the international dimension of firm activities. The IB stream of research can be conceived as generally based within this view. Importantly, the process of internalization of the MNC's ownership advantage brings about knowledge asymmetries that have powerful influences upon the issues of autonomy, control, knowledge management and innovation that are the concerns of this study.

The second phase of MNC development is then analyzed. This is concerned with the more established MNC, how it evolved and the strategies of cost minimization and product differentiation that were the result of an increasingly competitive environment. Again these strategies have important consequences for the subsidiary task and the HQ-subsidiary bond. The central studies are Vernon's (1966) product cycle thesis and Stopford and Wells' (1972) stages model. Theoretically this phase is driven by the ideas of Porter on competitive advantage as well as the contingency approach

Chapter 3 is a consideration of the recent MNC and the evolution towards a new organizational form driven by strategies founded upon global innovation and the demand for an ever-increasing stream of new products. This analysis is developed via Bartlett and Ghoshal's (1989) MNC strategy framework based upon their adaptation of the

Integration-Responsiveness (I-R) grid (Prahaled and Doz, 1987) and Hedlund's (1986) extension of Perlmutter's (1965, 1969) work. Strategies of innovation and their manifestation in the rise of the modern network MNC are examined. Chapter 3 also examines several literatures that provide new conceptual underpinnings for the subsidiary task and HQ-subsidiary relationship. A major distinction is made between subsidiary characteristics in hierarchical MNCs and the laterally/horizontally oriented MNCs that Hedlund (1986) labeled heterarchies. Elaborating this distinction requires the integration into the HQ-subsidiary model of insights from several other literatures especially those concerned with organizational knowledge. First, the tacit-explicit distinction is examined. Next, a description of the major theories of organizational learning and subsequent debates and empirical work are presented. Understanding how an organization learns is vital to the process of effectively creating, disseminating and leveraging a firm's knowledge resources. Nonaka (1991, 1994, Nonaka and Takeuchi, 1995; Von Krogh, Ichijo and Nonaka, 2000) set up a model of organizational learning in this area. The chapter then reviews and integrates the organizational memory literature. There are close links between organizational learning and the knowledge-based view of the firm and the next section reviews the knowledge-based view of the firm. The knowledge-based approach sees the firm as a collection of capabilities that must be deployed in a manner that brings about competitive advantage. Sustaining competitive advantage depends upon effective knowledge management – the process of extending old and developing new competences and capabilities. In the MNC the subsidiary's role in this process is vital. This section examines the basic characteristics of knowledge such as tacitness, codifiability, stickiness and imitability. Then an assessment is made of the emerging links between the knowledge-based view, strategic management and transaction cost approaches.

Chapter 4 first reviews the literature on classification of subsidiary tasks focusing upon the major conceptual and empirical studies and the few attempted syntheses. The various subsidiary task classifications that have arisen from all of this work are examined. The work is summarized, outlining the consistencies and drawing attention to the gaps in the developing frameworks.

Based upon the traditional and newer literatures, Chapter 5 presents a new model of the HQ-subsidiary relationship. It proposes that the nature of the strategy by which the MNC generates advantage determines three key aspects of the HQ-subsidiary relationship: the subsidiary task, the knowledge asymmetries between HQ and the subsidiary and whether the MNC takes a hierarchic or heterarchic form. These, in their turn, influence subsidiary autonomy, the types and strength of control and coordination mechanisms used by HQ, the use of knowledge management techniques and the subsidiary's embeddedness in innovation networks of the MNC. The logic that underpins the HQ-subsidiary relationship is presented and the genesis of the subsidiary tasks explained. The new conceptual HQ-subsidiary model suggests several broad research propositions that are examined in the empirical investigations.

The data collection process is described in the methodological appendix in Chapter 12 and Chapter 6 analyzes the data obtained using k-means cluster analysis to demonstrate the existence of distinct subsidiary tasks. The characteristics of these tasks are then shown to be congruent with the characteristics hypothesized by the model.

Chapter 7 explores the question of whether the levels of subsidiary autonomy for each subsidiary task accord with predictions that can be derived from the model. A series of hypotheses are generated regarding the likely levels of autonomy for each of the subsidiary tasks. These predictions are then investigated using ANCOVA (analysis of variance with covariates to control for other potentially predictive variables) with pairwise comparisons of estimated marginal mean scores of subsidiary autonomy for the various subsidiary tasks.

Chapter 8 continues the inquiry into autonomy. Subsidiary size was found to be insignificant as a predictor of subsidiary autonomy and this suggested a further investigation, in which Hedlund's (1981) hypothesis regarding the curvilinear nature of the subsidiary autonomy-subsidiary size relationship is tested.

Chapter 9 examines HQ's use of different mechanisms to control subsidiary activities. From the perspective of the subsidiary tasks, this investigation tests the Ouchi (1979) and Baliga and Jaeger (1984) characterization of the use of mechanisms of control by MNCs.

In Chapter 10 the subsidiary's use of knowledge management techniques and involvement in the innovations network of the MNC are scrutinized. In an investigation that assists in mapping this relatively new empirical domain, the predictors and associates of these variables are examined.

Chapter 11 is the concluding review that links the results of the investigations to the current knowledge base, examines the strengths and deficiencies of the research, and signposts the directions of possible future work. Despite the results of the investigations supporting the new model and some lack of support for previously well-accepted theory, it is argued that the present book is only the beginning of a potentially very fruitful research stream.

The book concludes with a methodological appendix in Chapter 12. This contains a detailed description of the collection and ordering of the data. The data are based upon a survey of foreign-owned Australian subsidiaries of US, UK, European and Japanese MNCs. The survey was carried out in 1999 and 2000. The processes covered include the sample selection procedure, design of the survey instrument, the mail-out and follow-up process, response rates and patterns, data entry and coding procedures and representativeness of the data. This is followed by details of the factor analysis procedure used to establish variables from the data, some validation information regarding the cluster analysis and a copy of the survey instrument.

Previous research investigating MNCs in Australia

The Australian context is distinctive in several ways. As a market it is relatively small and of limited importance but the overall economy is sophisticated and well-developed. The country is physically close and politically and economically linked to many of the South East Asian economies while being distant from the HQs of many of the MNCs in this study. In terms of Australia's historical relationships with the home countries of the MNCs in the study, there is a diversity of influences. The early historical antecedents of Australia have left a UK bias in its social and political institutions although intuitively this appears to be changing. More recent population changes caused by immigration from Europe and, even more recently, Asia, are producing a distinctly multicultural society. The Australian lifestyle and multicultural population suggest some similarities with the US. Ryan, Chan, Ployhart and Slade (1999) examined cultural and linguistic equivalence and their measure found Australia and the US to be very similar. This conclusion was largely consistent with earlier research by Jenner (1982). Australia is somewhat more dissimilar from the major European countries and very different from Japan. These issues of size, economic development and cultural similarity and difference are important since, as will be demonstrated, they may be significant determinants of the nature of the HQ-subsidiary relationship.

The earlier research focusing on Australia and MNCs falls into three broad categories. The first is concerned with the political, economic and, especially, employment effects of MNC penetration of the

Australian business environment. Beginning in the late 1970s and continuing periodically through the 1980s and 1990s, a series of studies (Bambrick, 1974; Crough, 1982; Crough, Wheelwright and Wilshire, 1980; Drysdale and Farrell, 1999; Fox, 1981; MacDonald, 1994; Ramsey, 1986; Renwick, 1988; Skully, 1976; Teo and Rodwell, 1998) investigated many of these concerns. Vernon (1971) first raised the general issue of MNC influence on host countries, analyzing the effects of US MNCs on issues such as growth, income distribution or technology transfer in host countries. He concluded that contextual issues, especially the value system of the foreign country, were the prime determinants of whether the tensions that inevitably arose produced positive or negative effects. In much of the Australian literature, MNCs were portrayed as predatory monolithic empire-builders, intent upon imposing their hegemony upon the industries of smaller nations. While the most pessimistic forecasts have not eventuated or have eventuated in more subtle ways, MNC influence on the Australian economy remains very strong. Fears remain that Australia will be reduced to a branch economy. Recent studies have been concerned with MNC effects upon the stability of the Australian industrial and employment infrastructure. This stream of research will not be examined in detail since, although it clearly examines important issues, it has only limited value for understanding the concerns of the present study. It does, however, indicate that within the academic community there was a noticeable hostility towards or, at least, a suspicion of, the motives and effects of MNC penetration of the Australian economy.

A second domain of concern has been a continuing interest in Japanese business activity in Australia. The Australia-Japan Economic Institute (Anon, 1989, 1992) has surveyed and directoried this activity and Edgington (1988) argued that the Japanese expatriate manager is both control tool and disseminator of tacit knowledge. Until recently, the Australian research in IM and IB has lacked a point of convergence but many of the studies above have arisen as a direct consequence of the recent development of two institutions – the Australian Centre for International Business (ACIB) and the Australia-New Zealand International Business Academy (ANZIBA).

Finally, a number of studies have examined the determinants and patterns of location decisions. The focus of interest was initially on the manner and characteristics of the FDI decision. For example, Merrett, Nicholas, Purcell, Whitwell and Kimberley (1996) concluded that Japanese FDI was driven by the nature of the MNCs particular competitive advantage and location criteria. They also provided detailed data on the motivation for FDI, the nature of the competitive advantage and the reasons behind the FDI decisions. Other studies from this research stream included Hutchinson and Nicholas (1994) that also focused on the rationale behind the FDI decision, Nicholas and Purcell (1998) on subcontracting relations, Nicholas, Gray, Purcell and Zimmerman (1999) on government incentives and Purcell, Nicholas, Merrett and Whitwell (1998) on transference of HR practices. Dedoussis (1995) also examined the perennial 'can Japanese management practices be transferred' debate in the Australian context and concluded that relatively low-cost practices were transferred but more costly welfare/tenure practices were not. Of somewhat more interest to this thesis, Merrett, Nicholas and Purcell (1999) followed up on Edgington (1988) and examined the duality of the expatriate manager role in Japanese MNCs. A notable feature of Australian industry is that, like Canada, it has an unusually high level of foreign ownership. An overall figure of greater than 33 per cent was quoted by Ratnayake (1993) and studies demonstrated figures of greater than 50 per cent in some industries. Parry (1974) found that, in manufacturing, MNCs with greater foreign operations and research intensity tended towards greater subsidiary size and greater concentration of foreign ownership. Ratnayake (1993) found foreign ownership higher in the skill and technology-intensive industries. Parry (1988) later demonstrated that foreign-owned firms had greater access to overseas technology.

It is clear that, while there is a reasonably strong research tradition on MNC activity in Australia, it has largely been at the aggregate national or industrial level, although some of the output from the Australia-Japan Institute, ACIB and ANZIBA studies mentioned earlier was at the level of the firm. This study took up the important opportunity that existed to extend our firm-level knowledge of MNC operations in Australia.

Terminology and semantics

A degree of semantic confusion may arise from the variation in labels used by different authors to designate MNC strategies, structures or organization types. For example, the label transnational originally had a specific meaning relating to a strategy that fitted a particular position on Bartlett and Ghoshal's (1987) reinterpretation of the I-R grid. It now is commonly used to mean any large MNC. In addition, Porter's (1985) term multidomestic refers to the nature of an industry, Cullen's (1999) multilocal refers to a strategy and Bartlett and Ghoshal (1987) use the term multinational to refer to another of their MNC strategy types in the I-R grid. Each author, however, is referring to essentially the same phenomenon – the MNC's need, in some instances, to focus on local responsiveness.

Second, there are many commonalities of meaning in the labels heterarchy, transnational, and differentiated network. For example, Bartlett and Ghoshal (1989: 17) stated: 'The transnational is not a specific strategic posture or a particular organizational form. In essence, the transnational is a new management mentality'. In general, this study will follow Bartlett and Ghoshal's (1987) framework (see the section on the modern MNC in Chapter 3 below) but use the term multidomestic to replace their multinational, since this latter word has more general application in the literature.

Further, it has been common practice to use the expressions subsidiary strategy and subsidiary role almost interchangeably and this misunderstanding has recently been further complicated by the advent of subsidiary mandates, charters, initiatives and other terms. Clearly, there are semantic differences with a charter more likely to be enshrined in a document, a strategy is usually the implementation of a policy and a role is a collection of behaviors and so on. The usage of these terms in the literature has usually been to indicate the tasks that the subsidiary performs on behalf of the MNC. Role would seem a more appropriate term when the subsidiary is relatively tightly controlled by HQ and strategy is more applicable for a more autonomous subsidiary. Since both situations are being examined here this presents a problem. Hereafter, the term subsidiary task will be used to cover both instances.

A final definitional problem arises in the use of the terms knowledge, information, know-how and other close synonyms. Kogut and Zander (1993: 631) touched upon this issue and attempted to clarify some of the subtleties of differences in meaning. These will be examined in some detail in the section on organizational knowledge in Chapter 3.

2
The Strategies of the Developing MNC

The next two chapters examine the strategies and theoretical under-pinnings of the developing and modern MNC. They provide the conceptual base of the study in that these strategies are the prime determinants of the subsidiary task and the characteristics of the HQ-subsidiary relationship.

The early years

The first part of this chapter examines the strategies that created the earliest form of the MNC. The material is presented and analyzed in the following way. First, the contextual explanation of the development of the early MNC and the links with many of the issues of this research is presented. As Chandler (1962: 42) explained, 'In those industries most affected ... growth came by going overseas and ... by diversification'. Chandler's focus upon strategies of geographical expansion and diversification is central to the analysis. Second, the rig-orous theoretical underpinning of the 'market failure' approach of internalization theory is applied (Buckley and Casson, 1976; Caves, 1996) to the Chandler explanation, giving that approach more predict-ive capability especially with regard to knowledge asymmetries and their effects on the HQ-subsidiary relationship. Internalization is a central concept to this research because it is the driving force leading to the creation of subsidiaries. The value of this theoretical perspective is shown by the concluding analysis in this section where Hennart's application of the transaction costs approach is applied to controls in the HQ-subsidiary relationship.

Related diversification and the link between strategy and structure

The crucial importance of Chandler's work is that it linked corporate strategy to the decentralized hierarchical organizational structure via a cost and coordination argument. The strategy-structure link is fundamental to an understanding of HQ-subsidiary relations. Chandler's expressed goal was 'to study the complex interconnections in a modern industrial enterprise between strategy and structure and an ever-changing external environment' (Chandler, 1991: 35). In this respect, his major contribution was to investigate and explain the change in operational structure from what he termed the multifunctional or U-form to the multidivisional or M-form organization. This is the prime source of understanding of the initial process of development of large firm structure. Although not directed specifically at the MNC, Chandler's work was a clear forerunner of many of the conceptualizations that have developed to date. His main theses were fully developed and extensively documented in Chandler (1962, 1964, 1977, 1990 and 1991). Briefly, the coming of the second industrial revolution in transport and communications generated the U-form's first competitive advantage by enabling the coordination and control of moves to new advantageous locations, such as new or large markets, where less or no competition existed. This geographical expansion relied upon the production and distribution of previously inconceivable volumes of product that resulted in mass production in food, drink, tobacco, electrical and mechanical engines, non-ferrous metals and chemicals. The challenge for management in both production and distribution was organizational rather than technological and, in the US, this gave rise to salaried managers and the managerial capitalism that replaced the owner-managers of the earlier era. Geographical and product diversification in the 1920s meant that the multifunctional or U-form organization, that had proved more than adequate up to that time, was unable to deal with the huge increases in information flows and ensuing expansion in volume and complexity of decision-making. The M-form or multidivisional form was developed at Du Pont, General Motors (GM) and other firms to deal with their planned expansion and diversification (see Chandler, 1962, esp. chapters 2–5) and this organizational innovation spread rapidly (Chandler, 1962, chapter 7).

In Chandler's analysis, the advantage of the M-form was derived from administrative cost reductions. Increasing size of U-form and M-form enterprises brought down production costs for both forms as economies of scale were achieved. However, in the M-form, adminis-trative efficiency was greatly superior. Hence, divisionalization in the M-form brought a superior *overall* cost structure than the U-form. At the time of Chandler's analysis, both the U-form and the M-form were hierarchical but the M-form was clearly more decentralized. It can be argued that decentralization was simply a response to the problems of the increasing volume of decision-making. For example, Chandler (1990: 43) stated 'senior managers realized that they had neither the time nor the necessary information to coordinate and monitor day-to-day operations and at the same time devise and implement long-term plans ... The administrative overload had simply become too great'. Too many decisions were being presented to top management for them to cope effectively. This single explanation is appealing but Chandler realized that the case for the M-form was more complex and there was contradictory evidence. For example, Ford was roughly equivalent in size to General Motors but it did not suffer from the same top manage-ment decision-making overload (Chandler, 1962: 301). The explana-tion lay in the dissimilar product lines of the two companies. Ford was producing only a single black Model T product while GM had many product lines. GM produced and sold cars, trucks, parts and accessories of many types. Chandler (1962) suggested that decentralization took place not simply because of the volume of decision-making but because of the diversity and complexity of the decisions that top man-agement had to make. Decentralization arose due to limitations on top management's cognitive and information/knowledge processing capa-bilities i.e. it was a bounded rationality problem (Simon, 1957, 1976) based, to a considerable extent, upon the knowledge asymmetries between HQ and subsidiaries.

With the operational top management overload reduced by the M-form structure, senior management was freed, in principle, to think more strategically. Senior management was encouraged to adopt strat-egies aimed at further long-term growth via diversification. It became easier, when firms were M-form, to move into new geographic areas or product markets. They simply created new divisions. The first new source of advantage open to the M-form corporation was to exploit its competitive advantage in locations of less or a total absence of com-petition. This included diversification into the international arena. Divisionalization can clearly be seen as one of a number of spurs to internationalization since a MNC was simply an M-form corporation with some subsidiaries established in new overseas locations and administered by an international division. If firms were not by now already multinational, it was now administratively more easily accomplished.

With regard to the link between strategy and structure, Chandler perceived administrative coordination to be the central advantage of the M-form structure. His first general proposition in *The Visible Hand* (Chandler, 1977: 6) stated 'administrative coordination permitted greater productivity, lower costs, and higher profits'. There were also, however, control implications because the shift from U-form to M-form demanded a fundamental shift in management style. In a typical U-form corporation the senior manager had direct, often hands-on, control in a single plant over all the functional areas of R&D, production, marketing and so on (Chandler, 1977). With the change to the M-form structure and the consequent multiple plants and sites, the newly freed up management was required to concede some important operational decision-making autonomy to the divisions. The direct result was that it became necessary to design new mechanisms to retain control over key variables and design and implement new methods to allocate the resources of the organization in line with corporate strategy. However, although Chandler's work convincingly ties context to strategy and demonstrates how the strategy of growth led to a new organizational structure, it does not examine the nature of the increasing knowledge asymmetries within that structure. Such a focus is central to an understanding of the HQ-subsidiary relationship.

In summary, therefore, for Chandler the firm's move overseas was just a further stage of the geographical expansion and internal divisional hierarchy that delivered the same cost effective method of coordination and control apparent in the domestic firm. While he outlined the importance of scale and scope economies and transaction costs, it was left to later theorists to build a more rigorous formulation to his essentially contingent approach to the strategy and structure of firm growth. In particular the links between HQ and the subsidiary divisions and firms were not developed.

Unrelated diversification

At this point, an additional growth strategy must be addressed since it gave rise to another variation on the multidivisional administrative structure. Chandler (1962: 42) stated 'diversification was primarily responsible for the development of the decentralized structure' and it is clear from his work that he was primarily concerned with both geographic and product related diversification. The latter is the generation of new but related products based upon the firm's extant technology, skills and know-how (or competences and capabilities in today's terminology). He later commented that 'managers occasionally purchased or merged with a company that provided a new or complementary product. Much more often such expansion resulted from internal growth' (Chandler, 1977: 474). Chandler was, however, aware of the rise in the 1960s of the financial conglomerate form of the multidivisional enterprise. In this corporate form 'The conglomerate expanded ... entirely by the acquisition of existing enterprises, and not by direct investment into its own plant and personnel, and it often did so in *totally unrelated fields*' (emphasis added) (Chandler, 1977: 481). The form remains relatively common today and, in some instances, has important implications for the nature of HQ-subsidiary relations.

While the potential for sustained competitive advantage via unrelated diversification remains questionable, Caves (1996) investigated international financial diversification behavior of MNCs and concluded that in both short and long-term markets it was possible for MNCs to 'enjoy opportunities for international arbitrage of funds and that investors recognize the value of international diversification built into the MNE's liabilities' (Caves, 1996: 144–146).

The financial conglomerates could 'concentrate more single-mindedly on making investments in new industries and markets and withdraw more easily from existing ones ... (but) on the other hand, ... were far less effective in monitoring and evaluating their divisions' (Chandler, 1977: 481). The last point clearly implies greater knowledge asymmetries than those found in the related diversification form and, hence, the subsidiary divisions and firms in this type of MNC will have a greater amount of decision-making independence.

The related vs unrelated diversification has not been satisfactorily resolved either on the basis of performance outcomes (see for example Rumelt, 1974; Bettis, 1981) or how easy it is in practice to make this analytical distinction in modern MNCs. For some recent contributions to the debate and the state of play see Capar and Kotabe (2003), Park (2003), Robins and Wiersema (2003), Helfat and Eisenhardt (2004), Li and Greenwood (2004) and Miller (2004).

Internalization, transaction costs and the principal-agent dyad

Knowledge asymmetries, within firms and between firms and their implications for the nature of organizational structure, are central to internalization theory and its transaction cost and agency components. Further, these approaches provide a rigorous underpinning to

Chandler's contingency explanation of firm growth and make it generalizable to the current organization of MNCs. The following analysis is based upon the works of Buckley and Casson (1976), Hood and Young (1979), Calvet (1981), Dunning (1988), Caves (1996) and Rugman (1996) that provide the theoretical underpinning for firm growth and internal organizational design. This section also introduces the key notion of the firm's, often knowledge-based, ownership advantage.

Market failure and internalization provide the theoretical core of the MNC and the subsequent HQ-subsidiary relationships. These explanations focus upon the results of markets failing to clear. Orthodox neoclassical economic theory had not successfully explained FDI or why firms engaged in overseas operations. However, when the underlying assumptions of perfect goods and factor markets did not hold, free trade was eliminated as a solution and replaced by second best solutions such as the MNC (Buckley and Casson, 1976; Rugman, 1996).

The modern understanding of FDI theory can be traced back to Coase (1937). His insight was that FDI and MNCs arose because there are circumstances when the market was a more costly and inefficient way to undertake certain types of transactions than the firm. When this logic was applied to the international arena, situations in which it was less costly to allocate resources internally within the firm than to use the market explained FDI and the MNC. The existence of an ownership advantage in the form of what Caves (1996: 3) labeled a proprietary asset (sometimes termed firm-specific asset or firm – specific advantage – FSA) and the internalization of this advantage within the firm but across borders, provided the MNC with its distinctiveness.

The role of the subsidiary was central because the efficacy of FDI lay in the firm, first, having and exploiting this ownership specific advantage and, second, perceiving and utilizing some foreign location specific advantage. 'It is the association of ownership – and locational-specific factors which determines whether ... the firm will exploit that advantage by producing abroad' (Hood and Young, 1979: 47). At the outset, a MNC operating in a foreign location was faced with a range of disadvantages *vis a vis* a local firm in the same location. The MNC had less knowledge of such factors as market conditions, was probably deficient in local business contacts and was less aware of and less competent to deal with, the entire legal, linguistic, social and cultural framework. The situation was exacerbated and hampered by having to do everything at a distance with ensuing communication difficulties and breakdowns. The ensuing costs have become generally known as the liability of foreignness and to overcome this liability and make a foreign operation viable, a MNC had to have its own, more than countervailing, advantage in relation to the local firm. This ownership advantage which was usually in the form of knowledge, know-how, techniques or technology, needed to be at least in part, firm-specific and able to be transferred within the firm to subsidiaries across distance (Caves, 1996: 4).

The early internalization theorists, notably Kindleberger (1969), Johnson (1970) Caves (1971) McManus (1972) and Hymer (1976, 1990), suggested many types of potential ownership advantage. These were mainly technological in nature although this label can be widely interpreted to include explicit and tacit knowledge (Johnson, 1970) concerning products, production processes, marketing expertise, organizational skills and management techniques. Ownership advantages may vary in terms of tangibility or specificity. They could take the form of a patented design or process or simply lie in the know-how shared by employees of the firm, embedded in the repertoire of skills and routines possessed by the firm's teams of human and other inputs (Nelson and Winter, 1982).

These ownership advantages alone, however, are still not enough to ensure that FDI is the best choice as a means of exploiting the firm's knowledge. The MNC does not need to create a subsidiary since it has the alternatives of exporting its home produced goods or of licensing production technology to a foreign producer. For foreign production in a wholly-owned subsidiary to be chosen, there must also be some location specific advantage, such as relative wage costs, trade or non-tariff barriers, government policies or some significant market characteristic, to add to the ownership advantage. Whatever the location factors may be, they will generally be available to, or at least affect, all firms in that locale. It is, therefore, the combination of the two types of advantage that determines, first, whether a particular firm has any advantage over other firms and, second, whether the firm will exploit this advantage by producing abroad, exporting or using some intermediate form of arrangement such as an alliance or licensing. Buckley and Casson (1976) proposed that there were additional gains (often in terms of knowledge growth) to be obtained from managing the ownership advantage within the owning firm – that the internalization process itself contributes economic rents – rather than leasing the asset at arm's length to another firm. Dunning (1980) argued that the results of this combination of ownership advantage, internalization advantage and location advantage constituted an eclectic theory of foreign investment.

In summary, while the literature has suggested that many factors might contribute to the FDI decision, the most commonly accepted theoretical stance is that market imperfections are the major explanation of why firms prefer FDI. This approach derives from Hymer's 1960 'seminal dissertation' (Dunning and Rugman, 1985: 228) and is espoused by most leading scholars (Casson, 1995, 1997; Hennart, 1982; Hymer; 1976; Rugman, 1981 and Teece, 1983). It is usually known as internalization theory. Because of imperfections in the market, firms elect to internalize their critical ownership advantages or firm-specific assets (FSA). All transactions in intermediate factors/products and knowledge related to the FSA are kept within firm boundaries by establishing proprietary production facilities in the target location. A subsidiary is born and while it may have many tasks, a primary role is always the protection of the FSA.

Transaction costs. The internalization decision and the creation of a subsidiary is based upon a cost-benefit analysis that is particularly concerned with transaction costs. Furthermore, transaction costs analysis is associated with the risks involved in various knowledge asymmetries. These formed the basis of many situations of market failure that led to internalization. While Chandler pointed to the general importance of transaction costs in the internalization decision (see for example, Chandler, 1990: 17), he did not develop this approach. The emergence of this specialized field of analysis, however, enabled the development of a transaction cost based interpretation of the Chandlerian link between strategy and organizational structure. First, the tenets of the theory are expounded. Second, literature is introduced that links transaction costs to the structure and functions of the MNC and the HQ-subsidiary relationship (Hennart, 1991, 1993).

Transaction costs analysis is the foundation of the internalization theory approach and it is prefaced upon the existence of costs in all economic transactions. These include *ex ante* costs such as drafting and negotiating contracts and *ex post* costs such as those incurred in monitoring or enforcing agreements. The relative levels of these costs in a given economic exchange dictate whether a market or a firm or some intermediate arrangement, such as licensing, franchising, a joint venture or strategic alliance in some form, will be the most advantageous governance structure. These general propositions were established by Coase in 1937 and Williamson (1975, 1985, 1996) has added substantially to the original arguments. The framework rests upon the interplay between two main external factors (uncertainty and asymmetric information), two assumptions of human behavior (bounded rationality and opportunism) and two dimensions of transactions (asset specificity and environmental uncertainty).

Bounded rationality is the term coined by Simon (1976) to describe the cognitive constraints and limited information processing ability of decision-makers. Their intended rationality is circumscribed by these deficiencies and in uncertain environments this leads to problems. The primary result of environmental uncertainty is an adaptation problem. If future circumstances cannot be specified *ex ante* then it leads to the need to modify agreements when external circumstances change. Another consequence of bounded rationality is that performance in accordance with the agreement cannot be easily verified *ex post*. Opportunism is the assumption that at least some decision-makers will unscrupulously seek to serve their own self-interests and that it is difficult to know *a priori* who is trustworthy and who is not (Barney, 1990; Hennart, 1991; Rindfleisch and Heide, 1997). Williamson defined opportunism as 'self-seeking with guile' (1985: 47) and suggested that cheating, lying and contract violation are typical opportunistic behaviors. In particular, if the transaction is supported by a specific asset that has less value outside the transaction than within it, then opportunism creates a problem in safeguarding the value of that asset. Transaction cost theory proposes that if adaptation, performance evaluation and safeguarding costs are relatively low or absent then economic actors will favor the market as governance mechanism. If these costs are high enough to exceed the production costs advantages of the market then organizations will favor internal (firm) or some intermediate form of organization. Firms, however, have three major advantages over the other available arrangements. First, because usually they can measure and reward behavior as well as output, firms are more powerful controllers of behavior than markets. Hence they can facilitate any necessary adaptation and detect opportunism more easily via the use of internal organizational structures. Second, by providing rewards that are more long-term, firms can reduce the payoff to opportunistic behavior. Third, firms can use corporate culture and socialization processes to create superordinate goals that reduce opportunism *ex ante*.

Hennart (1991, 1993) applied the transaction cost approach to the HQ-subsidiary relationship in the MNC. He was primarily concerned with the market vs hierarchy decision but extended the market failure arguments to apply to HQ and subsidiaries. He demonstrated how the bounded rationality of HQ management and the potential opportunism of the subsidiary management in the form of cheating or shirking, drove the design of hierarchical control mechanisms. Hierarchical control mechanisms are typically prescribed reporting systems and strict behavioral controls in the form of manuals, procedures and policies (Ouchi, 1977; Baliga and Jaeger, 1984). Hennart used the transaction cost approach to derive the mechanisms that the HQs of MNCs employed to control their subsidiaries by demonstrating that these were closely analogous to the processes that firms employed to impose controls over their employees. In doing so, he established the central role played by knowledge.

Within the firm, the extent to which management had knowledge of the employee's production function, together with information on the relative levels of shirking and cheating costs were used to categorize the available control mechanisms. The argument is summarized in Table 2.1 below. The logic for control of subsidiaries was exactly analogous (see Table 2.2). Hierarchy was used when HQ had a greater knowledge of the unit production function (usually this meant when the

Table 2.1   Employee control modes used in firms

Cheating costs/ shirking costs	Management knowledge of the worker's production function	
	Higher than workers	Lower than workers
High cheating, low shirking	1. Hierarchy	2. Selection and/or socialization
Low cheating, high shirking	4. No interaction within the firm	3. Price control (e.g. piece work)

Source: Hennart (1991: 84); adapted from Ouchi (1979).

Table 2.2   Subunit control modes used in firms

Cheating costs/ shirking costs	Headquarters' knowledge of the unit production function	
	Higher than local management	Lower than local management
High cheating, low shirking	1. Hierarchy 'centralization'	2. Selection and/or socialization
Low shirking, high cheating	4. No interaction within the firm	3. Profit centers

Source: Hennart (1991: 84).

subsidiary was simply implementing the FSA) and the subsidiary's performance was difficult to measure. Alternatively, when subsidiary output was easily measurable and the subsidiary had greater knowledge of the production function, then setting up a profit centre, with suitable transfer pricing arrangements, elicited the required behavior as long as subsidiary management remuneration and incentives were a function of profit. In both cases there was a mix of market and hierarchy. In the event of subsidiary management having greater knowledge of the production function and performance being difficult to evaluate, it became necessary to design more complex mechanisms to ensure the internalization of HQ goals by subsidiary management via selection and socialization processes.

Hennart's analysis was a crucially important extension of the strategy-structure and transaction cost approaches because it demonstrated the necessity of 'opening the black box' of the firm's internal functions. He demonstrated the need for a set of additional systems and structures, *internal to the firm*, that were congruent with the demands of the external environment and the consequent strategy and overall structure. These systems and structures had to be designed in a manner that made allowance for the existing knowledge asymmetries between HQ and the subsidiary. In the MNC, the knowledge asymmetries were even more problematic because the HQ-subsidiary relationship crossed national and cultural borders and was often accentuated by communications problems arising from language, multilocation and time differences.

Thus the transaction cost approach offers an explanation of the hierarchical organizational form (and the nature of the HQ-subsidiary relationship) that gives central place to the need for managers to institute structures to control employees possessing different and better knowledge than HQ. This is the basis of transaction cost theory in relation to the structure of the MNC.

Agency theory. Agency (or principal-agent) theory is also derived from the organizational economics paradigm and is similarly based in conceptions of risk and opportunism (see Eisenhardt, 1989, for a review and assessment). It is important for an understanding of the organizational structure of the MNC in that it stresses the principal role played by HQ *vis a vis* the agent role of the subsidiary and, thereby, demonstrates the power structure implicit in hierarchy. Jensen and Meckling (1976) proposed that organizations could be analyzed in terms of a conflict of interest between principals (the owners of the corporation) and agents (the executive management). Managerial interests may diverge from the interests of owners and consequently executive management may opportunistically use their superior local knowledge to serve their own interests at the expense of owners. This asymmetry of interests resulted in 'residual loss' for the owners. Curbing of this loss required the use of several devices. If the owners' prime control device, the board of directors of the firm, was considered to be analogous to the HQ in a MNC, the monitoring and control devices available were directly analogous to those in Hennart's opportunism and bounded rationality schema described above. Mechanisms such as monitoring and sanctions for non-compliance were hierarchical and fit into Hennart's cell 1. Profit-based incentives were market oriented and fit into cell 3. Cell 2 contained the selection or socialization (that is heterarchically-focused) mechanisms.

These market imperfection approaches have been used to increase understanding of several aspects of MNC management: foreign ownership decisions (Hennart and Park, 1994); foreign market entry decisions (Tihanyi, Ellstrand, Daily and Dalton, 2000); and subsidiary compensation strategies (Roth and O'Donnell, 1996). However, it is in the area of subsidiary control, that they are most illuminating and this is a point that allies the IB approach with the IM literature. O'Donnell (2000) demonstrated that agency theory acted as a good foundation for understanding monitoring mechanisms and incentive compensation in MNCs. She concluded, however, that to fully explain the phenomenon of subsidiary control in modern global interdependent firms, there was a need to include explanations of social control mechanisms including the heterarchic control mechanisms of the present study.

Summary

This section has examined the literature on geographic and product diversification in the early MNC and has dealt with the firm's first moves in a time of growth when cost reduction advantages led to expansionary policies via the achievement of massive throughput in minimum efficient scale plants (Chandler, 1990). This strategy was linked to organizational structure because the replacement of the multifunctional U-form (Chandler, 1990) by the multidivisional M-form when the diversification created problems of control and decision-making in the U-form. A further variation on the multidivisional form was then evidenced. The financial conglomerate based its advantage generation on unrelated portfolio diversification of its liabilities and assets. In consequence, the HQ-subsidiary relationship was likely to be substantially different from that in the related diversification form of MNC.

A transaction cost explanation was provided by Chandler but in contingency form. The development of transaction cost and principal-agent analysis was used to theoretically ground Chandler's empirical work and apply it in a more predictive way to different contexts. Further, it allowed the use of knowledge asymmetries and the imperative of the authority of the stewardship function to explain the hierarchical nature of the new M-form organizational structure. To date, however, this approach has been confined to the market-hierarchy choice (Hennart, 1991).

The established MNC

This section first examines the process of internationalization of the MNC and then deals with the strategies implemented by the established MNC in situations of increased competition. Over time the MNC began to have access to competitive strategies based upon the cost advantages that arise from the realization of experience curve economies such as learning effects and economies of scale and scope. Its developing expertise also enabled expansion and diversification of its range of products i.e. differentiation. This literature is not as fully developed or as cohesive as that which analyzed the development of the MNC in the previous section. It is presented in the following way. First, Vernon's (1966) product cycle model and Johanson and Vahlne's (1977) model of internationalization are used as contextual links between the early MNC and its established form. These two studies are significant for this research because they highlight two important features of the internationalization process. First, they bring into the spotlight the tasks that might be incumbent upon various subsidiaries and, second, they draw attention to the role of knowledge in the internationalization process. Next, the literature that seeks to deal with the organizational outcomes of the new cost minimization and differentiation strategies is presented. Stopford and Wells' (1972) stages model and the several empirical follow-ups are in this category. These studies raise the possibility of further subsidiary tasks. Porter's (1985, 1987) analysis of corporate and business level strategies is the conceptual framework for these two strategies. Bartlett and Ghoshal (1987, 1989) also illuminated these outcomes but, in addition, it is one of the studies that introduced the newer MNC form (labeled the transnational in their study) and hence is examined in the next chapter.

Vernon's product cycle theory

Vernon's product cycle theory (Vernon, 1966) is the link between the strategies of the early MNC and those of the established MNC. Vernon proposed that as geographic diversification takes place the products of a MNC pass through a series of production and distribution phases. First, products are manufactured and sold domestically. Second, output is produced domestically and then exported. Third, output is both produced and sold abroad. Fourth, products are manufactured abroad and re-exported to the domestic market. The third phase is congruent with the overseas diversification growth strategy as described in the earlier part of this chapter. The fourth phase is tied to the cost minimization and differentiation strategies of the established MNC that are examined shortly.

Vernon's (1966) analysis identified the central role played by cost factors, particularly labor (although transaction costs are also relevant), at home and in the host country and how these factors brought about shifts in the task of the subsidiary. Specifically, cost factors drove the change from export sales office to local producer and later to return exporter to the home country. Vernon did not analyze the types of organization that his internationalization model brought about but his work can be understood as part of the process of setting the scene for consideration of subsidiary tasks and characteristics of the HQ-subsidiary relationship.

In the context of this study the central importance of Vernon's work was to demonstrate how an initial growth strategy based upon moving to a new geographic location transformed into a different strategy based upon growth via low cost and scale economies.

The Uppsala model of internationalization

Johanson and Valne (1977) proposed that firms acquired knowledge about international operations by the simple expedient of beginning to operate in a new market. They learned incrementally thus gradually reducing uncertainty and reducing the perceived risk. Each successive step was postponed until the perceived risk was lower than the bearable risk (Johanson and Valne, 1977). The knowledge growth about internationalization was highly dependent upon individual acquisition of knowledge and was "therefore difficult to transfer to other individuals and contexts" (Forsgren, 2002: 259). Over time, the firm learned to carry out its international operations with increasing effectiveness. The Uppsala model did not imply any specific subsidiary task. It did, however, accentuate the importance of two types of knowledge in the HQ-subsidiary relationship. Increasing experience of operations in a host market brought increasing knowledge concerning the many social, cultural, legal and other characteristics of that market. The importance of individuals in the acquisition of that knowledge often resulted in that knowledge not being readily available to HQ. Headquarters did, however, on its part, develop knowledge of and competences in the management of the overall internationalization process.

Porter's generic strategies

Porter (1985, 1987) demonstrated that the multidivisional organization implemented strategy at two levels. At the corporate level, strategy concerned issues such as the type of business the firm should engage in and, importantly for this research, 'how to manage the array of units' (Porter, 1987: 47) to create advantage. Business level strategy (generic strategy) was concerned with how to create competitive advantage at the level of the individual business. The strategies Porter proposed were cost leadership (cost minimization) and product differentiation with the added strategic option that each strategy could focus on particular market segments or niches. Cost minimization is usually attained via volume production of a small range of standard products and brings a minimized selling price. The differentiation strategy is accomplished by selling an expanded range of products that have been adapted to suit a particular market segment. Strategies at both the corporate and business levels have repercussions for the tasks that are set for the subsidiaries and two of Porter's generic strategies are implicit in the two dimensions of the Stopford and Wells model that follows.

Stopford and Wells' stages model

The central importance of the Stopford and Wells model for the present study is that it extended Chandler's thesis by demonstrating that variation in the type of strategy adopted by the MNC led to variations in the internal structure of the MNC. Stopford and Wells (1972) argued that when firms engaged in a strategy of geographic diversification, regardless of whether they were U or M-form domestically, they typically grouped all their international activities under a single international division (Bartlett, 1981, 1983; Bartlett and Ghoshal, 1987). (Or, sometimes, as in the case of some Swedish MNCs used a mother-daughter structure, Hedlund, 1984.) This division tended to be subdivided geographically. There were inherent integration and coordination problems with the international division structure. While these difficulties may be attenuated via various mechanisms, as exemplified by the longevity of the international division in many Japanese MNCs (Bartlett and Ghoshal, 1989; Negandhi and Baliga, 1981a; Negandhi and Welge, 1984), continued overseas expansion often brought unsustainable strains to this structure. Stopford and Wells (1972) hypothesized that when the continued expansion was on the basis of greater volumes of a little-changing line of products, then the MNC tended to abandon the single international division and adopt a company wide area divisions structure. This structure facilitated the firm's much needed local responsiveness and consequently expanded extant location advantages. When the expansion was based upon increasing product diversity, the international division was abandoned and the MNC tended to restructure on the basis of product divisions. The advantages of this type of structure lay in its ability to consolidate value-creation in key locations and hence realize both location and scale/experience economies. They further proposed that if expansion took place on the basis of both strategies then a global matrix structure was necessary.

Stopford and Wells' formal matrix structure was based upon the two dimensions of product and geographic area and the configuration has been implemented in several high profile 'experiments'. In practice it appeared to be bureaucratic and clumsy with problems of accountability, creating greater problems than it solved (Bartlett and Ghoshal, 1986; Dwyer and Dawley, 1995). The decades since Stopford and Wells' analysis have seen the rise of other strategy-influencing factors of equal or more importance than geographic area or product line. The modern MNC must also consider innovation, critical interdependencies, knowledge flows, skill accessibility and many other factors (Nohria and Ghoshal, 1997; Ghoshal and Bartlett, 1997). It is possible that the frequent failures of matrix structure applications were a product of attempting to use hierarchically developed procedures for what was essentially a heterarchical organizational form.

The theoretical grounding of the Stopford and Wells model lay in structural contingency theory in the Chandler tradition. In consequence, Stopford and Wells were fully aware of the contingent nature of the control and coordination process.

> No one set of policies, instituted by management ... can be equally effective for all types of multinational enterprise (Stopford and Wells, 1972: 3).

As the international strategies of MNCs evolved, it became increasingly important and difficult to select and implement the most efficacious structure to complement those strategies.

The studies of the strategy-structure link in the established MNC were not usually theoretically grounded. In consequence, some of the studies based on the Stopford and Wells approach included variables that were not easy to place within an explanatory framework. It is therefore unsurprising that a cohesive pattern did not arise. Most importantly, the value and consequences of an area or product divisional distinction for the nature of HQ-subsidiary relationships were not explained. Hence, the major theme that emerges from these studies is that, as new strategies develop, they are demonstrating the inadequacies of the basic Stopford and Wells model. These inadequacies find some resolution in Bartlett and Ghoshal's extension of the Doz and Prahalad I-R grid that is a major topic of the next section.

3
The Strategies of the Modern MNC

This chapter shifts the analysis to the modern MNC and strategies based upon innovation and knowledge management. First, the central place of these issues in the transnational strategy and the organizational form of heterarchy are explained. Then, because the subsidiary's task, autonomy, control and contribution are intertwined with all aspects of knowledge, the remainder of this chapter examines the issues of organizational knowledge, learning and memory and the resource-based view of the firm to provide the conceptual base for understanding knowledge in the HQ-subsidiary relationship.

The transnational strategy and heterarchy

In recent work on MNC structure, the two strategies of cost minimization and differentiation are augmented or even replaced by an increased emphasis on innovation and the creation of new products and services. New product and innovation strategies have always been important to the MNC but the process of their generation was usually either centralized at HQ (or at a centre of excellence) or localized at the subsidiary level. Hedlund (1986) and Bartlett and Ghoshal (1987, 1989) have argued that a new strategy has emerged that stands in contrast to the highly structured command and control paradigm, focusing on efficient 'fit', that acts as the underpinning for cost minimization and differentiation. This strategy extends the MNC's innovative and entrepreneurial skills via the development of a multidimensional, distributed, integrated, flexible, interdependent, learning organization that generates locally leveraged and globally linked innovations (Bartlett and Ghoshal, 1989). The strategy stands as a major discontinuity in the evolution of the organizational form of the MNC that is as significant as the shift from U- to M-form examined by Chandler. The new organization is still emerging but there are some companies that excel at creating innovativeness and are very good at linking and leveraging pockets of resources and expertise and embedding organizational learning (Bartlett, interviewed in Stonham, 1992). The first study to examine this strategy and its congruent structure in the modern context was Bartlett and Ghoshal (1989).

Bartlett and Ghoshal's framework

Earlier studies had offered evidence that the type of divisional structure instituted by the MNC was linked to the need for global integration or the need for local responsiveness. Prahalad and Doz (1987) established the centrality of these two competing dimensions to an understanding of MNC strategy. The model they developed has become known universally as the I-R (Integration-Responsiveness) grid. They argued that firms competing in the global marketplace faced two types of competitive pressures, each of which placed differing demands upon the management of the resources of the firm. The need for integration is driven by the response to pressures to reduce costs that arose from sources such as technology and change in the external environment. This impelled the firm towards a strategy based upon factors such as scale economies, product standardization and low cost locations. Pressures for local responsiveness to suit unique local tastes, infrastructure or host government requirements had an antithetical effect. These pressures demanded product differentiation via local production, control of marketing, R&D and so on. The relative influence of these two factors has led a number of authors to consider the implications therein.

As the product of one of the few very distinct streams of research in the field (Bartlett and Ghoshal, 1986, 1987, 1989), Bartlett and Ghoshal (1989) shifted the focus from type of division to overall MNC strategy (see Figure 3.1). The framework used low and high levels of two pressures, global integration and local responsiveness, to hypothesize four possible MNC strategies, each with implications for organizational structure, resource allocation and HQ-subsidiary relations.

When global integration and responsiveness pressures were both low and the firm had a competence that the host country competition lacks, the international strategy was the rational option. The HQ developed a range of relatively standard products that were produced and marketed locally with perhaps some minor adaptation. However, all critical functions and knowledge were kept at HQ and tight control via

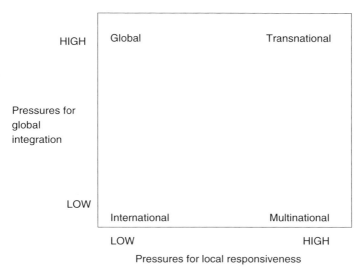

Figure 3.1   Bartlett and Ghoshal's interpretation of the I-R grid (adapted)

formal planning systems was kept over marketing and product strategy. Subsidiaries tended to become overseas appendages to HQ as units in a coordinated federation.

When pressure for local responsiveness was high and integration pressures relatively low, firms were likely to elect to follow the multinational strategy. In a manner similar to the international strategy, home developed skills and products were transferred to foreign markets but marketing and product development strategies were then extensively customized to fit local demand. Subsidiaries were relatively independent entities whose objectives were primarily local. There was a tendency to establish the full range of value-creation activities in each major market and headquarters only retained control of key financial indices and, in some instances, there was a distinct predisposition for the MNC to develop into a decentralized federation of firms with little more than a holding company at its centre. This strategy correlates with Porter's (1985) multidomestic industry.

Firms that pursued a global strategy were intent upon cost reduction via experience effects and location advantages. Primary activities – production, marketing and R&D – were centered in one or a small number of subsidiaries in beneficial locations and the standardized products produced there were then distributed and marketed through a worldwide subsidiary network. HQ maintained tight control of decision-making and significant knowledge.

Bartlett and Ghoshal finally argued that, for some MNCs, competitive pressures required that they simultaneously respond to both integration and responsiveness demands. Additionally, they argued that important capabilities might develop and reside anywhere in the MNC. Hence, they suggested that flows of advantage-generating skills, products and knowledge would be maintained between all significant units of the firm. Attempting to achieve this was the transnational strategy. Because it focused on lateral linkages and networks and rapid dissemination of knowledge, it was clear that the transnational strategy required a heterarchical organization, in contrast to the hierarchical orientation typical of the international, multinational and global strategies.

Several connections with earlier studies are evident. First, Chandler's geographic diversification into new markets is related to the international strategy. Vernon's (1966) focus upon the pressure to reduce production and other costs establishes a tie-up with the Bartlett and Ghoshal's strategies taxonomy where it is used as one dimension. The area and product divisional structures proposed by Stopford and Wells (1972) have some congruence with Bartlett and Ghoshal's (1989) global and multinational strategies.

Hedlund's development of Perlmutter's centric types and the heterarchy

Vernon's (1966) product cycle model was constructed from data collected during the heyday of the US's global economic dominance and his conclusions about internationalization had a strong ethnocentric (US) bias. This simple point links Vernon's work with that of Perlmutter. Perlmutter and his collaborators (1965, 1969) distinguished between three types of MNC – ethnocentric, polycentric and geocentric. Their taxonomy classified MNCs primarily on the basis of managerial attitude and, over time, Perlmutter's categories have become closely identified with human resource management (HRM) and staffing strategies in international business, rather than with structural types. From this perspective, the ethnocentric approach was described as having all strategic positions in the MNC including subsidiaries managed by home country nationals. The polycentric approach was to use host country nationals in the MNC's subsidiaries and home country managers at HQ. The geocentric approach utilized managers from any country who had become suitably widely experienced and attuned to the corporate norms of the particular MNC.

It was apparent to Hedlund (1986) that Perlmutter's proposals had many more implications than simply those related to HRM. The culmination of the Perlmutter taxonomy, the geocentric firm, remained firmly HQ-oriented, however, and Hedlund suggested that Perlmutter's analysis required extension in the light of changes that occurred in the two decades that followed the original propositions. Hedlund proposed that the modern MNC would also actively seek advantages deriving from the firm's global spread. Hedlund's developed geocentric firm – the heterarchy – has much in common with Bartlett and Ghoshal's transnational. Importantly, there is a clear convergence of analysis. Structurally, they were both networks that had many subsidiary nodes and every node was different from all others. Flexibility existed in the relationships between subsidiaries and with outside agents. The controls necessary to protect MNC interests were ensured primarily by normative mechanisms that brought about widely shared awareness of overall culture, values, goals and critical interdependencies. There were multiple organizing principles based upon function, product, geography and customer type but no single overriding dimension was superordinate to the rest. Each individual subsidiary brought to the overall MNC a unique collection of capabilities. Finally, subsidiary management was given a strategic role impacting on both the subsidiary and the MNC as a whole.

For the purposes of this study, the Hedlund and Bartlett and Ghoshal's studies make three important contributions. First, they further demonstrated the link between the changing external environment, corporate strategy and structure, although they did not extend the last part of the analysis to specifically examine the effects on HQ-subsidiary relations. Second, they introduced a new MNC strategy of global coordination of innovation via a process of leveraging the MNC's entire network of knowledge resources. Third, they emphasized that this new strategy had major structural implications for the MNC and HQ-subsidiary relations.

Two recent investigations specifically address the nature of this new organizational form. Both were spawned from Bartlett and Ghoshal's long stream of research giving them similarities but each has a differing perspective. Ghoshal and Bartlett (1997) had a distinct HRM orientation and an element of prescriptiveness that did not appear in Nohria and Ghoshal (1997). The latter study set up a new model of the MNC as a 'differentiated network' based upon linkages within subsidiaries, between HQ and subsidiary and between subsidiaries. They found that an MNC's ability to foster different types of innovation depends upon four factors. They were:

> the configuration of organizational assets and slack resources ... the structure of headquarters-subsidiary relationships ... socialization processes, and ... patterns of communication (Nohria and Ghoshal, 1997: 43).

While these studies were only the first steps to an understanding of this new organizational form, a number of important characteristics establish that this was a fundamentally new organizational form. First, the importance of 'slack' and autonomy in the organization as a stimulant to the creation, adoption and diffusion of knowledge and innovations contrasted with the traditional emphasis on efficiency and tight controls. Second, the structure was radically transformed from a hierarchy in which knowledge, resources and expertise are centralized (at HQ) or localized (at a specific subsidiary) into a network where they might be located anywhere but were able, via various communications systems, to be disseminated to any other subsidiary at need. Third, both studies stressed the role of socialization processes and a shared purpose that was based upon a trust culture rather than the formal mechanisms of control. Fourth, the novelty of this new form meant that the traditional modes of analysis, strategic contingency theory and the transaction cost approach (TCA), were now less relevant and had to be supplemented with insights from other domains such as organizational learning and the resource-based view.

Organizational knowledge

In the book that was the culmination of their understanding of the transnational (heterarchic) MNC form, Ghoshal and Bartlett (1997) stated 'The individualized corporation ... links dispersed initiatives and leverages distributed expertise, embedding the resultant relationships in a continuous process of organizational learning'. This concern with knowledge and learning in organizations can be traced back to earlier decades (Argyris and Schon, 1978; Bell, 1973; Daft and Weick, 1984; Dretske, 1981; Fiol and Lyles, 1985; Polanyi, 1967; Teece, 1987). The last few years, however, have seen a large number of published works on this general topic from almost every perspective. To organize this complex literature, the following discussion is set up as a series of distinct topics namely: the explicit-tacit distinction; organizational learning; organizational memory; the resource-based approach; and path dependence. This is clearly an artificial distinction for analytical convenience since, in reality, the boundaries between knowledge management, organizational learning and other domains is often diffuse and there is considerable overlap among them.

The explicit-tacit distinction

Nahapiet and Ghoshal (1998) argued that there are two central concerns when attempting to understand knowledge and knowledge processes in organizations – types of knowledge and levels of knowledge. With regard to types of knowledge, an important distinction is frequently made between practical, experience-based knowledge and the theoretical knowledge derived from reflection on and abstract conceptualization of that experience. The former is often labeled 'know-how' or procedural knowledge and concerns well-practiced skills and routines. It is analytically distinguished from the latter 'know-what' (or 'know-that') or declarative knowledge which is concerned with facts and propositions. Polanyi (1967) was exemplifying this 'knowing how' and 'knowing what' distinction when he described knowledge as either tacit or explicit. Tacit knowledge was tacit to the degree that it was incommunicable. Winter (1987) proposed that tacitness could be conceived as a variable with the degree of tacitness a function of the extent to which the knowledge could be codified. Polanyi (1967), however, indicated that some knowledge always remains tacit. He stressed the importance of knowing and the way it was shaped by experience. The explicit-tacit distinction is clearly important, especially for considerations of individual workers. The distinction is less clear and hence less obviously useful in the context of HQ-subsidiary relations because the knowledge flows in this relationship are likely to be complex mixtures of both types.

The second issue is the extent to which it is possible to consider the idea of an organization's knowledge as being in some way different from the sum of the knowledge held by the organization's members. The question of the social vs the aggregation of individual phenomena has a worthy lineage, back to Durkheim, at least. At one end of the spectrum, Simon (1991: 176) stated 'all organizational learning takes place inside human heads; an organization learns in only two ways: (a) by the learning of its members, or (b) by ingesting new members who have knowledge the organization didn't previously have'. This view would not garner much support among modern researchers. Nelson and Winter (1982) argued that technical knowledge is an attribute of the firm as a whole, embedded to a large extent in its routines and procedures, and not reducible to what an individual knows or even to some simple aggregation of the competences and capabilities of the people and equipment. They suggested that an organization might know more than it can tell. Weick and Roberts (1993) and Brown and Duguid (1991) reported similar views. It is a debatable point whether the learning that takes place or the knowledge that resides in Nelson and Winter's routines and procedures can be considered 'inside human heads' as Simon suggested.

Spender (1996) developed a matrix of four types of knowledge based upon these two dimensions – explicit/tacit and individual/collective. Individual explicit knowledge (conscious knowledge to Spender) is comprised of facts, concepts etc that can be stored in and retrieved from repositories such as personal memory or records. Individual tacit knowledge (automatic knowledge) was found in many forms of tacit knowing such as the performance of various technical, artistic and other skills. Organizations need people with these abilities and they are often a key element of successful organization performance. Social explicit knowledge (objectified knowledge) is manifest as the shared corpus of knowledge of any specialist knowledge community – medical, philosophic, legal and so on. This tends to be the focus of many of the current attempts to share and leverage knowledge that can be seen in the business community. Social tacit knowledge (collective knowledge) is the knowledge that is embedded in organizational practice. Difficult to access, it is sustained through the continual interaction of those in the organization. Frequently this knowledge is manifest only in the performance of highly trained and experienced teams. It is the essence and product of their well-oiled 'routines' (Nelson and Winter, 1982). Spender's four types of knowledge collectively constitute the intellectual capital of the organization.

These concepts highlight the heterarchic organizational form literature that focuses on issues such as organizational memory, the dynamic nature of knowledge, competences and capabilities, the path dependent character of innovation and other processes and the significance and complexity of organizational learning.

Organizational learning

The next literature of relevance to the heterarchic organization is that concerned with organizational learning. These analyses bring the unit of analysis explicitly to the level of the organization. The idea that organizations as a whole were capable of learning has sometimes been traced back to the 1930s when Wright (1936) developed learning curve theory from observations of airframe manufacture. The primary source of present understanding, however, is the behavioral theory of the firm as presented initially by Simon (1957) and March and Simon (1958). These ideas have been variously extended and developed. Levitt and March (1988) was an eclectic review of the literature to the mid-1980s. Their observations were not greatly optimistic concluding that 'it is possible to see a role for routine-based, history-dependent, target-oriented organizational learning … (but) … the design … must recognize the difficulties of the process' (Levitt and March, 1988: 338).

Since that time there has been a considerable increase in research in this field and while the domain remains disparate, some synthesizing work has begun. Miller (1996), for example, set up a preliminary typology of organizational learning and generated some testable hypotheses. As yet, however, organizational learning appears to remain a rather haphazard and eclectic notion and 'it remains unclear just what learning is, how it takes place, and when, where and how it occurs' (Miller, 1996: 485).

Until some recent developments the most important studies of organizational learning in the 1990s were Argyris and Schon (1978, 1996), Senge (1990) and Nonaka (1991, 1994). While coming at the problem with different intellectual equipment, all of these centered upon the processes whereby individual knowledge could be transformed into organizational knowledge. Argyris and Schon (1996) was an extension of their original ground-breaking work (Argyris and Schon, 1978). They suggested that organizational learning occurred when individuals or groups experienced a problematic, inquired into it, found a mismatch between actual and expected results, thought about the causes of the problem and consequently restructured activities. If these new activities were then embedded in the routines of the organization, learning had taken place. A central insight was the differentiation between what they call single loop learning – learning which changes strategies and actions but leaves values unchanged – and double loop learning which brought about value change. The other major treatise in this 'learning loops' paradigm, Senge (1990), caused a major impact in its heyday. Senge argued in this book (and its companion Senge, Roberts, Ross, Smith and Kleiner, 1994) that learning organizations continually expand their capacity to create the future. They achieved this by the use of five core disciplines. These were: (1) personal mastery – clarifying values and goals and striving towards one's highest aspirations; (2) identifying and questioning our unconscious assumptions – mental models; (3) building a shared vision; (4) mastering team learning; (5) learning to see and use the underlying systems and patterns – systems thinking (the fifth discipline of the book title). The learning loops perspective has not impressed everyone. Ross (1992: 112) described it as 'the silly world of circle babble' but, while there may be some merit in Ross's position, Senge's (1990) five disciplines, despite their florid exposition, were generally considered to have relevance for understanding learning, processes, structure and other dimensions of the MNC.

Also of concern to this study are the works of Ikujiro Nonaka (Nonaka, 1991, 1994; Nonaka and Takeuchi, 1995). He developed a model of the knowledge-creating company based upon the practices of the innovative Japanese manufacturers such as Matsushita, Canon and Honda. Nonaka and Takeuchi (1995) began with the distinction between tacit and explicit knowledge and developed a model that proposed four fundamental processes by which new knowledge was created – tacit to explicit (externalization), tacit to tacit (socialization), explicit to tacit (internalization), explicit to explicit (combination). It was proposed that a 'knowledge spiral' facilitated the interaction of these processes and amplified knowledge. Their detailed analysis substantiated Lipshitz's assertion that 'it is easy to see that analogies between individual learning and organizational learning are superficial, inasmuch as the former can be adequately described as a cognitive process, whereas the latter is essentially a process of social interaction.' (Lipshitz, 2000: 458). Gupta and Govindarajan (2000) supported this last point by arguing that there was a need to build an 'effective social ecology' (the social environment within which people operate) in order to acquire, create, share and mobilize knowledge through the corporate network. Nonaka and Takeuchi's (1995) emphasis on the social dimension was central to their analysis of organizational learning because it was in social situations that the four fundamental knowledge transformation processes (tacit to tacit – socialization; tacit to explicit – externalization; explicit to tacit – internalization; explicit to explicit – combination) that brought about organizational learning took place.

Nonaka's work has proved the most enduring to date. For Nonaka, the central players in the knowledge creation process are the middle managers that are intimately involved in the processes mentioned above. While Nonaka's studies were important, a distinctive problem lay in their provenance in that they were produced from within a

Japanese scenario. As such, they did not address the specific problems of knowledge dissemination across borders or the implications for other home countries. Nevertheless the Japanese model of Sony, Canon and so on was presumed to be operable elsewhere.

While concepts such as Argyris and Schon's (1996) double-loop learning, Senge's (1990) personal mastery or Nonaka and Takeuchi's (1995) externalization were relatively easily explained or defined, they were not orderly or straightforward processes in practice. Organizational learning remains problematic because of the difficulty of reconciling neat academic conceptualizations with messy practical realization (Lipshitz, 2000). Particularly messy in the context of the cross border transfer of learning and its enabling practices and environment.

Moran and Ghoshal (1996) argued, following Schumpeter, that all new resources, including knowledge, were created either by exchange or by combination. The view that combinations of existing knowledge are the prime stimulant of economic activity appears to have been the major starting point for current work. This combination process takes place either via incremental change and development from existing knowledge or via more radical change. While his original ideas have been somewhat commodified, in the philosophy of science Kuhn (1970) saw development as occurring by two mechanisms. Incremental change within the paradigm (normal science) was the major mode of progression and changes of paradigm were radical leaps forward that were relatively rare. Whether the process was incremental or radical, in both cases, the new knowledge was the product of novel combinations of known elements.

When the knowledge to be combined was held by different parties (as was often likely in the case of MNCs), exchange was a necessary prerequisite for new combinations. The creation of new knowledge then required facilitation by communication mechanisms of various kinds such as scientific conferences, the Internet, or by the day-to-day interactions of shared working experience. As Penrose (1959: 53) observed 'such experience develops an increasing knowledge of the possibilities for action and the ways in which action can be taken ... by the firm. This ... also contributes to the "uniqueness" of the (productive) opportunity of each individual firm'. The relationship of this view with Conner (1991) and her resource bundle uniqueness thesis is very apparent.

Moran and Ghoshal (1996) also pointed out that the creation of new knowledge had a number of preconditions. The first of these was the existence of opportunity. Combinations and exchanges required that the knowing communities or individuals were able to come together. The conferences and technological developments mentioned above were examples of such mechanisms. They further contended that the history of science demonstrated that new combinations were often unplanned and they argued that there was a case for creating environments that allow for serendipitous, emergent processes. This has resonances in Nohria and Ghoshal's concept of 'slack' (1997) and Barney's 'luck' (1986).

The second precondition was embedded in expectancy theory. The parties involved had to expect that new knowledge would be created (Barney, 1986). They may have been uncertain of what would be produced or how but they had to proceed confident that the combination/exchange process would produce something. This anticipation of success has been argued by Hamel (1991) to be a factor in the success or otherwise of international strategic alliances.

The third precondition concerned expectations also. The parties had to be motivated to become involved on the basis that they believed the engagement would be worth their while. Szulanski (1996) in his research on the internal 'stickiness' of best practices found that, as well as 'stickiness', lack of motivation also inhibited their transfer. Szulanski also found that a much more important barrier was the lack of capacity to assimilate and apply the new knowledge. Cohen and Levinthal (1990) labeled this fourth precondition the recipient's 'absorptive capacity'. It was essentially the ability of the organization to recognize the value of the new knowledge and to assimilate it. This depended crucially upon the existence of related prior knowledge and Cohen and Levinthal argued that the capacity to absorb knowledge resided in a mosaic of individual and group capabilities.

As a final point, if a firm or, in particular, a subsidiary was to innovate, it had to somehow generate new knowledge. The subsidiary was unable to generate new knowledge from any domain whatsoever. It must develop new knowledge from the starting point of its current knowledge and resources bundle. Hence it was clear that the direction of future learning trajectories would be strongly influenced by its current knowledge and resources endowments. There would undoubtedly be strong path dependencies in the organizational learning process.

In summary, the major insights from this literature are that organizational learning and the generation of new knowledge required substantial groundwork by the MNC. It needed to develop a learning and knowledge management regime and supportive culture that offered opportunity and positive expectations, as well as systems that enabled storing, accessing, combining, exchanging and sharing of knowledge.

Organizational memory

An important aspect of organizational knowledge and organizational learning is the notion of organizational memory, since it is in this memory that organizational knowledge is stored. As Ackerman and Halverson (2000) argued, it is intuitively entirely reasonable to expect that an organization should be able to store and retrieve traces of information and knowledge of its past activities and, on the basis of this belief, the term organizational memory has passed into common business parlance. This is in line with Ackerman's (1994) catchy, but less than complete, definition: 'Organizational memory is organizational knowledge with persistence'.

Despite the increasing use and general familiarity of the term, Walsh and Ungson (1991) stated 'it is not clear that we have understood the concept or its implications for the management of organizations ... a myriad of unexamined conjectures has defined (organizational memory)' (Walsh and Ungson, 1991: 84–85). Walsh and Ungson (1991) went on to perform a valuable task in examining the history of the concept, producing a definition, and detailing its structural, content and process attributes. Their definition was 'stored information from an organization's history that can be brought to bear on present decisions' (Walsh and Ungson, 1991: 61). Walsh and Ungson added substantially to the analysis by proposing that there were three key elements for understanding organizational memory: the structure of the retention facility; the information contained in that facility; and the processes of acquisition, storage and retrieval. These three elements are central to the following analysis.

It is possible to distinguish three uses of the term organizational memory from the literature. Each type of organizational memory distinguished has a particular retention facility, each contains distinctive information or knowledge and each encompasses particular processes of acquisition, storage and retrieval.

In the first use of the term, organizational memory conveys what Bartlett and Ghoshal (1989) termed 'administrative heritage', what Spender (1996) described as social tacit knowledge (or collective knowledge) and what David (1994) was encapsulating by describing 'institutions as the carriers of history'. All of these perspectives are concerned with the 'role of historical experience in forming mutually consistent expectations that permit coordination of individual agent's behaviors without centralized direction' (David, 1994: 205). The storage facility for this type of organizational memory is the corporate culture that is embedded in the thoughts and actions of individuals and groups – the 'common knowledge' or 'organizational code' (David, 1994: 209 and 213) that suffuses the organization and enables coordination and the mutual understanding of expectations. For example, this common knowledge brings about the shared norms of performance and shared philosophy of management that are central to Baliga and Jaeger's (1984) analysis of control systems that is examined in Chapter 9. The information or knowledge found in this form of organizational memory is derived from the influence of factors such as the founder's values and the embedded procedures, policies or conventions that have arisen as the result of contingent solutions to historically earlier problems. As a consequence, change and the input of new knowledge into this form of organizational memory and subsequent modification of the corporate culture is a slow process. Arrow (1974: 56) stated 'Since the code is part of ... the organization's capital ... [it] will be modified only slowly over time'. As this type of knowledge is stored in conventional ways of thinking and behaving, its retrieval is generally automatic and unconscious, although it may be made manifest (externalized – Nonaka and Takeuchi, 1995) in various forms such as induction course presentations and mission statements.

The second type of organizational memory contains what Nelson and Winter (1982) termed the organization's technical knowledge. It is the knowledge embedded in the organization's routines and procedures, exemplified by the activities of well-trained and experienced teams. This knowledge is partly explicit and partly tacit in nature and the organization acquires more when new procedures are developed and formalized (consistent with Argyris and Schon's single loop learning) or when individuals develop new work experience and 'learn by doing'. The storage mechanism for this memory is partly in the written manuals and operating procedures but, more importantly, in the competences and skills of the workforce. If this knowledge is to be retrieved by an individual, the explicit knowledge may lie in the manuals but the tacit element must be learned from experienced co-workers.

A third type of organizational memory is the set of consciously designed and installed systems, instituted to more efficiently access the types of knowledge described above. This memory may contain all types of tacit or explicit knowledge that has been acquired by organization members in the course of their experiences. It may be stored in the form of project reports, standard operating procedures, data compilations or individual experience of past tasks or ways of doing things. It can be retrieved via hard copy reference manuals, IT databases or interpersonal contacts.

While the three types are analytically separable, in any given organization, they are intricately interlinked and often mutually supportive. The 'routines' that have developed in any organization will undoubtedly have been influenced by that organization's conventions and codes. In addition, when any individual accesses the organization memory system, the knowledge they obtain will be influenced by the database or the interpersonal source they select or to which they are directed. There is also a clear link here between organizational memory and bounded rationality given that the acquisition, storage and retrieval of knowledge involves individuals.

The broad purpose of knowledge management, as conceived in this research, is to access the organizational knowledge stored in these types of organizational memories in order to develop the organization's capabilities, and generate innovations, thus creating and sustaining the firm's competences and competitive advantage. In the heterarchic/transnational MNC, the knowledge repositories may reside anywhere among the subsidiaries within the corporate network.

Part of the empirical work in this investigation is concerned with various structured systems, consciously installed by firms, to collect, store and retrieve organizational knowledge that has been accumulated over time. The process is simple in principle but intricate in practice. The techniques are used to enable organizations to generate products and processes but these innovations are powerfully influenced by embedded values about what are appropriate products for the firm and how things should be done. The organization's capabilities are dynamic but the paths that are available for development are constrained by the nature of the knowledge that is already embedded in the organizational memory. Path dependence is again an issue.

The resource-based view

Introduction

The central tenet of the RBV is that a firm's competitive position and advantage in an industry is defined by its unique bundle of resources and most recent conceptions see knowledge as the firm's primary resource. The Resource-Based View (RBV) has been posited to allow a firm to obtain a competitive advantage at least partially independent of its competitive environment (Mehra, 1996). Thus, emphasis has moved away from the idea that the industry in which a firm competes is the primary determinant of a firm's profit potential and sustained competitive advantage (Porter, 1980; Barney, 1997). Stemming from Wernerfelt's (1984) influential article, this perspective is becoming increasingly well developed (see for example, Barney, 2001; Grant, 1996; Kogut and Zander, 1992, 1993, 1996; Mahoney, 2001).

Drawing on the notion that the key characteristic of a firm is that it consists of unique bundles of tangible and intangible resources (Collis and Montgomery, 1995; Peteraf, 1993), firms with superior systems and structures, firm specific assets and capabilities, as well as the existence of isolating mechanisms, will be capable of gaining efficiencies in firm performance and entrepreneurial rents (Black and Boal, 1994; Teece, Pisano and Shuen, 1997). These characteristics center on the key issues of resource heterogeneity (Barney, 1991), the uniqueness of resource bundles (Conner, 1991), resource immobility (Dierickx and Cool, 1989; Szulanski, 1996), dynamic capabilities (Teece, Pisano and Shuen, 1997) and firm boundaries (Teece, Rumelt, Dosi and Winter, 1994).

An accumulation of unique resources will impede current and potential competitors from quickly replicating the firm's resource base. However, superior earnings and a competitive advantage will only be achieved once the firm's resources satisfy a number of criteria, the most important of which are value, inimitability and causal ambiguity (Foss and Knudsen, 2003). These resources must be scarce, appropriable and specialized, allowing a firm to adjust itself to potential opportunities and threats presented by its competitive environment (Amit and Schoemaker, 1993). Furthermore, these resources must have no equivalent substitutes (Barney, 1991; Peteraf, 1993).

'A resource-based approach views a firm's performance as resulting from the simultaneous interaction of at least three forces: the firm's own asset base, the asset bases of competitors and constraints emanating from the broader industry and public policy environment' (Conner 1991: 145). This suggests that resources be defined relative to the industry, customers and competition, as the value of resources is ultimately determined by the interaction of these factors. To be able to take full advantage of the opportunities presented by the external environment, a firm must place particular emphasis on fully exploiting its current resources and developing new capabilities that are able to keep a firm in harmony with its environment (Wernerfelt, 1984). This argument sees the RBV as being driven by the broad themes of strategic contingency theory.

Resources are viewed as a broad classification encompassing all of the firm's valuable attributes, including assets and skills. Tangible resources are easily identifiable and capable of being quantified and evaluated (Grant, 1996; Collis and Mongomery, 1995). In principle, the RBV focuses on the importance of *all* resources in allowing a company to achieve superior performance (Hunt and Morgan, 1996; Peteraf, 1993). However, most recent works have emphasized the importance of intangible resources for superior performance (Itami and Roehl, 1987; Hall, 1993; Hunt and Morgan, 1996). Intangibles must be built, using a number of resources simultaneously (Teece et al., 1997; Collis and Montgomery, 1995), illustrating the importance of resource bundles. Unlike tangibles that wear away over time and depreciate in value, intangibles often improve with use (Itami and Roehl, 1987; Grant, 1991; Collis and Montgomery, 1995).

Intangible resources are 'non-physical assets' (Sanchez, Heene and Thomas, 1996: 7) and include knowledge of processes (Hall, 1993). Some have classified intangibles as being either assets or capabilities (Amit and Schoemaker, 1993). Whilst assets can be transformed into products and services, capabilities are the firm's ability to deploy these resources to reach a desired outcome (Teece, 1998; Collis and Montgomery, 1995).

Thus the resource-based view of the firm is grounded in the belief that sustained competitive advantage derives from having a dynamic, continuously developing configuration of resources and assets that bring about the desired stream of new products and innovations. In this sense it is clearly linked to the internalization of know-how perspective of the market failure approach. It is also clearly akin to the heterarchic/transnational standpoint. Bartlett and Ghoshal (1989: 57), for example, stated that the transnational has 'the ability to develop and exploit knowledge on a worldwide basis'. Several aspects of this approach illuminate the heterarchic form and its effects upon the HQ-subsidiary relationship.

Change over time

First, it has been argued that the firm specific advantage(s) that combines with location advantages to bring economic returns to the MNC is not eternal. Over time this competitive advantage is likely to erode in some way due to the nature of the initial advantage, the activities of other firms in the market place, demographic changes, input scarcity, product saturation or a host of other factors (Ghoshal and Westney, 1993; Kogut, 1983; Dunning, 1988). Headquarters might respond with various strategies and tactics such as R&D programs, marketing initiatives, moves to new or more locations (Chandler's geographic diversification) to further exploit and renew existing advantages. Or, as the subsidiaries developed useful capabilities of their own, HQ could, in its search for innovativeness, tap into, coordinate and leverage these subsidiary resources and competencies that lay within the MNCs global network. By following the latter course, HQ concedes not just some local autonomy of decision-making, as in the case of the multidomestic MNC, but a significant strategic role in the overall corporation.

If a firm has been successful, then the bundles of resources, capabilities and routines that had evolved over time were necessarily sufficient for that success. However, when the context changed, these bundles often restricted further growth (see Leonard-Barton, 1992) giving rise to the imperative for innovation. New bundles needed to be constructed to deal with the changes in the environment. In many cases, MNCs needed to encourage autonomy throughout the network to advance innovation. This brought the risk of opportunism by affiliates. Such a situation clearly generated issues of trust and organizational commitment. The costs of engineering the necessary trust were the costs of aligning the goals of subsidiary management with those of the MNC. Buckley and Casson (1998) suggested that the costs were those of flattening the corporation and opening up horizontal and vertical communication channels. This process increased knowledge flows and gave visibility to procedures. In doing so, it emphasized the role of due process and procedural justice issues that Kim and Mauborgne (1988, 1991, 1993a, 1993b) and Taggart (1997a) suggested led to voluntary cooperation and altruistic knowledge sharing.

Peteraf's RBV-TCA link

The second point is taken from a model of competitive advantage proposed by Peteraf (1993). The model that will be developed later proposes that the type of strategy developed to generate advantage was the determinant of the HQ-subsidiary relationship and of the underlying hierarchical or heterarchical structural form of the MNC. Peteraf's model paralleled this argument because it demonstrated axiomatically that advantage could be analytically derived via resource-based theories of the firm, while at the same time showing that advantage could also be drawn from the market failure analyses discussed earlier.

Peteraf's model (1993) is clearly linked to the general resource-based theoretical literature (see, for example, Barney, 1991; Conner, 1991; Dierickx and Cool, 1989; Dosi, Teece and Winter, 1992; Teece et al., 1994; Teece et al., 1997). It was deceptively simple and parsimonious (see Figure 3.2). She hypothesized that competitive advantage arrived and was sustained if four environmental conditions were met. These conditions were as follows: (1) heterogeneity of resource bundles and capabilities between firms. These ensured that firms with superior resources would earn rents; (2) *ex post* limits to competition. These ensured that after a superior position was attained the rents were sustained; (3) imperfect resource mobility (or 'stickiness' as in Szulanski, 1996). This ensured that the rents were bound to the firm and shared by it; (4) *ex ante* limits to competition was a situation in which prior to a firm establishing a superior position, there was limited competition for that position. In effect this prevented the costs of establishing the position from offsetting the rents obtained.

The model is important for two reasons. First, it is a synthesized resource-based approach providing an important bridge between resources, information and market imperfections approaches to the firm. Conditions (1) and (3) are fundamental premises of the resource-based view, conditions (2), (3) and (4) are clear examples of market imperfections and condition (1) also underpins the Hymer (1976) and Johnson (1970) conceptualizations of the MNC. Second, it demonstrated that

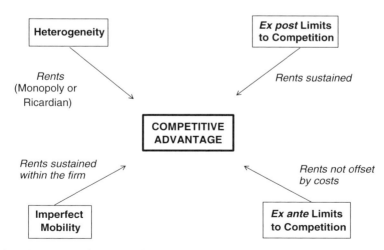

Figure 3.2   Peteraf's model of competitive advantage

advantage can arise and be sustained (at least over the short term) in several different ways.

Kogut and Zander (1993) argued that the knowledge-based approach arose particularly to question a prevailing assumption that firms exist to internalize markets. They stated that 'the prime casualty of this (knowledge-based) view is the belief that the boundaries of the firm can be explained only by the creation of governance mechanisms to curb the opportunism of individuals' (Kogut and Zander, 1993: 626). Their argument is easily extended to apply to the creation of departments in the U-form or divisions in the M-form or subsidiaries in the MNC. Nevertheless, as Barney (1996) pointed out in his exordium to a dialogue on the relative merits of knowledge-based and transaction cost-based theories of the firm (this debate appeared in various issues of *Organization Science* Volume 7 during 1996), newly proposed theories not only have to explain the existence of firms but must also explain why new theories themselves are needed. The internalization approach had several variants. While Williamson (1975) focused on the failure of intermediate product markets, others emphasized the failure of markets for knowledge (Johnson, 1970; Hymer, 1976; Hennart, 1982; Buckley and Casson, 1976). The overall view was, however, well embedded in the literature and it was to be expected that any alternative theory would be contentious. It is perhaps unsurprising that Kogut and Zander described the review process of their 1993 (Kogut and Zander, 1993) article for the *Journal of International Business Studies* as 'raucous' (Kogut and Zander, 1995: 419). Kogut is probably the leading protagonist in this cross-examination of current theory and the following is a partial summary of his overall position:

the design of the governance mechanism is not equivalent to the capabilities of the firm and what individuals know how to do. Cooperation within an organization leads to a set of capabilities that are easier to transfer within the firm than across organizations and constitute the ownership advantage of the firm (Kogut and Zander, 1993: 627).

It was differential capabilities derived from varying internal organizing principles that gave one firm the advantage over another and the key resource to be organized is knowledge.

Two notions touched upon earlier were introduced in the process. First, Kogut and Zander (1993) made specific reference to tacit knowledge. This is knowledge that was difficult or even impossible to codify and hence was impracticable to transfer via market mechanisms. Second, they stressed not just the transfer but also the recombination of knowledge. There were clear links here with Buckley and Casson's (1998) propositions as well as Hennart (1982) who argued that through repeated interactions individuals and groups in firms develop a common understanding, embedded capabilities, by which to transfer knowledge. It was the firm's efficiency in this respect, relative to other firms, that determined the firm's competitive advantage as well as the firm boundary (Teece et al., 1994). The rules, documentation, procedures and manuals that permeate the firm were its mechanisms to reduce the tacitness of the key organizational knowledge.

Moran and Ghoshal (1996) shifted perspective by pointing out that the approach brought a shift in focus from value appropriation (Casson, 1995; Hennart 1982) to one of value creation. They labeled this ability to create and share knowledge as 'the organizational advantage'. Nahapiet and Ghoshal (1998) argued that the particular capabilities that generated this advantage derived from a number of factors, many of which were touched upon earlier in this review. They included:

> the special facility organizations have for the creation and transfer of tacit knowledge (Kogut and Zander, 1993, 1996; Nonaka and Takeuchi, 1995; Spender, 1996); the organizing principles by which individual and functional expertise are structured, coordinated, and communicated, and through which individuals cooperate (Conner and Prahalad, 1996; Kogut and Zander, 1992; Zander and Kogut, 1995); and the nature of organizations as social communities (Kogut and Zander, 1992, 1996) (Nahapiet and Ghoshal, 1998: 243).

Finally, Kogut and Zander (1993) concluded by stating:

> The sequential expansion of a firm's activities after the first entry into a country is an expression of the evolutionary acquisition and recombination of knowledge. In its more advanced evolution, this process alters the global knowledge of the firm and may result in its transformation towards a network of subsidiaries characterized by the cross-border transfer of learning .... Firms compete on the basis of the superiority of their information and know-how and their abilities to develop new knowledge by experiential learning (Kogut and Zander, 1993: 640).

Recently, occasional attempts have been made to reconcile the TCA and RBV approaches. Combs and Ketchen (1999) argued that in many instances both perspectives agreed on likely managerial actions but when deciding whether or not to engage in interfirm cooperation, resource based concerns were foremost. Even Williamson (1999) made an equivocal move in this direction by challenging the competence perspective to 'apply itself more assiduously to operationalization' (Williamson, 1999: 1087).

Summary

This chapter has presented a detailed analysis of many manifestations of knowledge in organizations because asymmetries in the organization's knowledge are the central concept in understanding the HQ-subsidiary relationship in the MNC. There are several aspects to this assertion.

First, following the Hymer, Johnson, Hennart et al. variant of the transaction cost approach, it was the failure of the market for knowledge in the international context, that led to the rise of the MNC via the internalization of the firm specific advantage. However, while understanding the centrality of knowledge, this perspective took the existence of the knowledge-based advantage as given. It made no suggestions as to how this advantage arose. One of the contributions of the resource-based approach has been to begin the task of illuminating how knowledge advantages are created, sustained and renewed in the first place.

Second, the move towards the heterarchic organizational form evidenced in some MNCs, in conjunction with the globally innovative transnational strategy, is prefaced upon facilitating and leveraging the knowledge resources of the organization. Again, the resource-based approach, in conjunction with constructs such as organizational learning, organizational memory and path dependence, has been the prime source of illumination.

Third, the several strategies of the MNC used to achieve competitive advantage in the marketplace bring about knowledge asymmetries between HQ and the subsidiary. An understanding of these asymmetries is necessary to comprehend issues of subsidiary autonomy and the types of control mechanisms instituted by HQ. Theoretically, the transaction cost approach suggests that this monitoring and control of subsidiary activities is best understood in terms of the potential for opportunistic behavior intrinsic to the HQ-subsidiary relationship. In addition, many aspects of organizational knowledge are brought into play in these asymmetries. These generally focus upon the interplay between HQ and subsidiary regarding the knowledge embedded in the FSA, the knowledge the subsidiary has of the host environment and the knowledge flows that arise from the need for innovation.

Overall, these developments can be summarized as having shifted the focus of theoretical concern from the hierarchy and command and control to the heterarchy and the learning and innovating organization.

4
Subsidiary Tasks

The literatures examined in the previous two chapters have centered upon understanding the development of MNC strategies and their theoretical underpinnings. However, particular tasks for the subsidiaries are implied in each of the MNC strategies and subsequent organizational designs considered. The subsidiary task question is important and there have been a number of attempts to model this construct directly. The major studies in the literature consist of six classifications of subsidiary task and two attempted syntheses but see, for example, Birkinshaw and Hood (1998) for several others. It is evident that the studies that generated the six classifications could generally be placed within the contingency perspective but, for the most part, the authors did not give any of them a specific theoretical grounding. They were based upon either an analysis of a particular business context or derived from the use of one of several conceptual frameworks such as the Integration-Responsiveness (I-R) grid.

The first two of the six classifications – the studies of D'Cruz (1986) and White and Poynter (1984) – were extracted from the Canadian government policy context of the early 1980s. Both were contingent in nature, viewing subsidiary task as a product of HQ's perception of the most effective response to external forces in the business environment. The third, Jarillo and Martinez (1990), was a direct extension of Prahalad and Doz's I-R grid (Prahalad and Doz, 1987), using that framework to examine subsidiary task on the basis of formal and informal control and coordination mechanisms. The fourth analysis, Bartlett and Ghoshal (1986), also stemmed from the I-R grid but they utilized both capabilities and contingency themes to construct a framework on the basis of subsidiary competence and host market importance. Gupta and Govindarajan's (1991) fifth classification was constructed from an analysis of knowledge flows in and out of the sub-sidiary and hence was buttressed by the resource-based approach. The sixth study, Taggart (1997a), extended Jarillo and Martinez's control/coordination framework by using Kim and Mauborgne's (1993a) procedural justice construct.

In addition to the six studies above, a further two, Birkinshaw and Morrison (1995) and Hoffman (1994), were attempts to produce frame-works that encompassed all subsidiary task types. All eight investiga-tions will be scrutinized in turn in the following review.

Task classifications

Two classifications from the Canadian context

As Taggart (1997a) pointed out, much of the impetus for research on subsidiary task appears to have developed in smaller economies, espe-cially those subject to the influence of substantial foreign ownership. The first significant modeling attempts appeared in the middle of the 1980s and were Canadian in origin. This Canadian concern for sub-sidiary task was driven by policy requirements to adapt to the expected dramatic lowering of tariff barriers generated by the forthcoming General Agreement on Tariffs and Trade (GATT) round in Tokyo. In 1981, 59 per cent of output from the medium and large firm sector of the Canadian economy was accounted for by foreign-controlled (mostly US) subsidiaries. These subsidiaries were usually under interna-tional minimum efficient scale and heavily protected by tariffs. Academic work was primarily aimed at offering proactive policy options to the Provincial and Federal governments. In the process, D'Cruz (1986) and White and Poynter (1984) produced classifications of subsidiary task. These frameworks were constructed using data col-lected from interviews with subsidiary managers.

D'Cruz (1986) reported a subsidiary mission grid drawn from the strategic planning system of a subsidiary that had been in Canada since the late 19th century. While having commonalities with Vernon's (1966) product cycle model, D'Cruz's growth stages perspect-ive focused solely upon developments in the host country. The dimen-sions of the model were the subsidiary's decision-making autonomy (high vs low) and its extent of market involvement (Canada vs North America vs World). The model proposed that MNC development in Canada had begun by importing and the setting up of a simple sales office subsidiary. Price and non-price competition was countered by the development of a satellite firm that assembled lower tariff rated components, provided a local service business or, the most common development in Canada, acted as a branch plant. As the focus on the world market grew, the move could then be made to function as a globally rationalized producer or to a full world product mandate. The value of this model to subsidiary managers was the presentation of a range of proactive mechanisms to develop the subsidiary's task and position in the corporate network. More generally, the subsidiary mission grid highlighted a number of issues. First, it suggested a range of available task options and grounded these in case study evidence. Second, it called attention to subsidiary autonomy as a key variable. Third, it emphasized the value of the subsidiary perspective in considering analytical or policy issues. On the deficit side, D'Cruz's schema was primarily manufacturing-oriented, distinctly ethnocentric (although possibly of more general applicability) and the taxonomy, while logical, lacked a theoretical grounding.

White and Poynter's (1984) much-quoted article grew from the same policy milieu as D'Cruz (1986) and like D'Cruz they used market scope, as one dimension in their model. However, by installing product scope and value-added scope on the second dimension, they were able to generate a more detailed inventory of subsidiary tasks. White and Poynter's marketing satellite, rationalized manufacturer and product specialist are familiar from D'Cruz (1986) but the delineation of three types of miniature replica – adopter, adapter, innovator – was a useful reflection of reality if somewhat difficult to discriminate in practice. Further, their strategic independent category was distinctive since no other categorization finds a place for these types of subsidiaries so typical of conglomerate MNCs. The deficiencies of the White and Poynter classification were similar to those of the D'Cruz model.

Classifications from the I-R framework

The third model (Jarillo and Martinez, 1990) was based upon an extension of the I-R grid. Jarillo and Martinez (1990) postulated an adapted version of the I-R grid using degree of integration and degree of localization as their dimensions. The study hypothesized three out of four possible classifications of subsidiary: receptive (high integration-low localization), autonomous (low integration-high localization) and active (high integration-high localization). They successfully tested the existence of the categories using a sample of 50 Spanish subsidiaries. Although they did not find any subsidiaries in the low integration-low localization quadrant, this inadequacy was later remedied by Taggart's

(1997b) study using foreign subsidiaries in the UK. The Jarillo and Martinez (1990) study had a number of important characteristics. First, it clearly linked the analysis of subsidiary tasks to the mainstream MNC process literature and demonstrated the value of integration and autonomy as analytical variables. Second, it identified the active subsidiary as occupying an important node in the MNC network. The framework did not, however, present a very discriminating catalogue of subsidiary tasks. The receptive classification, for example, would certainly include marketing outlets as well as globally integrated subsidiaries in both vertically and horizontally structured MNCs. Theoretically, the model was clearly grounded in the strategic contingency approach that has at its core the concept of 'fit' between environment, strategy and structure.

The global strategy literature (exemplified by Prahalad and Doz, 1987, and Bartlett and Ghoshal, 1989) has usually employed a Head Office perspective and taken as its unit of analysis the overall MNC, in contrast to the subsidiary focus of the three studies above. Nevertheless, the next subsidiary task model (Bartlett and Ghoshal, 1986) was also logically derived from the I-R perspective. In this study the role of the subsidiary was seen from the standpoint of the MNC's attempts to deal with the simultaneous and often conflicting pressures for global integration and local responsiveness. The material for much of Bartlett and Ghoshal's work of the 1980s and 1990s had been obtained from detailed case study of a relatively small number of large MNCs. By the mid-1980s, Bartlett and Ghoshal (1986) claimed to have verified the existence of differentiated subsidiary roles. They mapped subsidiary role on the basis of the competence of the local organization and the strategic importance of the local environment. This produced four roles. The strategic leader was high on both dimensions and they saw this subsidiary acting as a partner to HQ. A strategic leader was clearly capable of taking the active subsidiary role envisaged by Jarillo and Martinez (1990). The contributor had a distinctive capability but acted in a minor market. It had to be encouraged to contribute its capability for the benefit of the entire MNC, rather than remain locally focused. The implementer was low on both dimensions but had just enough competence to maintain its local operation. This type of subsidiary delivered the company's value-added. The black hole subsidiary had a position in an important market but lacked the competence to deliver much of value. The task here was to manage its transformation to strategic leader status.

The two dimensions of the Bartlett and Ghoshal (1986) model have implications for understanding what forces drive subsidiary task. First, the level of competence that the subsidiary brings to its task clearly had implications for its relationship with HQ. Low local competence implied a dependence upon HQ for technology, finance or other resources. If the local organization was particularly competent then dependence might be replaced by autonomy and HQ could be required to handle the relationship in a more subtle manner. The formal controls probably used for the implementer might give way to socialization and normative integration mechanisms for the contributor and strategic leader. Second, a market could be strategically important for a number of reasons. It could be a competitor's home market, it could be technologically advanced or it might simply be large enough to warrant special attention. Whichever was the case, it was important that the subsidiary had first, the competence and, second, the freedom to respond quickly to market signals. Autonomy was once again an issue.

Knowledge flows

In the fifth model, Gupta and Govindarajan (1991) introduced a fresh perspective on subsidiary task. Extending the basic ideas of Egelhoff's (1982) information-processing approach, they conceived the MNC as a network of information or knowledge transactions with the magnitude and direction of transactions varying depending upon the subsidiary's strategic context. Their framework proposed that high and low values of outflows and inflows of knowledge between the subsidiary and the rest of the MNC would discriminate between subsidiary tasks. Low flows in either direction predicted the existence of a local innovator in which innovation autonomy and idiosyncratic knowledge had resulted in a high degree of independent action. The global innovator was charged with innovating on behalf of the rest of the MNC. The role could be limited to specialist functions or areas or it might encompass the entire R&D function. In either case, there were relatively high outflows to and low inflows from the remainder of the network. The integrated player also implied a responsibility for creating knowledge but it did not have self-sufficiency in its own needs and, consequently, inflows and outflows were both high. Low outflows and high inflows produced the implementer classification that has appeared in some of the other studies.

Several points arose from Gupta and Govindarajan's study that might have relevance to the present research. First, the study was set up from a purely subsidiary perspective. Second, the munificence of transactions between units was clearly directly related to the interdependencies within and degree of integration of the MNC. Third, inflows and outflows of knowledge from the rest of the corporation had obvious implications for the understanding of the subsidiary's level of decision-making autonomy.

Procedural justice

Finally, a study by Taggart (1997a) used subsidiary autonomy as one dimension of a framework and, building upon the insights of Kim and Mauborgne (1988, 1991, 1993a,b), utilized the concept of procedural justice as the other dimension. Simply expressed, procedural justice can be understood as a measure of fairness of treatment across subsidiaries. It was measured by asking subsidiary managers questions such as the extent of effective communications between HQ and subsidiary, the extent to which the subsidiary could challenge HQ decisions, the degree of HQ sensitivity to the subsidiary's local situation and the uniformity of decision-making across subsidiaries.

Kim and Mauborgne (1993a) demonstrated that procedural justice enhanced subsidiary management's compliance with HQ strategic decisions. As such, procedural justice can be understood as an explicit or implicit attribute of the normative integration process. Taggart (1997a) hypothesized and found four types of subsidiary task. The partner subsidiary had high autonomy and high procedural justice, the militant had high autonomy and low procedural justice, the collaborator was low autonomy/high procedural justice and the vassal subsidiary was low on both dimensions. This was not the end of the story, however. Taggart (1997a) summarized the empirical characteristics found in his four types. From this summary, it appeared that high and low levels of procedural justice could occur with either high or low levels of integration. In this study, integration was calculated using Kobrin's (1991) measure that centred upon the degree of integration of the manufacturing value chain. Integration might have several meanings in these contexts and it was evident that there was little congruence between the formulation of integration as expressed by Taggart and Kobrin and the normative integration construct that encapsulated procedural justice. A further finding of note was the indirect proportionality between autonomy and the Taggart and Kobrin integration formulation. High Taggart and Kobrin integration was consistently coupled with low autonomy and vice versa. Since the sample was comprised entirely of manufacturing MNCs this was not unexpected. The greater the degree of intermediate and final product flows between units the less scope each unit had for individual action. Taggart did not link the analysis to MNC home country or Bartlett and Ghoshal's MNC types but he did mention the possibility of a host country/national culture effect, commenting that this would limit the generalizability of the results. The present study has a single host country and this comment must be considered when its results are analyzed.

Attempted syntheses

Two attempts have been made to encapsulate the existing range of subsidiary types. Birkinshaw and Morrison (1995) examined the existing literature and induced a three-part classification – local implementer, specialized contributor and world mandate. They acknowledged several significant limitations. First, each of their categories required the collapsing of several tasks into one with considerable loss of discrimination, such as placing the 'pure implementers' with the 'local adapters'. Second, they were unable to classify some roles. They conceded that Barlett and Ghoshal's (1986) 'black hole' type (low competence in a strategically important market) was difficult to incorporate into their model. Although, in their defense, this role was hardly a subsidiary task and would be difficult to incorporate into any model. There were also several strategically-oriented roles hypothesized in other studies that sat uncomfortably in the Birkinshaw and Morrison (1995) classification or were left out altogether. Finally, the manufacturing orientation prevented the overt inclusion of any distribution or marketing type roles, such as White and Poynter's (1984) marketing satellite. At best, Birkinshaw and Morrison's classification was incomplete.

Hoffman (1994) developed a three factor contingency model. These dichotomous factors were global vs. multidomestic MNC strategy, few vs. many subsidiary capabilities and constrained vs. accommodating local environment. This produced eight generic strategies for subsidiaries and examples were presented. The model had a number of limitations. First, while the model was derived from the extant literature, it lacked a specific theoretical grounding. Second, it was designed solely on the basis of an analysis of global and multidomestic MNC strategies. Third, the model was not validated in any empirical manner (other than by typical cases) and, importantly, no suggestions were made as to how measures of each dimension might be operationalized.

Discussion

As we have seen there have been several previous attempts to classify subsidiaries on the basis of subsidiary task. Most studies lacked a tightly-argued theoretical derivation but as a research field they high-lighted the importance of the MNC strategy-subsidiary task link. Overall, these studies produced a considerable assortment of subsidiary categories but each study generated a limited number and its applicability was restricted by contextual factors such as conceptual focus, range of industries, timeframe, MNC type and home and host country. It is likely that a particular perspective may be well suited to a particular research question or business issue but the centrality of the HQ-subsidiary tie and the consequences for issues of control and autonomy argue for the usefulness of a more general framework.

All of these studies that classify subsidiaries 'categorize phenomena into mutually exclusive and exhaustive sets … (on the basis of) … a series of discrete decision rules' (Doty and Glick, 1994: 232). The variability in context and analytical focus has resulted in a wide assortment of decision criteria being used in developing sets of subsidiaries: extent of market involvement (Canada/North America/World) vs subsidiary autonomy (D'Cruz, 1986); market scope vs product scope and value-added scope (White and Poynter, 1984); subsidiary competence vs strategic importance of the local environment (Bartlett and Ghoshal, 1986); inflow and outflow of subsidiary knowledge (Gupta and Govindarajan, 1991); integration vs localization (Jarillo and Martinez, 1990; Taggart, 1997b); procedural justice vs subsidiary autonomy (Taggart, 1997a); and MNC strategy type vs subsidiary capabilities vs level of accommodation in the local environment (Hoffman, 1994). They were usually presented as 2×2 or other matrices and the variability ensured that there was little consensus on the categories derived. The issue of the extent to which classifications such as these might be acceptable as theory has been debated (Scott, 1998; Bacharach, 1989; Doty and Glick, 1994) but the examples above were clearly classification schemes or taxonomies in the sense proposed by Doty and Glick (1994). They assigned subsidiaries to groups on the basis of high and low levels of the decision criteria. Having done so, the studies then took one of several routes. Some provided descriptions of their categorizations but did not supply the statement of a relationship between constructs or variables that constitutes theory (White and Poynter, 1984; D'Cruz, 1986; Bartlett and Ghoshal, 1986; Hoffman, 1994). Others empirically examined the classifications to assess the extent to which the types existed in reality and thus confirmed their status as classification schemes only (Jarillo and Martinez, 1990; Taggart, 1997a, b). Only Gupta and Govindarajan (1991) use their analysis to derive research hypotheses. They hypothesized associations between their four subsidiary type and various control mechanisms. Their study was a major step forward but the hypotheses were derived from what was, in the final analysis, an essentially ad hoc classification of types and the study was restricted by their 'decision to focus only on knowledge flow patterns' (Gupta and Govindarajan, 1991: 772). As a result, their control implications related primarily to the innovation process.

Many of these studies have been cited widely but few have been the progenitors of further empirical investigations. A major exception is Gupta and Govindarajan (1994) that evaluated the conceptual analysis in Gupta and Govindarajan (1991). Hence, despite some effort and the importance of the issue, the prevailing models of subsidiary type are incomplete and there remains potential for a more inclusive framework.

The analysis above has suggested that any classification of subsidiary tasks ought to incorporate a number of features. First, the framework should attempt to encompass the range of subsidiary tasks derived in the research above. Second, the model should be more universal than previous models, in the sense of having wider applicability in terms of industries, home and host countries and MNC types. Third, it should be developed from a subsidiary perspective since this study is attempting to learn more about Australian subsidiaries. Fourth, it should have a strong theoretical base grounded in the MNC literature. Fifth, it should give due attention to the importance of first, subsidiary autonomy and, second, the extent to which the subsidiary is embedded within the network.

Finally, there are two further important temporal and contextual issues that affect understanding of the above review and the usefulness of any subsequent classifications. First, the time and place of a study can influence the types of subsidiaries that are to be found. For example, Taggart (1997a) in the UK was able to detect the quiescent subsidiary that had eluded Jarillo and Martinez (1990) in Spain and the Canadian policy context of the early 1980s prompted the 'world product mandate' theme of D'Cruz (1986) and White and Poynter (1984). Second, as described in these last two studies, subsidiaries go through stages of evolution, they evolve over time through a path dependent upon factors such as the local business environment, the subsidiary's resources and capabilities and the MNC/subsidiary administrative heritage. The current study and the empirical studies above are single cross-sectional snapshots through a given time and context. The phenomenon of subsidiary task, however, is dynamic. Some of the implications of the cross-sectional nature of the research will be discussed in Chapter 11.

5
A New Model of the Headquarters-subsidiary Relationship

The several literatures presented in the Chapters 2 and 3 above have not made much progress in extending their analysis to include HQ-subsidiary relations. This is because the picture has become more complex in recent times. As international competition grew, so did proliferation of strategies. The extant research was generally based upon detailed examination of relatively small numbers of firms. For example, few if any large-scale studies in this literature linked strategy with particular industries or product markets in the manner of Porter. The classifications that have emerged were therefore simply descriptive, providing labels for the outcomes of a given context. The hierarchical form and its various local and global subsidiary tasks remained unexplained and the new dimensions introduced by the arrival of the transnational/heterachy have not yet been convincingly assimilated into the previous work.

It is unsurprising that the link between strategy and structure cannot be explained by simple classifications because the crucial issue of internal structure and functioning of operations was not considered. There was no attempt to link asymmetries of knowledge and the consequent need for HQ direction with the issue, for example, of local initiative and product differentiation/focus strategies. Nor were associated policies of control or external factors such as culture considered. For the same reasons, it is also unsurprising that the various subsidiary task taxonomies were unconvincing. There is a need for a new model that integrates all the relevant issues: strategy, structure, task, control, co-ordination and knowledge.

This chapter develops an integrated model of HQ-subsidiary relationships in MNCs. The model is integrated in two senses. First, it brings together the three primary theoretical approaches reviewed earlier –

strategy-structure, transaction costs and knowledge-based approach – as they refer to this topic. Second, the HQ-subsidiary relationship is multi-facetted and the model incorporates many of these facets. The purpose of the model is to explain the development of a series of particular subsidiary tasks that arise from overall MNC strategy. These tasks are then investigated as clusters of actual firms. For each subsidiary task, the model is used to clarify the nature of the relationship between HQ and the subsidiary, on the basis of HQ-subsidiary knowledge asymmetries and flows, control mechanisms, subsidiary autonomy, knowledge management and innovation networks.

The fundamental underpinning to the model is the strategic contingency approach that allows for the influence of an array of economic change, cultural effects and other contextual factors. Within this broad approach, transaction cost analysis is adapted to a dynamic rather than a static situation. It is used to analyze circumstances of advantage generation rather than the single event of the failure of the market for knowledge. The approach provides a view of the firm that focuses on knowledge asymmetry and also explains hierarchical and heterarchical relations in the MNC. Once internalization of the FSA has occurred, a number of optional organizational designs are available to the MNC. Two major general forms have appeared to date: divisional hierarchy and heterarchy. Divisional hierarchical structures have been associated with five of the advantage generating strategies that will be proposed below. The heterarchic form is distinctive of the sixth strategy that focuses upon new products and innovation.

The chapter is organized in the following manner. First, the major studies are examined to identify the range of subsidiary tasks arising from them. Then, following Porter (1985, 1987) and Chandler (1962, 1977, 1990), the central role of the MNC's advantage-generating strategy in determining the major characteristics of the HQ-subsidiary relationship is examined. Different MNC level advantage-generating strategies bring about different subsidiary tasks. With each subsidiary task, the attendant knowledge asymmetries, autonomy, control, knowledge management and innovation implications are then explained. Finally, the overall model is presented and the some research propositions derived.

Subsidiary tasks

The first step in the conceptual logic is to demonstrate the existence of distinct subsidiary tasks. In the literature, the link between HQ strategy and subsidiary task has not generally been examined directly. Rather, scholars attempted to explain MNC strategy and structure, from which subsidiary character, and thereby the subsidiary task, may be deduced. It is possible, therefore, to identify in some of the major studies, examples of a range of subsidiary tasks. The value of these particular analyses lies in their insights into subsidiary tasks consistent with the changing form of (mostly US) MNCs as they have developed.

Chandler's (1962, 1977) did not address the MNC specifically but his work is a progenitor of many more recent studies. First, among various pre-multidivisional business structures Chandler's (1977) described the use of trusts and holding companies in various industries in the late 19th and early 20th centuries. As mechanisms for management of a federation of *independent* subsidiaries, these devices predate today's portfolio diversified conglomerates. Second, his focus upon diversification and subsequent geographical expansion will prove to be important to this analysis since, as Chandler (1962: 42) explained, 'Growth came by going overseas and ... by diversification' into new geographic areas or product markets. Multidivisional corporations grew initially via exploitation of their ownership advantage domestically but a major source of further growth was to exploit this advantage in locations of little or no competition in the international arena. In this domain, Chandler did not concern himself in detail with the nature of the subsidiary task or the HQ-subsidiary relationship but his studies indicated that the move overseas brought into existence subsidiaries that acted first as sales or distribution units (*distributors*) and then developed into affiliates that implemented the domestic innovation in the new overseas environment (*implementers*).

Closely linked to Chandler's theme, Vernon's (1966) perspective on the life cycle of MNC products proposed that they passed through a series of phases: domestic production and sale; domestic production and export; international production and sale; and, eventually, international production and re-export to the domestic market. Vernon did not analyze the subsidiary tasks that this cycle brings about but, as above, his study implied the existence of subsidiaries that distributed and coordinated output from other parts of the MNC (*distributors*) and others that were *implementers* of the domestic transformation process in the host country.

Stopford and Wells (1972) proposed that when organizational expansion was made on the basis of larger volumes of a relatively narrow line of products, the MNC tended to adopt an area divisions structure. When the expansion was based upon increasing product diversity, product divisions were implemented. In terms of subsidiary task, the importance of the Stopford and Wells model was the emphasis placed upon local responsiveness, location advantages and scale economies. Local responsiveness implied subsidiaries that generated products adapted to the unique demands of the local market (*adapters*). This adaptation might require anything from very minor modifications such as local language labeling to major alterations to conform to overseas tastes, legal constraints, religious demands, climate or some other criterion or criteria. Location advantages and scale/experience economies suggested either a subsidiary that simply implemented the domestic advantage in a foreign location (*implementer*) or a more complex configuration of a series of vertically integrated subsidiaries (*contributors* to the value chain) that combined to generate a product destined for various, possibly worldwide, markets. This analysis is an extrapolation of the Stopford and Wells perspective but it is undoubtedly compatible with Stopford and Wells' intellectual descendant, the Bartlett and Ghoshal (1989) interpretation of the I-R grid. The importance of their conceptualization for this study is that it was the first to provide a direct analytical link between the corporate and business level strategies of the MNC and the task of the subsidiary.

Bartlett and Ghoshal (1989) predicated low and high levels of two pressures, global integration and local responsiveness, to hypothesize four types of MNC strategy. They presented several examples of MNCs that have had various levels of success in implementing these strategies. First, when global integration and local responsiveness pressures were low and the firm had a FSA that was lacking in the host country, they suggested the international strategy. With this strategy a range of relatively standard products were produced and marketed locally with perhaps some minor adaptation. The subsidiary was simply an *implementer* of the firm's domestic ownership advantage. All critical functions and knowledge were kept at HQ and tight control was kept over marketing and product strategy. When pressure for local responsiveness was high and integration pressures relatively low, the multinational strategy was proposed. The implementation of this strategy required that home designed and developed product knowledge was transferred to the overseas market and product design and marketing were customized in the host country to fit local requirements. The subsidiary was an *adapter* of the HQ processes and while headquarters retained control of some key indices, knowledge of host market characteristics and of the needs of the local adaptation process was held within the subsidiary. When firms faced high pressures for global integration and low pressures for local responsiveness they should adopt a global strategy based upon location advantages and cost reduction via experience effects. The logic of this strategy was to establish primary activities in one or a small number of beneficial locations and distribute and market the standardized products worldwide. The production units were either large single units (*implementers* located at home or abroad) or vertically integrated chains of subsidiaries (*contributors*) working in combination. The vast majority of subsidiaries, however, were simply delivery pipelines for the corporate output (*distributors*). Most significant knowledge of product development, the transformation process and overall coordination of distribution and marketing was held at HQ with perhaps some of the contributing units holding unique knowledge of their particular segment of the overall process. Finally, when competitive pressures required that the firm simultaneously respond to both cost (integration) and location (responsiveness) demands, a transnational strategy was recommended. This strategy necessitated the utilization of the many important capabilities that might have been developed and implemented anywhere in the MNC. The MNC needed to ensure that the flows of advantage-generating resources and factors that brought about new products and other innovations were maintained throughout the significant units of the network of subsidiaries.

Subsidiaries in the transnational/heterarchy might have many tasks but their major contribution lay in their input to the ongoing system of product and process innovation. They were *innovators*. The major nodal subsidiaries were expected to be hubs of innovation at the local and global level despite the reality that significant knowledge might reside anywhere within the network.

Overall, these studies reveal the probable existence of six subsidiary tasks – independents, distributors, implementers, adapters, contributors and innovators – that now require a more detailed derivation.

A typology of subsidiary tasks

Conceptually grounded in the theoretical insights into strategy presented by Porter (1985, 1987), Caves (1996) and Bartlett and Ghoshal (1989), the central theme of this section is that the strategy employed by a MNC, at either the corporate or business level, imposed a particular task upon a subsidiary. While a given subsidiary may perform several tasks or a particular strategy may require some differentiation of tasks among subsidiaries, it is proposed that there are only a limited number of subsidiary tasks.

Porter (1985, 1987) argued that the multidivisional organization implemented strategy at two levels. At the corporate level, strategy concerned issues such as the type of business the firm should engage in and 'how to manage the array of units' (Porter, 1987: 47) to create advantage. The firm's three choices of corporate level strategy were vertical integration and unrelated and related diversification. Business level (generic) strategy was concerned with how to create competitive advantage at the level of the individual business. The available generic strategies were cost leadership, differentiation and focus on particular geographic, product or customer segments or niches. The focus strategy could be applied via either cost leadership or differentiation. Since competition between firms existed primarily at the business level, the term competitive strategy should properly be reserved for strategies employed at this level. In the present study, since the analysis deals with strategies employed at both levels, a more convenient term advantage-generating strategy is used when necessary.

Congruent with Porter's corporate level strategies, Caves (1996) distinguished three types of MNC. He labeled them vertical, portfolio diversified and horizontal. Since, as will be demonstrated later, the horizontal MNC might gain advantage from any of four different business level strategies, it is possible to identify six separate advantage-generating strategies, each of which leads to a particular subsidiary type.

Vertical integration

Caves' vertical MNC employed Porter's vertical integration strategy. In the archetypal form of this strategy, each subsidiary performed a single task, was simply one link, within the product or service value chain. In a MNC the production units might lie in different countries due to some important locational pressure (e.g. raw materials in one place, energy in another, markets somewhere else) or technical non-separabilities such as economies of scale. Williamson (1975) proposed that vertical integration came about because the parties adopt it in preference to the *ex ante* contracting costs and *ex post* monitoring costs that arise with arms length transacting. Thus the firm was persuaded to internalize the transactions in intermediate products so typical of this MNC form. The subsidiary congruent with this strategy is termed a value chain contributor subsidiary (for convenience, *contributor* hereafter). This brief statement oversimplifies a complex reality. Of the six subsidiary tasks that are proposed in the present study this is the most elusive in practice. Clarifying exactly what constitutes vertical integration is problematic. In the modern MNC, vertical integration elements are so deeply embedded in the global and transnational corporate forms, in particular, that they are difficult to disentangle. This is not necessarily detrimental analytically, however, since ideal types are 'theoretical abstractions' (Doty and Glick, 1994: 233).

Unrelated diversification

Diversification occurs when firms acquire or develop businesses that are either related or unrelated to current businesses within the MNC. Related diversification has generally been associated with the cost minimization, differentiation or focus strategies. Unrelated diversification, however, brings about a distinctive *modus operandi* for the MNC. When implementing this strategy, MNCs acquired firms that they considered represented a good financial investment in some way (Thompson and Strickland, 1992). This may have had either a short or long-term intent depending upon factors such as growth potential, asset value or the timing of the industry economic cycle. Any competitive advantage lay in the prospect of various short or long term economic gains and/or the minimizing of risk exposure (Caves, 1996). It was likely that the business of the acquired firm would not be well understood by HQ and all knowledge central to the transformation process was held in the subsidiary. If autonomy is considered to be the subsidiary's decision-making power in the light of the knowledge asymmetries of the HQ-subsidiary relationship then, in this case, high levels of subsidiary autonomy would be evidenced. In addition there would be considerable potential for agency problems. Head Office's solution was essentially to manage the MNC as some combination of an asset stripping, cash harvesting and/or investing portfolio. Control of this subsidiary type was likely to be primarily via the setting up of a profit center with tight financial reporting mechanisms augmented by senior subsidiary management remuneration based upon performance incentives. This is the only suitable mechanism available given the knowledge asymmetry in the HQ-subsidiary relationship. Thus Caves' portfolio diversified MNC utilized Porter's unrelated diversification strategy based upon managing the growth, harvesting and divestment opportunities of a portfolio of independent firms. Except for some strategic and financial guidance by HQ the subsidiary usually acted autonomously. Hence the archetypal subsidiary matching this strategy is the *independent*.

Related diversification

Caves' horizontal MNC is the outcome of Porter's corporate level strategy of related diversification. It is argued that with this strategy, competitive advantage arises at the business level via four possible strategies: making a first move into a new overseas market, cost leadership, differentiation and global innovation. These are all derived, either singly or in combination, from Porter's generic strategies. Four subsidiary types are produced.

First move into a market. The term first mover advantage has usually referred to the advantages derived from being the first firm to develop minimum efficient scale production units and the subsequent problems that this presents for challengers. However, as Chandler's analysis explained, a first mover advantage may also arise as a result of the overseas geographical expansion of the firm. Chandler (1990: 39) demonstrated how firms with the strongest domestic competitive advantage were the first to go abroad in order to expand market share. He argued that the desire to establish plants abroad was based upon a calculus that balanced the costs of producing in plants of optimal size at home with the costs of travel, distribution, tariffs and other regulatory measures abroad. Acting as a first mover is chronologically often the first strategy available to the expanding MNC. It is a move into a host environment where the subsidiary acts as the extractor of value from the MNC's firm specific advantages by generating products similar to those produced at HQ. While relatively competition free markets were probably more common in the early decades of the 20th century that were Chandler's concerns, they do still exist today, although it is likely that the strategy will only be evident in some specialized niches. With the move overseas the subsidiary was probably a sales office initially, facilitating export, but had some likelihood of developing into a relatively simple implementer of the MNC's technology via assembly of ckd (completely knocked down) imported subassemblies or some similar process (D'Cruz, 1986, Vernon, 1966; White and Poynter, 1984). The advantages generated by this strategy were illustrated by Urban, Carter, Gaskin and Mucha (1986) who calculated that the first entrant into a market will have a market share that is $\sqrt{n}$ times as large as the nth entrant.

In the first move into a market strategy, all the significant knowledge flows were from HQ to the subsidiary with the subsidiary's role restricted to sales and/or assembly. Knowledge of the local environment was of little concern at HQ since the MNC's basic products were unopposed in the market. The subsidiary could be expected to have minimal autonomy of action. However, since the subsidiary was merely implementing the HQ's FSA once the transformation process was running smoothly there would seem to be little requirement for extensive controls. With an organization structure that was centralized and hierarchical, it would be expected that the subsidiary would be controlled and coordinated via basic reporting and procedures manuals and the nature of any intermediate product flows. The risks from agency problems were limited since HQ's total control over significant knowledge generally precluded opportunistic behavior by the subsidiary. Thus the *implementer* subsidiary ideal type arose when geographic diversification had taken place and a domestic product or process innovation was exploited in a new overseas location (Chandler, 1990: 39).

Cost minimization. Absence of competition in a host environment rarely endures and when competition arrived the subsidiary had to regain or sustain its advantage via cost leadership or differentiation-based focus (Porter, 1985).

The advantage-generating strategy of cost minimization was based upon attaining volumes of production of standardized products that brought about economies of scale. This could be accomplished in various ways but commonly the strategy meant developing a global network of subsidiaries that produced and distributed the standard product at low cost throughout the world. Key knowledge was held at HQ and production took place at one or a few highly efficient central plants (*implementers*) or through a chain or network of locationally-advantaged plants (*contributors*). Knowledge of the local environment was important only in terms of ensuring correspondence and coordination with global marketing and distribution policies. Most overseas operations were seen as delivery pipelines distributing to a unified global market. The structure was again highly centralized and hierarchical but the global spread of operations demanded that tight central control was executed to allay possible agency problems. This combination of factors logically demanded detailed policy and procedures manuals as core control and coordination mechanisms. These manuals enforced adherence to the HQ behavioral demands that facilitated global integration. Autonomy of decision-making was likely to be negligible. While there was likely to be some manufacturing either centralized or vertically-integrated on the basis of advantaged location, by far the most numerous subsidiaries matching this competitive strategy have a task that is best described as a *distributor*.

Differentiation. The differentiation/focus strategy was accomplished by selling products that have been differentiated from other similar products to enhance their perceived value. Differentiation is accomplished by a firm 'when it provides something unique that is valuable to buyers beyond simply offering a low price' (Porter, 1985: 13). In the international arena this meant a strategy founded upon geographic market segmentation. Products were adapted variations of overall MNC products, tailored to suit local market tastes. The product was distinguished from other products on the market by focusing on the needs of particular country or region – the multidomestic strategy. It was thus the focus strategy from the Porter types with a differentiation emphasis (Porter, 1985). Knowledge of the basic FSA probably remained at HQ but the detailed knowledge of the local environment that brought much of the advantage from the strategy resided with the subsidiary. In addition, the subsidiary was likely to have developed a degree of innovation capability to enable the adaptation. There was, thus, some potential for opportunistic behavior. The subsidiary required substantial autonomy of action and trust became a major issue. Consequently, subsidiary managers were often selected from a coterie of long-serving trusted employees. The logic for this subsidiary task suggested that the primary control and coordination tool should be detailed reporting but supplemented via informal personal controls based upon close relations between managers at HQ and subsidiaries. With HQ's limited knowledge of the local aspect of total transformation process, formal procedures and manuals were not likely to be evident for design or manufacturing but might appear in other areas such as accounting, customer relations, corporate philosophy and so on. A subsidiary that was locally focused and adaptive – the *adapter* – was the archetypal associate of this strategy.

Innovation. The sixth subsidiary task is the outcome of a distinctive extension of all of the above strategies. Most firms engage in a degree of product differentiation, via new product development and innovation but, from the 1980s, according to many authors (Bartlett and Ghoshal, 1989; Birkinshaw, 1994; Casson, 1997; Hedlund, 1986; Nohria and Ghoshal, 1994, 1997), there were indications of a new organizational form appearing in MNCs. While there is room for debate as to whether it is even yet truly manifest, it was argued that this form was the result of a need for a new competitive strategy based upon a new pattern of innovation. This subset of MNCs gained particular advantage from leveraging the global knowledge resources of its entire network to generate innovations. These innovations were generated via a process of knowledge management that encompassed the entire global network of the firm. All subsidiaries that were capable contributed their knowledge to the innovation process via a vast array of inter-unit communication and knowledge management linkages.

Innovation and new products were the products of a complex interplay between all parts of the MNC. While there might be centers of innovation excellence set up these usually acted as foci for tapping the knowledge of the total network.

With this strategy, key knowledge might be found at HQ or in any subsidiary within the group. Subsidiaries required considerable autonomy of action but were also embedded in the knowledge and innovation networks of the MNC. Formal procedural and reporting controls were in evidence but the obvious agency problems that the strategy generated required attenuation via cultural controls and socialization processes. These were designed to engender commitment and motivation towards the goals and values of the overall corporation. The need to leverage all the knowledge resources of the MNC meant that the coordination demands of this strategy were intense. It was likely that these MNCs would contain well-developed mechanisms to facilitate knowledge and innovation sharing and inter-unit communications. The nature of this strategy ensured that there was no single distinctive subsidiary task. Any given subsidiary might perform any one or several of a range of tasks. They could act as suppliers to other subsidiaries, specialist foci of particular expertise, local agents or developers of group products and so on. The subsidiaries most characteristic of this strategy, however, were the relatively large, resource-rich firms that act as key nodes in the MNC network. They performed many tasks on behalf of the MNC but their key task was linked to their contribution to innovation. For the purposes of description in this research they will be labeled *innovators* to coincide with the overall strategy.

Compared to the relative simplicity of the other four hierarchical strategies, the structures and processes that are required to facilitate the heterarchy and knowledge leveraged innovation are complex and, as yet, not well described. The heterarchic form, however, is based upon the premise that knowledge is the most significant resource available to any organization. The literature on organizational knowledge reviewed earlier generated some insights into the characteristics of the heterarchic organization, particularly in its contrast with the hierarchic form.

Summary

Changing economic contexts meant that MNCs adopted different strategies, depending upon their particular product market, bundles of assets and resources and other factors. Vertical integration was the progenitor of one subsidiary task while the Chandlerian focus upon diversification was central to understanding the rise of the other five tasks. Diversification may be related or unrelated and related diversification may focus upon geographic scope or product lines. Diversification into new geographic locations by the early multidivisional corporation was a first mover strategy that generated advantage based upon the absence of any significant competition in these markets. In their turn, the increasing number of new geographic locations and markets presented the MNC with the opportunity to develop scale and scope economies and hence advantage via a strategy of cost minimization. Alternatively, if the MNC continued diversification on the basis of new but related product lines, focused upon particular international market segments, then a strategy of focus/differentiation was the basis of advantage generation. Increasingly, in some industries, it has become necessary to apply the focus/differentiation strategy in combination with cost minimization strategy for the purpose of gaining advantage via a continuous stream of new products and innovations. This fourth strategy is based upon leveraging the knowledge attributes of the entire corporate network. Concurrent with these developments, unrelated diversification has been utilized in some MNCs to develop a fifth form of strategic advantage based upon portfolio diversification of assets and resources. Geographic, product line and portfolio diversification are thus the progenitors of five corporate level and business level strategies. These are in addition to the sixth strategy of vertical integration.

In summary, at the corporate level, the MNC can create advantage by managing its subsidiaries as a vertically integrated value chain or as a portfolio of investments. Alternatively, at the business level, it can generate advantage by having a strategy that presents the market with the first product of its kind or the cheapest or a market segmented version or a continuous stream of new products. Each of these imposes a distinct task upon the subsidiary.

Knowledge asymmetry, control and autonomy

The following section links subsidiary task to the knowledge asymmetries that arise between HQ and subsidiary and examines their implications for issues of autonomy, control, knowledge management and innovation. Knowledge asymmetries are derived from the interplay between several categories of knowledge. These are the knowledge gained from and how to implement the internationalization process, the knowledge embedded in the HQ's ownership advantage (or FSA), the internalization advantage that subsequently arises, the subsidiary's knowledge of the host environment and the knowledge that the subsidiary holds as a result of its part in the transformation process. Several perspectives illuminate this issue.

The Uppsala model of internationalization described in Chapter 2 drew attention to the importance of two types of knowledge in the HQ-subsidiary relationship. Knowledge of the host market tended to be individually accrued and hence not easily available to HQ. Headquarters did, however, hold knowledge of the management of the overall internationalization process.

The internalization of the FSA brought reduction of the risk of competitor appropriation of that advantage but not without a price. Within the MNC, HQ-subsidiary knowledge asymmetries are particularly problematic because the relationship crosses national and cultural borders and the problems are often aggravated by communications problems arising from issues such as language, multilocation and time differences. Appropriate control systems must be developed to ameliorate these problems.

Chandler's work (Chandler 1962, 1977, 1990) firmly established the relationship between strategy and structure but it did not clarify the internal mechanics of the relationship, particularly with regard to control of MNC subsidiaries. Control has been approached from many directions but several studies help to remedy the deficiency in the case of the MNC. For Baliga and Jaeger (1984; Jaeger and Baliga, 1985; following Ouchi, 1977, 1979) the central issue of subsidiary control is the asymmetry of knowledge about the transformation process in the subsidiary. Hennart's (1991, 1993) further development demonstrated how the bounded rationality of HQ management and the potential opportunism of the subsidiary management influenced the design of the control mechanisms.

The agency perspective adds to understanding of the HQ-subsidiary relationship because it reveals how the role of principal is played by HQ *vis a vis* the agent role of the subsidiary. Curbing the HQ's potential residual loss (Jensen and Meckling, 1976) that might arise from the subsidiary's opportunistic use of its superior local knowledge requires the use of one of several devices depending upon circumstances. The implication from the brief recap of these studies is that subsidiary context, defined in terms of various knowledge asymmetries, is a major justification for using a particular control mechanism. Different contexts will lead to different control mechanisms.

Control and autonomy are clearly related, albeit inversely. Subsidiary autonomy is the antithesis of HQ control. The control mechanisms adopted by the MNC to proscibe potential opportunistic behavior in the subsidiary have important effects upon the subsidiary's autonomy. A significant amount of research has been done on subsidiary autonomy in the last 25 years and the list of factors that scholars have suggested will influence the level of subsidiary autonomy is very long. (Simoes, Biscaya and Nevado, 2000; Young and Tavares, 2004). From the perspective of the HQ-subsidiary relationship, subsidiary autonomy is likely to be primarily associated with the subsidiary's superiority over HQ with regard to knowledge of the host environment, the subsidiary's transformation process and assorted marketing, procurement, distribution and other issues.

The amount, type and asymmetries of knowledge flows associated with each of the advantage-generating strategies considered dictate the nature of the HQ-subsidiary relationship. The subsequent subsidiary task is developed to facilitate these knowledge flows. Each subsidiary task is then operationalized via a suitable organizational structure and set of control and coordination mechanisms. As we have seen, however, the demands of the new products/innovation strategy, as conceived here, lead to a fundamentally different organizational form from the other strategies. Each of these strategies and their outcomes are considered separately.

An integrated model

The analysis above examined the HQ-subsidiary relationships that developed as a result of six different HQ level advantage generating strategies. Separate analyses were performed for each HQ strategy but there was a general overall pattern discernible. In each HQ-subsidiary relationship, the HQ strategy is the prime determinant of a distinctive subsidiary task. The particular knowledge asymmetries appearing in the HQ-subsidiary relationship and arising from the overall MNC strategy, create the need for matching control mechanisms. The overall MNC strategy also determines whether the MNC will have a hierarchic or heterarchic organizational form and hence the embeddedness of the subsidiary in the knowledge management and innovation networks of the MNC. Five of the six subsidiary types were hypothesized to be found in hierarchical MNCs while the sixth was proposed to be typical of the heterarchic organizational form. Figure 5.1 is a model summarizing the theoretical logic presented above. This model suggests a series of general propositions and these propositions preface the series of empirical investigations that comprise the rest of this study.

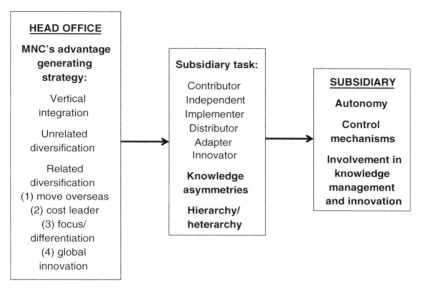

Figure 5.1   An integrated model of the HQ-subsidiary relationship

First, it is proposed that the six HQ level advantage generating strategies discerned in the literature are each typically associated with a particular subsidiary task that can be identified as clusters of firms. Hence:

P1: Six distinct subsidiary tasks will be identified.

Second, the knowledge asymmetries associated with each subsidiary task, in conjunction with contextual variables, imply differing levels of autonomy for the different subsidiary tasks. Hence:

P2: Differing levels of subsidiary autonomy will be associated with each subsidiary task.

Third, on the basis of the differing subsidiary tasks, their knowledge asymmetries and the organizational form, specific control mechanisms can be expected to be associated with each of the range of subsidiary tasks. Hence:

P3: Differing frequency of use of various control mechanisms will be associated with each subsidiary task.

Fourth, due to the differences between the hierarchic and heterarchic MNC forms, it is expected that:

P4: Subsidiaries performing the innovator task, typical of heterarchic MNCs, will be more deeply embedded in the knowledge management and innovation processes of the MNC than subsidiaries performing the other tasks.

Each general proposition above will be articulated into more specific hypotheses as they are developed and embedded in the empirical literature in the forthcoming chapters.

For each empirical investigation the data and methodology will be described and explained as they arise. The details of the basic data collection procedure are presented in Chapter 12, a methodological appendix. In addition this appendix also contains some information on the factor analysis procedures, the survey instrument and the validation procedures for the cluster analysis. Chapters 6 through 10 consist of separate empirical investigations. In Chapter 6 k-means cluster analysis is used to examine Proposition 1 and establish the validity of the subsidiary tasks typology. The study in Chapter 7 investigates the determinants of the level of subsidiary autonomy (Proposition 2) using the ANCOVA technique. Chapter 8 uses hierarchical linear regression to explore the specific relationship between subsidiary size and subsidiary autonomy as proposed by Hedlund (1981). Chapter 9 investigates the extent to which control mechanisms are associated with each of the subsidiary tasks (Proposition 3). Finally Proposition 4 is investigated in Chapter 10 where the relationships of the subsidiary tasks with knowledge management and innovation coordination mechanisms are examined.

Part II
Empirical Investigations

6
MNC Strategies and Subsidiary Tasks

In Chapter 5 a model was developed that hypothesized the existence of six distinct subsidiary tasks each of which was derived from the advantage-generating strategy embraced by the MNC parent. Each subsidiary task was proposed to be manifest as a group of firms. The relevant section of the basic model is shown in Figure 6.1 below.

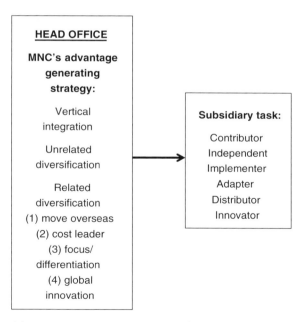

Figure 6.1   Advantage generating strategies and subsidiary tasks

This gave rise to a proposition that it will be possible to empirically identify distinct subsidiary tasks.

Identifying subsidiary task

Three basic methods have been used to ascertain the task that subsidiaries perform within the MNC. Jarillo and Martinez (1990) and Kobrin (1991) inferred the nature of the task from quantitative measures of diverse activities including percentage of inputs received from other group companies, percentage of local R&D out of total R&D and so on. Roth and Morrison (1992) and Taggart (1997a) deduced the task from managerial perceptions of the extent of issues such as heterogeneity of customers, dependence upon other units in the MNC and degree of standardization of production technology. O'Donnell (2000) directly asked respondents the extent to which certain statements accurately described the role of the subsidiary in the MNC. Direct questioning of respondents was the method arrived at independently in this research and subsequently employed.

The variables used in the investigation were the responses to a series of statements that ascertained the respondent's perception of how well those statements described the subsidiary's role within the MNC.

The question asked:

What is your company's PRIMARY role in the overall corporation?
Please consider that question and then rank the following statements as to how well they describe that role. Please select from a scale where:

1 = not accurate/important   through   5 = very accurate/important

S.1. Sales/distribution of goods produced elsewhere in the group
S.2. Generation and marketing of similar products to Head Office
S.3. Adapting product or its delivery for the local market
S.4. Product or process innovation
S.5. Generation of a range of products/services largely from our own resources.
S.6. Performing a single value-adding activity in the production process of the corporation's leading product

The questions were derived directly from the theoretical model. The intention was to capture – via a scale – the extent to which each subsidiary was involved in a particular process, for example, sales or innovation. The resulting pattern or combination of patterns of ratings would reflect the task of that subsidiary and allocate each case to a subsidiary task. While some subsidiaries at least were likely to carry out a range of tasks, it was expected that a dominant specific task for the subsidiary would be identified by a distinctive mix of responses. It was presumed that distributor subsidiaries, essentially disseminators of group products, would score above the mean on statement S.1. Implementer subsidiaries generate and market similar products to HQ so they should score above the mean on statement S.2 only. Because they adapted group products for the local market, adapter subsidiaries would score above the mean on statement S.3 and probably on S.1 also. Contributor subsidiaries would score above the mean on S.6 concerning the performance of a single value adding activity. Independent subsidiaries should rate high on statement S.5 – generation of a range of products/services largely from our own resources. Innovator subsidiaries were proposed to perform one or several of a range of tasks and would hence be expected to rate quite high on most or all statements but would rate the highest of all the groups on the innovation statement S.4.

The six statements shown above were then presented followed by a 1 to 5 scale. The descriptive statistics for the responses to the six statements are shown in Table 6.1. The mean value for S.6 was very low and a cause for further examination. The value of 1.79 was significantly

Table 6.1 Descriptive statistics for subsidiary role statements

The primary role of the subsidiary is:	n	Mean	s.d.
S.1. Sales/distribution of goods produced elsewhere in the group	313	3.45	1.66
S.2. Generation and marketing of similar products to Head Office	313	2.62	1.59
S.3 Adapting product or its delivery for the local market	313	2.97	1.40
S.4. Product or process innovation	313	2.43	1.30
S.5. Generation of a range of products/services largely from our own resources	313	2.69	1.50
S.6. Performing a single value-adding activity in the production process of the corporation's leading product	313	1.79	1.20

($p < .001$) less than 2.43, the next lowest (S.4). The purpose of statement S.6 was to identify the contributor subsidiary task typical of the vertical integration strategy. This very low score brought up the possibility that there might be very few or perhaps no subsidiaries performing the contributor task as their primary function. Since cluster analysis aims to derive the most internally consistent clusters across all variables, then the inclusion of irrelevant variables can create validity problems (Aldenderfer and Blashfield, 1984). Hence it is advisable to use as few variables as possible to obtain the solution. Including attributes that do not differentiate among clusters has been shown (Punj and Stewart, 1983) to have adverse effects upon clustering method performance. As a consequence, the decision was made to consider the possibility of searching for five as well as six clusters in the forthcoming cluster analysis, bearing in mind the possibility of excluding the contributor task and statement S.6 from the analysis.

Cluster analysis

K-means cluster analysis was employed to interpret the data. This technique allocates cases to clusters based upon their responses to the questions.

Cluster analysis is a generic term for a range of techniques used to create subsets from a population of entities based upon their similarity across a set of attributes (Everitt, 1980; Lorr, 1983). They are essentially heuristic techniques unsupported by extensive statistical theory. With large and complex data sets, it is quite possible for different clustering techniques to generate different solutions.

Lorr (1983: 4) states that cluster analysis can be used to 'test hypothesized classes believed to be present within a certain group of cases'. However, while cluster analysis usually aims to be structure seeking it can, in fact, be structure imposing. As a consequence, it is important to guide the clustering of the data on the basis of theory (Aldenderfer and Blashfield, 1984) and to statistically validate the clusters obtained as the best available solution. Clustering techniques are widely used in disciplines such as medicine and in marketing research (Lorr, 1983) but are somewhat less common in management (see, however, Harrigan, 1985; Cool and Schendel, 1987; Jermier, Slocum, Fry and Gaines, 1991; Arthur, 1994; Nohria and Ghoshal, 1997; Forsgren and Pederson, 1998; Gordon and Milne, 1999; Osborne, Stubbart and Ramaprasad, 2001; Harzing, 2002; Kim, Hoskisson and Wan, 2004).

There are many subtle differences in clustering strategies leading to varying procedures but there are only two basic techniques – agglomerative hierarchical and k-means non-hierarchical. The former is the most commonly used but when there are large quantities of data and the data has been derived from five point Likert-type responses, the k-means clustering technique is more appropriate (Aldenderfer and Blashfield, 1984). This technique begins by specifying a tentative set of cluster centroids as seed points. The number of seed points is set by the number of clusters predicted by the theory underpinning the research. Each data point is then assigned to its closest seed point. The distances between points are measured using simple Euclidean distance. The cluster centroids are then recomputed and updated. Another pass is then made through the data to reassign each element to its nearest revised cluster centroid. The process is then repeated until no reassignments occur or the maximum number of iterations is reached. In contrast to hierarchical clustering where once a data point is allocated it cannot be moved to another cluster, any data point in k-means clustering can be moved to any cluster at any time. This flexibility is the major strength of the technique. 'K-means appears to be more robust than other methods ... and is least affected by the presence of irrelevant attributes or dimensions in the data' (Hair, Anderson and Tatham, 1992: 277).

There are several important data considerations concerned with k-means clustering. First, scaling of variables is sometimes required but, since the variables in this research were derived from questions that used identical scales, the usual standardization procedure was unnecessary. Second, the number of clusters was theoretically specified in advance by the model derived in Chapter 5. Third, the technique can sometimes be sensitive to the accuracy of the initial seed points. There were, however, only a small number of independent variables (five or six were used at different stages of the analysis) and random allocation of seed points would be unlikely to influence the final solution.

In cluster analysis, there are no statistical or mathematical guidelines for the choice and number of clusters or variables. This is solely at the discretion of the investigator and is based upon judgement and theory. Aldenderfer and Blashfield (1984) suggest that sometimes a theoretical relationship may suggest a natural number of clusters. Ketchen, Thomas and Snow (1993) argued that methodological research showed it was often wise to use deductive theory to guide variable choice. The theoretical model derived in Chapter 5 gave the solid theoretical foundation recommended by Ketchen et al. (1993).

Following Jermier et al. (1991) it can be argued that the subsidiary differences derived from clustering algorithms may be viewed in two different ways. They may be seen as statistical artifacts (analytical fictions) that represent nothing more than minor dissimilarities in respondents' ratings. Or, alternatively, they may be viewed as groupings of subsidiaries that perform similar tasks and practice similar methods of doing things. In this case, there will be commonalities of activity that arise from the practical demands of the environment. In the final analysis, the value of the investigation and which view prevails, will be resolved by the ability of the clustering to, first, produce a set of meaningful classifications and, second, to compare the subsidiary tasks on the basis of relevant criteria.

Results of the cluster analysis

As a consequence of the earlier analysis that detected potential problems with statement S.6, it was decided to run two k-means cluster analysis. The first was run on the basis of the six statements and set up for six clusters. The second analysis removed the sixth statement (S.6) and was run on the first five statements and set up for five clusters.

The six clusters solution proved to have no obvious compatibility with the logic of the research. In addition, detailed inspection of the individual cases where S.6 scored 4 or 5 found that none of these cases had the other five statements scoring 3 or less. Together these results strongly suggested the absence of contributor subsidiaries in the sample.

In contrast, the five clusters solution produced combinations of ratings that appeared to be very clearly in line with the proposed five remaining subsidiary types. In addition, a 4 clusters solution was generated using the five statements and the reasons for discarding both 4 and 6 clusters are detailed in the methodological appendix in Chapter 12.

The initial 5 clusters solution is shown in Table 6.2. The distinctiveness of the clusters in the solution indicates the probable existence of

Table 6.2   Initial cluster solution

	Cluster 1	Cluster 2	Cluster 3	Cluster 4	Cluster 5
Statement 1	5	4	2	3	1
Statement 2	2	1	4	4	1
Statement 3	2	4	2	4	2
Statement 4	1	3	2	3	3
Statement 5	1	3	3	3	4

Table 6.3   Expanded cluster solution – statement means for the five
clusters solution

	Cluster 1 Distr	Cluster 2 Adapt	Cluster 3 Imple	Cluster 4 Innov	Cluster 5 Indep
S.1 Sales/distribution of goods produced elsewhere in the group	4.82[a]	**4.46**	1.65	**3.35**	1.42
S.2 Generation and marketing of similar products to Head Office	2.39	1.46	**4.15**	**4.31**	1.40
S.3 Adapting product or its delivery for the local market	2.41	**4.03**	2.37	**4.22**	1.91
S.4 Product or process innovation	1.44	2.85	2.37	**3.46**	2.68
S.5 Generation of a range of products or services from own resources	1.36	2.58	2.85	**3.41**	**4.34**

[a] All statement means above the mid point 3 are shown in bold.

five clusters. The solution was then saved as a variable in the SPSS data editor. This variable indicated which cases were in each cluster. The mean values for each statement in each cluster were then calculated. This is the expanded solution, shown in Table 6.3. Simple inspection of Tables 6.2 and 6.3 did not support Proposition 1. However, five of the six proposed subsidiary task clusters were revealed.

Detailed examination of Table 6.3 showed that cluster 1 was dominated by the variable denoting a primary task of selling or distributing products produced elsewhere in the group (S.1 = 4.82). This was significantly the highest in the cluster ($p < .001$) and was combined with relatively low values for all of the other ratings (S.2 = 2.39; S.3 = 2.41; S.4 = 1.44; S.5 = 1.36). The pattern is notably congruent with the proposed distributor task.

The primary task of subsidiaries in cluster 2 was the sale and distribution of group products that had been adapted for the local market. This cluster demonstrated high mean values (4.46 and 4.03) for the variables S.1 and S.3 respectively. Both were significantly higher than S.4 the next highest score (2.85) in the classification (S.1 > S.4, $p < .001$; S.3 > S.4, $p < .001$). In addition, as expected, they exhibited a low rating in terms of generating products similar to Head Office (S.2 = 1.46), they performed some innovation (S.4 = 2.85) to support the adaptation process and worked from their own resources to some extent (S.5 = 2.58).

Overall, the pattern of ratings was convincingly similar to the expected values for the adapter subsidiary task.

In the cluster 3, the substantially highest mean value was for the variable indicating a primary task of generating products similar to those produced by Head Office (S.2 = 4.15). This was significantly the highest rating in the classification ($p < .001$). This group of subsidiaries do very little selling of products from other group companies (S.1 = 1.65), only a small amount of adapting (S.3 = 2.37) and innovation (S.4 = 2.37) but have a modicum of dependence on their own resources (S.5 = 2.85). There was a clear concordance with the implementer subsidiary task.

The combination of values in cluster 4 was generally congruent with the innovator subsidiary task. This cluster demonstrated the highest value for the product and process innovation statement of all the clusters (S.4 = 3.46). It was significantly the highest *between* clusters (cluster 4 > cluster 2; $p < .01$) and differed again from all of the others in having values above the mean for all variables (S.1 = 3.35; S.2 = 4.31; S.3 = 4.22; S.5 = 3.41). This is an important finding because, overall, this result demonstrated that these were subsidiaries with a considerable degree of resources and competences, yet they were still linked with other firms in the group in terms of selling, producing and adapting common group products. Bartlett and Ghoshal (1989: 71) described the overseas operations of the transnational strategy as differentiation of roles and responsibilities so as to make contributions to integrated worldwide operations. The subsidiaries represented by the innovator task fit comfortably with this conceptualization.

The values for cluster 5 were a very good match to those that might be expected for the independent subsidiary task. The primary task of the subsidiaries in this cluster was to generate products from their own resources (S.5 = 4.34). This was significantly the highest score in the cluster ($p < .001$). They perform some innovation (S.4 = 2.68) as might be expected of a firm functioning independently but rated low on the other variables, having little concern for the products from other group companies either as seller/distributor (S.1 = 1.42), producer (S.2 = 1.40) or adapter (S.3 = 1.91). Again the congruence with expectations was very good.

The pattern of scores shows considerable face validity in matching the predicted subsidiary tasks very well. In combination, the data offered persuasive statistical support for five of the six subsidiary tasks proposed.

On the deficit side, this study found little evidence for the existence of the proposed (value chain) contributor subsidiary. This may have been a result of inadequacies in the survey design or it is possibly simply another attribute of the Australian environment. Alternatively it may be that, in the modern MNC, vertical integration elements are so deeply embedded in the corporate structure that they are difficult to disentangle as a single subsidiary task and hence difficult to extract from the data on the basis of a single survey question.

These five clusters were closely comparable with the hypothesized subsidiary tasks. However, since the analysis was set up to generate five clusters, it was the uniqueness of the clusters rather than their number that was important. It was also necessary to demonstrate the reliability and external validity of the solution as well as its statistical significance (Hair et al., 1992). Detailed analysis of the reliability and validity of the cluster solution are presented in the Methodological Appendix in Chapter 12.

A comparison between the present and previous studies

The review of the literature on subsidiary strategy typologies in Chapter 4 concluded that the attempted syntheses by Hoffman (1994) and Birkinshaw and Morrison (1995) had considerable limitations. Both lacked a theoretical foundation, had limited application and did not present any empirical validation. The present study and typology is superior on all three of these criteria. This research derived the subsidiary tasks from well-grounded strategy theory and empirically verified them using a satisfactorily large sample of subsidiaries from manufacturing and service firms in a wide range of industries.

Importantly, it was also argued that any satisfactory typology ought to encompass the range of subsidiary tasks identified in the six major studies on the topic. This is a demanding criterion since these studies were derived from very different contexts, produced from many differing perspectives and used subsidiary characteristics dissimilar from those in this study. Comparison of tasks between studies therefore cannot be exact but broadly-based similarities will be noted and dissimilarities explained. Comparisons between the five subsidiary tasks elicited from this study's theoretical model and the previous studies are summarized in Table 6.4 and briefly commented upon below.

In D'Cruz's (1986) study the satellite subsidiary that assembles low tariff components is an implementer and the branch plant which has more local focus is probably an adapter. D'Cruz's import subsidiary is

Table 6.4 Comparison of present classifications with previous studies

Independent	Contributor	Innovator	Adapter	Implementer	Distributor
W&P: strategic independent	W&P: rationalized manufacturer	J&M: active	D'C: branch	D'C: satellite	J&M: receptive
G&G: local innovator	D'C: rationalized manufacturer	G&G: integrated player	W&P: miniature replica-adapter type	W&P: miniature replica-adopter type	T: collaborator
T: militant	B&G: contributor	B&G: strategic leader	W&P: miniature replica-innovator type	B&G: implementer	D'C: import
	T: partner		J&M: autonomous	G&G: implementer	W&P: marketing satellite
	G&G: global innovator			T: vassal	

D'C: world product mandate and W&P: product specialist are either implementers or adapters that are present alongside the more numerous distributor subsidiaries; B&G: black hole is not categorized

D'C = D'Cruz; W&P = White and Poynter; J&M = Jarillo and Martinez; B&G = Bartlett and Ghoshal; G&G = Gupta and Govindarajan; T = Taggart the distribution first phase of the first move into a market competitive strategy and precedes the implementer. The globally rationalized producer and the world product mandate are probably best categorized as the production units in the cost minimization competitive strategy and, as such, they are present alongside the much more numerous distributors. The rationalized producer is probably a contributor to the value chain while the world product mandate may be an implementer or an adapter.

White and Poynter's (1984) proposed three miniature replica types – adopter, adapter and innovator. The first is an implementer and the second and third are two variations on the adapter strategy. White and Poynter also proposed a strategic independent type that is clearly similar to this study's independent. Their marketing satellite, rationalized manufacturer and product specialist are similar to D'Cruz's importer, globally rationalized producer and world product mandate above and should be categorized similarly.

Jarillo and Martinez's (1990) receptive, autonomous and active subsidiaries are similar to the distributor, adapter and innovator, respectively.

The strategic leader of Bartlett and Ghoshal's (1986) taxonomy has many of the characteristics of an innovator. Their contributor also has high levels of resources and capabilities and is probably best considered as an innovator that is simply operating in a less important market. Their implementor is similar to this study's implementer. The black hole, however, might be the residue one of several failed MNC strategies. It defies comparison with the present study.

The lack of knowledge flows between the subsidiary and the rest of the MNC typical of Gupta and Govindarajan's (1991) local innovator indicates some similarity with the independent subsidiary task (or possibly the adapter). Their integrated player is an innovator and their implementer similar to this study's implementer. They also hypothesize a subsidiary that is charged with innovating on behalf of the rest of the MNC. This is a global innovation role typical of hierarchic rather than heterarchic MNCs and probably fits into the contributor category.

Taggart's (1997a) study proposed partner, collaborator, militant and vassal subsidiary types. These are generally similar to the innovator, distributor, independent and implementer types, respectively, although the comparisons are less clear than with the other taxonomies.

This brief description demonstrates the close relationship of this study's six proposed and five demonstrated subsidiary tasks with those derived from previous work.

Summary

A considerable range of subsidiary classifications has been postulated in the literature. These have been derived either from considerations of subsidiary business context or via extrapolations of frameworks such as the I-R grid. The present study has demonstrated the empirical validity of five of the six proposed types in a more theoretically derived typology of subsidiary tasks. In addition, this typology has been argued to encompass the majority of previously proposed tasks. The investigation has thus established the beginnings of theoretical and empirical integration to this field of study.

Several issues were noteworthy. First, as expected, the evidence suggested that, in reality, subsidiaries were rarely single task entities and they usually performed various tasks on behalf of the MNC. This undoubtedly added some 'noise' to the data.

The second consideration lay in the nature of Likert-type scales generally and their ability to accurately capture differences in perceptions. This was a general caveat that related to many sections of this study. The validity and reliability of Likert-type scale responses has been extensively researched (see, for example, Armstrong, 1988; Albaum and Murphy, 1989; Rasmussen, 1989; Albaum, 1997; Ommundsen and Larsen, 1997; Maurer and Pierce, 1998). The primary concerns have been that Likert scales appeared to under-report high intensity responses and they also suffered from some common psychological tendencies such as central tendency, leniency and proximity. The response intensity issue should not have been problematic in this study since this issue is only evident with very strongly held perceptions. While some respondents might have held very strong views on a given topic, it was unlikely that, given the subject matter, strongly held views were widespread and they probably did not constitute a substantial part of the data. The leniency, proximity and central tendencies were probably in evidence but Albaum (1997) and Maurer and Pierce (1998) stated that the Likert scale meets all available reliability and validity criteria. These tendencies should not have affected the results.

Third, it was not clear that it was always easy to identify the subsidiary's primary role even for the senior executive in the firm.

These caveats notwithstanding, it was evident that the data offered strong support for the suggested typology providing an extremely robust result.

Criteria of evaluation

Miller (1996) proposed three criteria by which to measure the significance of a typology. First, it must capture important conceptual distinctions. The present study fulfils this criterion, first, by distinguishing subsidiary task on the basis of the MNC's advantage-generating strategy and, second, by further expanding knowledge of the hierarchy/heterarchy distinction as it applies in MNCs. Miller's second criterion was that it should derive types that occur regularly in reality. The existence of the subsidiary tasks was demonstrated in the analyses of MNC strategies in Chapter 4. The third criterion was that the model should generate testable hypotheses. In forthcoming chapters, a series of hypotheses will derived from the model and then examined and tested. The present model fulfils all of Miller's (1996) criteria.

In addition to the Miller criteria, it was argued earlier that any new categorization of subsidiary types should fulfil a number of further, more specific, conditions. First, the framework should encompass a greater range of subsidiary tasks than any previous study and, ideally, should encapsulate all the types derived in the current research. In this respect, the present study is more efficacious than any former investigation but the framework was still unable to embrace all of the earlier types. There is, however, potential to expand the basic model to encompass more subsidiary types. If the basic MNC strategy-subsidiary task link is accepted, then the number of subsidiary types is determined by the number of strategies available to the MNC and the subsidiary tasks that derive from each. Some of these possibilities will be explored later in Chapter 11.

Second, the model should be more universal than previous models, in the sense of having wider applicability in terms of industries, home and host countries and MNC types. The 313 subsidiaries in the present study came from nine of the fourteen major groups in the Australian Standard Industrial Classification system and covered 59 of the subgroup classifications. No previous study covers such a wide range of industries. MNCs were examined from seventeen home countries but only from one host country, Australia. In terms of MNC type, since the study was totally subsidiary focused no categorization of overall MNC type was made.

Third, most analyses of HQ-subsidiary relationships have been derived from a HQ perspective. This view illuminates the MNC's overall form and structure but does little to help understand the subsidiary's viewpoint. This study was developed from a subsidiary perspective for two reasons. First, it was attempting to learn more about the place of subsidiaries from a particular host country, Australia, in foreign MNCs. Second, examining the MNC from the subsidiary perspective gives a better perception of the subsidiary's overall place in both the hierarchical (HQ-subsidiary) and heterarchical (subsidiary-subsidiary) elements of the MNC structure. The subsidiary is seen to be at the nexus of many vertical and horizontal linkages.

Finally, it was argued that the investigation should have a strong theoretical base grounded in the MNC literature. This criterion was a major objective in the development of the model in Chapter 5.

These criteria were, in total, a very demanding set of conditions for the model but they have been adhered to closely. In the process of satisfying these criteria, a solid theoretical base has been created from which to tackle the issues of autonomy, controls, knowledge management and innovation in later chapters.

7
Subsidiary Task and Subsidiary Autonomy

It was argued in Chapter 1 that the relationship between headquarters and subsidiaries is central to the understanding of the functioning of multinational corporations and, as several authors have pointed out (Birkinshaw, Hood and Jonsson, 1998; Enright, 2000; Edwards, Ahmad and Moss, 2002), the subsidiary is playing an increasingly important role in generating competitive advantage for the overall MNC. The sometimes conflicting and sometimes cooperative nature of this connection has become a significant concern in international management. The ambivalence in the relationship frequently arises because the subsidiary requires or desires a degree of autonomy of decision-making that the HQ is not always disposed to concede. Over the last two decades, subsidiary autonomy has been the subject of considerable academic research. An important outcome of the nature of the task that the subsidiary performs on behalf of the overall corporation is its connection with the subsidiary's level of autonomy. The first contribution of this chapter is to investigate the relationship between level of subsidiary autonomy and subsidiary task in the context of the range of strategies available to the MNC. The second results from subsidiary autonomy being a phenomenon independent of the factors used to derive the subsidiary task clusters in Chapter 6. Hence, by testing hypotheses regarding the task-autonomy relationship the investigation also adds important external validation to the clusters derived in Chapter 6.

The chapter begins by briefly reviewing the literature on subsidiary autonomy and presents a series of hypotheses that link that variable to the range of subsidiary tasks. The empirical section investigates the subsidiary task-subsidiary autonomy association. First the subsidiary tasks derived from unrelated and related diversification are compared and then the four related diversification subsidiary tasks are examined.

Literature and hypotheses

Subsidiary autonomy

The earliest approaches focused on identifying the factors that influenced the level of autonomy in the subsidiary. Several studies (Skinner, 1968; Stopford and Wells, 1972; Picard, 1977; Hedlund, 1981) proposed that the diversification process, both related and unrelated, led to subsidiary autonomy. Hedlund (1981) also argued that HQ influence was usually strongest on decisions involving access to central resources, when long-term obligations result or when common frameworks and organizational routines and practices were involved. Garnier (1982) proposed that MNC philosophy and perceptions of the local environment also influenced subsidiary autonomy. Gates and Egelhoff (1986) argued that MNC-wide conditions were more important than subsidiary specific factors although the latter could not be ignored. These studies were essentially early attempts to map the domain and, as such, they provide some basic indicative information.

From the standpoint of what Birkinshaw (1994) labeled the 'process school', subsidiary autonomy was seen as one factor in a dynamic pattern of forces that drives the MNC's evolution (see for example, Prahalad and Doz, 1981a, b). In particular this approach emphasized how subsidiary autonomy was linked to MNC strategy with regard to the local environment. Closely allied to this perspective was the contribution by Bartlett and Ghoshal (1986). They examined the effects of developing subsidiary capabilities, the subsequent establishment of a mutually agreed strategy for the subsidiary and the required coordination techniques. For example, subsidiary autonomy was identified as a necessary condition for adoption of a world product mandate (Rugman and Bennett, 1982; Poynter and Rugman, 1982; White and Poynter, 1984). More recently, Birkinshaw, Hood and Jonsson (1998) demonstrated how the initiatives of subsidiaries were able to contribute to the firm specific advantages of the MNC. Young, Hood and Dunlop (1988) called attention to the subsidiary's ability to make strategy-supportive decisions and, in a similar vein, Taggart (1996) demonstrated the contribution that subsidiary autonomy made to the MNC's strategic evolution. Taggart (1997a) modeled subsidiary strategy using autonomy in conjunction with procedural justice (Kim and Mauborgne, 1991, 1993a,b) and linked the classifications to a subsidiary's shift from one strategy state to another. Bartlett and Ghoshal (1989) examined the link between subsidiary autonomy and innovation. Greater subsidiary autonomy was proposed to facilitate the creation of local innovations.

The direction of causation between MNC strategy and subsidiary autonomy is not consistent in these studies. Some have tended to examine the role of autonomy as one determining variable in an array of forces that influence MNC strategy while others saw autonomy as a direct outcome of MNC strategy.

From an alternative viewpoint, autonomy is the antithesis of control and there is a considerable literature relating to what determines the amount of control imposed by HQ. Many factors have been proposed and investigated: home country of MNC (Hedlund, 1981; Negandhi and Baliga, 1981a, b; Welge, 1981; Egelhoff, 1984; Dunning, 1986; Bartlett and Ghoshal, 1987; Hennart and Larimo, 1998); degree of formalization of MNC control procedures (Hedlund, 1981; Egelhoff, 1984; Young, Hood and Hamill, 1985); the subsidiary's contribution to R&D and innovation creation (Negandhi and Baliga, 1981a, b; Negandhi and Serapio, 1991; Bartlett and Ghoshal, 1989; Birkinshaw, Hood and Jonsson, 1998); size of subsidiary both absolute and relative to the overall corporation (Negandhi and Baliga, 1981b; Welge, 1981; Tomita, 1991); and industry characteristics (Cray, 1984; Negandhi and Welge, 1984; Bartlett and Ghoshal, 1987; Birkinshaw and Hood, 2000).

The literature on subsidiary autonomy, while extensive, is fragmented (see however Simoes, Biscaya and Nevada 2000 and particularly Young and Tavares, 2004 for reviews). However, as the examination above demonstrates, it is possible to identify a dominating theme that there is an intimate association of subsidiary autonomy with various aspects of the MNCs overall strategy.

Subsidiary tasks and subsidiary autonomy

Building upon the literature above the present study proposes that the differing advantage-generating strategies employed by the MNC bring about knowledge asymmetries between HQ and the subsidiary and are thus highly influential in determining of the level of subsidiary autonomy. There are several categories of knowledge that influence these asymmetries but the two primary types are knowledge of the transformation process employed in the subsidiary and knowledge of the characteristics of the host country environment. On the basis of these knowledge asymmetries, it is hypothesized that different subsidiary tasks are associated with different levels of subsidiary autonomy, *ceteris paribus*.

Because the advantage-generating strategies employed by the MNC are implemented at both corporate and business levels within the organization, the analysis is divided into two phases. First, it is necessary to investigate the levels of subsidiary autonomy associated with related and

unrelated diversification strategies, that is to compare the level of subsidiary autonomy of the independent subsidiary with the overall level of
autonomy for the four related diversification subsidiary tasks – distributor, implementer, adapter and innovator. The second phase examines
the levels of subsidiary autonomy between the latter four tasks.

Unrelated vs related diversification

Unrelated diversification is the strategy of the portfolio diversified
MNC and it occurs when the MNC assembles collections of unrelated
businesses. Competitive advantage lies in managing the portfolio to
elicit various short and long term economic gains and/or the minimizing of risk exposure (Caves, 1996). The independent subsidiary task is
associated with this strategy. In these cases it is highly unlikely that the
details of the business of the subsidiary firms will be well understood
by HQ and hence HQ is likely to leave day-to-day management to the
subsidiary management team. In addition, these subsidiaries probably
generate their output primarily from their own resources and have few
linkages with the products of the rest of the MNC. All knowledge of
the transformation process is held in the subsidiary as is the important
knowledge relating to the subsidiary's business context. These subsidiaries are predicted to be more autonomous than the subsidiaries
associated with related diversification.

> **Hypothesis 7.1:** The subsidiary task associated with unrelated
> diversification – independent – will demonstrate higher levels of sub-
> sidiary autonomy than the four subsidiary tasks – distributor, adapter,
> implementer and innovator – associated with related diversification.

The four related diversification subsidiary tasks are now examined.
Having established that the four discrete subsidiary tasks associated
with related diversification exist in the dataset, the following analysis
predicts that subsidiary autonomy means of these will follow a specific
pattern. The innovator will demonstrate the highest level of subsidiary
autonomy, the adapter will be next, followed by the implementer, and
the distributor will have the lowest autonomy value.

Related diversification: Cost leadership

The distributor is the most common subsidiary type in MNCs that
produce large volumes of low cost standardized products for the global
market. The subsidiary's task is that of a delivery pipeline for goods
produced elsewhere in the group with little further contribution. The

subsidiary has less knowledge of the transformation process than HQ and any important knowledge of the host environment will be held at HQ to inform the global coordination of the distribution of the product. For these subsidiaries, knowledge of the local environment is important only in terms of ensuring correspondence and coordination with global marketing and distribution policies. These subsidiaries are predicted to have the lowest level of autonomy.

> **Hypothesis 7.2:** The distributor subsidiary task will demonstrate the lowest level of subsidiary autonomy among the four related diversification subsidiary tasks.

Related diversification: Domestic innovation and the move into a new overseas location

The implementer task is associated with subsidiaries that are exploiters of the MNC's ownership advantage in a new, relatively competition-free, overseas location. While the export/sales phase may give rise to a distributor subsidiary, the archetypal subsidiary strategy congruent with this advantage generating strategy is best described as an implementer of the HQ's firm specific advantage.

The subsidiary produces a similar product to HQ, is likely to be involved only slightly in innovation or adapting the product for the local market but, in many instances, will depend upon its own resources to some extent. The subsidiary has knowledge of the transformation process but somewhat less than HQ and knowledge of the host environment is relatively unimportant. On the basis of this analysis it is expected that the implementer will exhibit very low levels of autonomy. However, the task of the implementer is likely to be relatively routine and it may be that if the subsidiary is well established and performing satisfactorily, it is left undisturbed. In addition, there are probably greater constraints imposed on the implementer strategy by the physical distance of Australia from HQ than on some of the other types. On balance these factors suggest:

> **Hypothesis 7.3:** The implementer subsidiary task will demonstrate the second lowest level of subsidiary autonomy among the four related diversification subsidiary tasks.

Related diversification: Focus/differentiation

The adapter subsidiary task is linked with subsidiaries that tailor group products for the local market. It is likely that the adapter subsidiary will have some innovative capacity and some need to work from its own resources. The basic transformation process was probably developed at HQ but the knowledge of the host environment that enables suitable adaptation and brings much of the advantage from the strategy resides with the subsidiary. A key question is exactly what is involved in the adaptation process. This may constitute anything from merely minor adaptation of a product produced elsewhere (little more than a distributor) to full-scale production of an adapted product. On balance it is predicted that

> **Hypothesis 7.4:** The adapter subsidiary task will demonstrate the second highest level of subsidiary autonomy among the related diversification subsidiary tasks.

Related diversification: Global innovation

While there are many variations on the nature of the knowledge asymmetries in the four HQ-subsidiary relationships detailed above, all of them so far have been hierarchical in nature. Even if HQ knows little or nothing of the subsidiary's business, the strategic configuration of the MNC is centralized. The final strategy and subsidiary task to be discussed are congruent with the new hierarchical organizational form.

The innovator is the subsidiary task associated with the global innovation strategy. Innovator subsidiaries are called upon to perform a variety of tasks on behalf of the MNC, including contributing to the innovation process. Innovations are generated via a process of knowledge management that encompasses the entire global network of the firm. Knowledge management is no longer a simple cooperative process instigated and directed by HQ. All subsidiaries that are capable of innovation contribute to the innovation process via a vast array of, often electronic, inter-unit communication and knowledge management linkages. Innovation and new products are the products of a complex interplay between all parts of the MNC. There might be centers of innovation excellence set up and these often act as foci for tapping the resources of the total network (Birkinshaw and Hood, 2000). As with the domestic innovations considered earlier, these globally developed innovations bring initial advantages but these advantages too are ephemeral and must, in their turn, be rebuilt and extended via cost reductions and/or differentiation. The entire process is iterative. The need to leverage all the knowledge resources of the MNC means that the coordination demands of this strategy are intense. These firms have a considerable range of capabilities and, on occasions, independence of action although key knowledge might be found at HQ or in any subsidiary within the group. Since they are deeply embedded in the corporate network, they are not likely to be more autonomous than the independent subsidiary task but they are, nevertheless, expected to show substantial autonomy and be the most autonomous of the subsidiaries associated with related diversification.

> **Hypothesis 7.5**: The innovator subsidiary task will demonstrate the highest level of subsidiary autonomy among the four related diversification subsidiary tasks.

Method

The empirical investigations examined the relationship between subsidiary tasks and level of subsidiary autonomy, controlling for a range of contextual variables. The relationship was investigated using ANCOVA, analysis of variance with covariates using the general linear model (GLM), treating the several control variables as fixed factors or covariates as appropriate. The univariate version of the GLM provides a regression-like procedure that removes extraneous variation in the dependent variable due to the fixed factors or covariates. Then a standard ANOVA is carried out (Hair et al. 2002: 328). Importantly for this investigation it also enables the provision of estimated marginal mean values of the dependent variable for each of the categories in a categorical predictor or control variable. The subsidiary autonomy means obtained for individual and groups of subsidiary tasks can then be compared to test the hypotheses presented above.

Dependent variable

It is implicit in the Aston Studies and their derivatives that a measure of subsidiary autonomy is also a measure of MNC centralization or, more correctly, decentralization. This, however, is only true in the event that all subsidiaries are delegated the same amount of autonomy. Implicit and explicit in most of the more recent examinations of HQ-subsidiary relations is the presumption that the amount of subsidiary autonomy is contingent upon factors such as the complexity of the host environment, the level of subsidiary capabilities, the nature of the firm specific advantage, and so on. Measures of subsidiary autonomy used in the literature have been based upon this conception of degree of decentralization of decision-making authority to the individual subsidiary. Definitions by Brooke (1984), O'Donnell (2000) and Young and

Tavares (2004) have all emphasized the decision-making aspect. Researchers have either taken the inverse of measures of centralization (Ghoshal, Korine and Szulanski 1994; Nohria and Ghoshal 1997; Picard, Boddewyn and Grosse 1998) or have asked respondents to rank the level of the subsidiary's input into a range of hypothetical decisions *vis-a-vis* the influence of HQ (Birkinshaw and Hood 2000; Bowman, Duncan and Weir 2000; Ghoshal and Bartlett 1988; Roth and Morrison 1992; Taggart 1996). Measuring autonomy in this latter manner has been the most commonly used in the literature but there is not yet a generally accepted scale. Previous studies have used as few as three questions but, for this study, nine were selected from Hedlund (1981) relating to operational, marketing, financial and human resource decisions. Ghoshal and Bartlett (1988) discuss the issue of whether there is a need for separate measures of strategic and operational subsidiary autonomy but conclude that a single overall measure is adequate.

Respondents were asked how much influence head office would have on the following decisions: (1) extension of credit to a major customer; (2) product introduction to the local market; (3) training programs in the company; (4) choice of advertising agency; (5) setting the aggregate production schedule; (6) hiring of operational personnel; (7) setting sales targets; (8) return on investment criteria; and (9) quality control norms. Individual scale items were summed to create an aggregate measure of the level of subsidiary autonomy. The reliability analysis (α = 0.81 exceeding the .70 level recommended by Nunnally, 1978) suggested that the measure was valid as a single construct. The scale in each question ran from 1 (totally HQ decision) to 5 (totally subsidiary decision). Thus the overall score from 9 to 45 gave a measure of the subsidiary's decision-making autonomy (see the Methodological Appendix in Chapter 12 for details of the questions and factor analysis).

Predictor variable

The subsidiary tasks were coded to reflect the expected levels of autonomy. In the first investigation the unrelated diversification subsidiary task (the independent) was coded 2 and the combined related diversification subsidiary tasks were coded 1. In the second investigation they were coded in hypothesized descending order: 4 = innovator; 3 = adapter; 2 = implementer; 1 = distributor. The subsidiary autonomy means for each subsidiary task without controlling for the various fixed factors and covariates are shown in Tables 7.1 and 7.2.

Table 7.1   Uncontrolled subsidiary autonomy means for unrelated and related diversification subsidiary tasks

Subsidiary task	n	Mean	s.d.
Unrelated diversification – independent	52	37.02	6.77
Related diversification – distributor, adapter, implementer and innovator	258	34.07	6.63

Independent > distributor/implementer/adapter/innovator combination: $p < .01$ (two-tailed test)

Table 7.2   Uncontrolled subsidiary autonomy means for related diversification subsidiary tasks

Subsidiary task	n	Mean	s.d.
Innovator	53	35.42	6.94
Adapter	65	33.66	6.88
Implementer	46	35.76	5.91
Distributor	94	32.76	6.38

Innovator > distributor; $p < .05$
Implementer > distributor, $p < .01$ (two-tailed tests)

Control variables

The literature suggested that many factors, not necessarily associated with subsidiary task, were likely to affect level of autonomy. These were categorized as knowledge and capability factors, MNC cultural factors, local environment factors and size. It was not possible to incorporate all factors suggested in the literature in the analysis but a number are included and presented briefly here. Details of the scales appear in the methodological appendix in Chapter 12.

1. *Knowledge and capability factors*: technology level – What is the level of technology your company utilizes in its primary operations? (scale values 1–5; very basic – leading edge); amount of R&D – How much R&D does your company perform on behalf of the rest of the firm? (scale 1-5; none – virtually all); creation of innovations – What is the frequency over the last two years of the following event: creation of significant product or process innovations within your company? (scale 1–5; never – very frequently)

2. *MNC characteristics*: parent nationality – What is the home country of your parent corporation home? (categorical 1–11: UK, US/Canada, Japan, Sweden, Germany, Italy, Switzerland, Netherlands/Belgium,

Table 7.3 Descriptive statistics and intercorrelations for control variables

Variable	(1)	(2)	(3)	(4)	(5)	(6)	(7)	(8)	(9)
1. Mentor	—								
2. Corporate culture	-.02	—							
3. Industry: retail/distr	.11	.12	—						
4. Level of technology	.00	-.06	.07	—					
5. Amount of R&D	-.02	-.10	-.27	.15	—				
6. Creation of innovations	.00	-.07	-.28	.09	.39	—			
7. Ln Size (employees)	-.06	-.10	-.38	.03	.10	.26	—		
8. Training availability	.13	-.09	.03	.12	.01	.03	.18	—	
9. Industry innovativeness	.03	-.01	-.04	.18	.23	.33	.18	.02	—
Mean or proportion	.36	—	—	3.82	2.00	2.79	4.47	2.54	2.94
s.d.	—	—	—	.89	.90	1.06	1.59	1.40	.99
N	303	307	308	304	305	306	298	307	300

Correlation coefficients of > .11 are significant at $p < .05$ (two-tailed tests)

France, Denmark/Norway, Other); corporate culture – Does the corporate culture of your firm make you feel that you work for a corporation from the parent's home country? (1/0 dummy); mentor – Did you have a mentor at Head Office? (1/0 dummy); training – Are suitable employees encouraged and enabled to attend non-vocational training courses: in house; at HQ at other venues in the corporation at external venues? (scale 0–4).

3. *Local environment characteristics*: industry innovativeness – What is the rate of generation of product and process innovations characteristic of the local market for your most important products? (scale 1–5; very slow – very rapid); industry – industry variable indicating retail/distribution (1/0 dummy)

4. *Firm size*: natural logarithmic transformation of number of employees (continuous) – There is some evidence (Grinyer and Yasai-Ardekani, 1980, 1981) that number of employees is the preferable measure of firm size when examining autonomy.

The means and standard deviations for the continuous/scale variables, proportion of total sample for dummy variables and intercorrelations are shown in Table 7.3.

Testing and results

Investigation 1. The ANCOVA procedure was performed for the unrelated vs related diversification subsidiary tasks. Table 7.4 presents the

Table 7.4 Analysis of covariance summary – unrelated diversification vs related diversification subsidiary tasks

Variable	df	F	Partial eta
Subsidiary task	1	7.05**	.026
Parent nationality	10	4.25***	.139
Mentor	1	5.18*	.019
Corporate culture	1	4.38*	.016
Industry (retail/distribution)	1	0.03	.000
Technology level	1	4.44*	.017
Amount of R&D	1	4.40*	.016
Creation of innovations	1	4.83*	.018
Ln size (employees)	1	0.26	.001
Training	1	3.31†	.012
Industry innovativeness	1	1.06	.004
Intercept	1	286.43***	.521
Model	20	4.27***	.245
Mean square error	263	–	–

*** $p < .001$; ** $p < .01$; * $p < .05$; † $p < .10$ (two-tailed tests)

Table 7.5   Estimates of subsidiary autonomy marginal means for subsidiary tasks of related and unrelated diversification strategies

Subsidiary tasks	n	Mean	Standard error
Unrelated diversification – independent	45	35.82	1.10
Related diversification – distributor, adapter, implementer, innovator	239	32.93	0.69

Difference between means significant at $p < .01$ (two-tailed tests)

analysis of covariance summary and Table 7.5 the estimated marginal means for these tasks. Table 7.4 indicates that, controlling for a range of variables, subsidiary task was a significant predictor of level of subsidiary autonomy ($F[1,263] = 7.05$, $p < .01$) being responsible for 2.6 per cent of the variance in subsidiary autonomy. Table 7.5 shows the subsidiary autonomy mean of 35.82 for the independent task is greater than the 32.93 for the other tasks ($p < .01$). Hypothesis 7.1 was supported.

As suggested in the literature many of the controls were also significant. Table 7.6 shows the estimated marginal means for the level of subsidiary autonomy for the categories of the parent nationality variable. The last category, other, was significantly less than all the nationalities at varying levels of significance but more interestingly

Table 7.6   Estimates of subsidiary autonomy marginal means for parent nationality

Parent nationality	n	Mean	Standard error
1. UK	53	35.50	.99
2. US/Canada	136	33.70	.78
3. Japan	17	38.19	1.63
4. Sweden	11	36.55	1.88
5. Germany	32	38.18	1.28
6. Italy	12	38.11	1.96
7. Switzerland	11	32.12	2.05
8. Netherlands/Belgium	12	35.27	2.10
9. France	9	35.29	2.20
10. Denmark/Norway	14	32.19	1.78
11. Other	6	23.09	3.04

Pairwise comparisons ignoring the Other category (two-tailed tests):
$p < .001$: 5>2
$p < .01$: 5>10; 3>2
$p < .05$: 5>7; 3>7; 3>10; 6>2; 6>7; 6>10

Table 7.7   Analysis of covariance summary – four related diversification subsidiary tasks

Variable	df	F	Partial eta
Subsidiary task	3	3.10*	.041
Parent nationality	10	3.44***	.137
Mentor	1	4.06*	.018
Corporate culture	1	1.15	.005
Industry (retail/distribution)	1	2.34	.011
Technology level	1	2.76†	.022
Amount of R&D	1	2.96†	.013
Creation of innovations	1	3.08†	.014
Ln size (employees)	1	0.47	.002
Training	1	0.75	.003
Industry innovativeness	1	1.78	.008
Intercept	1	233.64***	.520
Model	22	3.24***	.248
Mean square error	216		

*** $p < .001$; ** $p < .01$; * $p < .05$; † $p < .10$ (two-tailed tests)

German, Japanese and Italian MNCs ceded significantly more autonomy to subsidiaries than those from US/Canada, Switzerland and Denmark/Norway. In addition, the respondent having had a mentor at HQ, a home country corporate culture in the MNC, level of technology, amount of R&D performed and frequency of creation of innovations were all significant predictors of subsidiary autonomy at the $p < .05$ level.

Investigation 2. Table 7.7 presents the analysis of covariance summary the four related diversification subsidiary tasks. Subsidiary task was significant ($F[3,216] = 3.10$, $p < .05$). Table 7.8 presents the subsidiary autonomy means for the four related diversification subsidiary tasks controlling for several variables. As hypothesized in Hypotheses 7.2

Table 7.8   Estimates of subsidiary autonomy marginal means for subsidiaries of related diversification strategy

Subsidiary tasks	n	Mean	Standard error
Innovator	48	35.14	1.14
Adapter	62	31.97	1.03
Implementer	42	34.34	1.23
Distributor	87	31.59	0.94

Pairwise comparisons (two-tailed tests):
Innovator > distributor, $p < .01$; innovator > adapter, $p < .05$

and 7.5 the distributor demonstrated the lowest score for subsidiary autonomy and the innovator the highest although only some of the differences from all the other tasks were significant. This indicated some support for Hypotheses 7.2 and 7.5.

The implementer and adapter subsidiary tasks were in the reverse of the expected ordering. Hypotheses 7.3 and 7.4 were not supported.

Although the major focus of these investigations was on subsidiary tasks, the results for many of the control variables add value to the research. They often confirmed the expectations apparent in the literature and thus the robustness of the dependent variable measure. In particular, the importance of MNC home country variable presents as expected (F[10,216] = 4.25 and 3.44 in the two investigations, $p < .001$). Interestingly, the insignificance (F[1,216] = 0.26 and 0.47, $p > .1$) of the size (employees) result in both investigations offered some support for Hedlund's (1981) somewhat neglected contention that the size-autonomy relationship is non-linear.

Discussion and conclusions

This study investigated the HQ-subsidiary relationship in MNCs by examining the links between firm strategy, subsidiary task and subsidiary autonomy. Neither of the two steps in this sequence is particularly controversial since both have been foreshadowed in earlier studies. The firm strategy-subsidiary type link was implicit in the classic studies of Chandler, Vernon, Stopford and Wells and Bartlett and Ghoshal and the task-autonomy association in, for example, Hennart (1993) and Jarillo and Martinez (1990). While some of the specific hypotheses were not supported the overall tenor of the study was in line with the predictions. The major contribution was some empirical evidence of an association between subsidiary autonomy and subsidiary task on the basis of a representative and appropriately sized sample of Australian subsidiaries of largely triad-based MNCs. In addition, while this study did not test deductive hypotheses regarding the firm strategy-subsidiary task link, it also contributed by acting as external validation of the cluster analysis in Chapter 6 that established the existence of five subsidiary tasks theoretically associated with HQ's advantage-generating strategies. This study may have merely scratched the surface of the complexities of the HQ-subsidiary relationship but, by presenting and validating a conceptually developed framework, a new tool is offered with which to investigate this important phenomenon.

The major discrepancies in the results concerned the lower than expected score for the adapter and the higher mean score for the implementer subsidiary tasks. Possible explanations of these have been presaged in earlier discussions. The nature of the actual adaptation task is clearly important. The adapter's score was very close to that of the distributor and hence suggests that, in many cases, the adaptation involved was probably quite limited. Only further data collection and analysis can resolve that question.

A particular aspect of subsidiary autonomy that this investigation highlighted was the extent to which it might be determined by characteristics of the host country. The Australian business environment is economically well-developed and relatively small (and therefore not of major importance to HQ) and the subsidiaries are generally staffed by local personnel (albeit trained or mentored by HQ) that are likely to exhibit a considerable levels of expertise. Hence, *a priori*, a broad-based argument can be made that the HQ might be prepared to accept and encourage high levels of autonomy, as long as the subsidiary's results fulfilled expectations. This issue is discussed in detail in Chapter 12.

Future research

This study is important from the local Australian perspective as it is the first major study of the HQ-subsidiary relationship within foreign-owned MNCs that has been conducted in that country. It should act as a stimulus for future research. More generally the work demonstrates the value of the single host country design as it acts a consistent baseline to measure effects.

While quite commonly used, the construct of subsidiary autonomy is not particularly well-developed in the literature. It was conceived here as a product of the knowledge asymmetries arising from the MNC's utilization of a particular advantage-generating strategy and characteristics of the MNC, the local environment and individual characteristics of any particular subsidiary. This is in line with much of the literature (Taggart and Hood, 1999; Harzing, 1999). This is one starting point but there appears to be a need for a better understanding of subsidiary autonomy. The influences examined here and elsewhere provide some groundwork but a more complex and nuanced analysis is necessary. For example, in this study the innovativeness of the industry might influence the level of capabilities likely to be found in the firm. Which of the variables are directly causal and which are intervening relationships must be ascertained.

From a practical point of view this study has control connotations. The HQ-subsidiary relationship can be conceived in a principal-agent format and the differing knowledge asymmetries between HQ and the subsidiary not only bring about autonomy differences but may also demand that differing control mechanisms be implemented. Following Ouchi (1977), Baliga and Jaeger (1984) and Hennart (1993) consideration may need to be made of output vs behavioral controls and bureaucratic vs cultural mechanisms. However, while more modern perspectives suggest the preponderance of the use of all-embracing cultural or socialization controls, the question of whether the use of controls relates specifically to context remains unresolved. It will however be addressed in Chapter 9.

8
Subsidiary Size and Subsidiary Autonomy

As was demonstrated in the previous chapter, over the last two decades, subsidiary autonomy has been the subject of considerable academic research but the specific relationship between the subsidiary's size and its decision-making autonomy has not been the primary subject of research since a preliminary investigation more than two decades ago (Hedlund, 1981).

The purpose of this chapter is to build upon Hedlund's (1981) study and to shed light upon the subsidiary size-subsidiary autonomy relationship in MNC subsidiaries. For several decades now it has been common practice to relegate firm size to the status of a control variable in organization studies. However, with the escalating interest in firm attributes such as resources, knowledge, competences and capabilities, firm size, in the form of number of employees, merits close attention. It may, for example, be a useful proxy, *ceteris paribus,* for the level of these attributes. In addition, an understanding of the size-autonomy relationship in MNC subsidiaries would be valuable as a template against which to base other studies of subsidiary autonomy.

Drawing on Hedlund's (1981) theoretical proposition, a three-phase model of the effect of subsidiary size on subsidiary autonomy is proposed and tested. Extending linear and quadratic perspectives, the investigation captures the cyclical behavior of the size effect and identifies three distinct phases. The literature on subsidiary autonomy was reviewed in Chapter 7. Hence, after a review of the limited literature on subsidiary size, a series of analyses of subsidiary size as a predictor of subsidiary autonomy are presented, controlling for a number of contingent variables. On the basis of these analyses, Hedlund's (1981) proposition regarding the relationship between subsidiary size and subsidiary autonomy is explored.

Conceptual background and hypothesis

Subsidiary size

The literature pertaining to size as a variable in organizational studies goes back at least to the Aston Studies but is almost entirely focused upon overall firm size. The few studies primarily concerned with subsidiary size were investigating other phenomena (for example, Duhaime and Baird, 1987, as predictor of likely divestment). Some studies have, however, included subsidiary size as a control or secondary predictor variable.

Hedlund (1981) suggested that a large subsidiary would *ceteris paribus* have greater resources than a small subsidiary and increasing size should lead to less dependence upon HQ and thus more autonomy. He cited Aylmer (1970), Peccei and Warner (1976) and Picard (1977) in support of this argument. These studies examined HQ vs subsidiary influence on decision-making in various domains of MNC operation. They were, however, all exploratory and limited in scope and it is far from clear that they demonstrated Hedlund's contention. In contrast, both Negandhi and Baliga (1981b) and Welge (1981) found a direct relationship between subsidiary size and control and coordination intensity over the subsidiary. Contradicting both these sets of results, Egelhoff (1988), focusing on centralization rather than autonomy *per se*, concluded that subsidiary size had no significant influence on organizational design generally, except that large subsidiaries tended to experience a higher degree of manufacturing control than smaller ones. On the basis of these studies the role of subsidiary size as a predictor of subsidiary autonomy remains unclear. The situation is exacerbated by the substantial age of most of the studies that are available.

Hypothesis

Hedlund (1981: 53) offered an explanation that enables a resolution of all of the above equivocality. Figure 8.1 is a direct reproduction of his model of the subsidiary size-autonomy relationship. Three phases are identifiable. While the subsidiary is small and building up resources, it becomes less dependent on HQ and autonomy increases (Phase 1). However, as a subsidiary becomes larger its importance to the MNC, as a whole, increases and then HQ could be expected to impose greater control over it (Phase 2). Combining these ideas would result in a quadratic, inverted U-shaped relationship.

Theoretically both the transaction cost/agency approach and the resource-based view can be brought to bear to support this argument. While the subsidiary is small, the potential costs to the overall MNC of

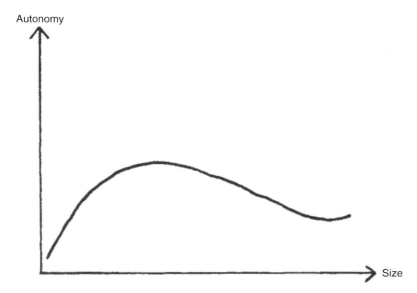

Figure 8.1   Hedlund's (1981) proposed relationship between size and autonomy

subsidiary opportunism remain small. As the subsidiary size increases, the risk of opportunism costs intensifies and the likelihood of HQ imposing progressively more hierarchical controls on the subsidiary grows accordingly.

From a resource-based view, it is to be expected that the increasing size of the subsidiary will bring about an expansion in the subsidiary's unique bundle of tangible and intangible resources. As these become more valuable they must be isolated and retained within the MNC boundary so that their value can be more easily appropriated by the whole corporation.

The inverted U-shape proposition will be explored but, in addition, there might be grounds to extend the logic to argue that, at some stage, the subsidiary reaches such a size that it is able to reassert its autonomy. A possible explanation is that, at some point, diseconomies of scale arise that substantially affect the control and coordination costs for HQ and, consequently, it delegates decision-making autonomy to the subsidiary unit management for all but the most important decisions (Phase 3). In line with these ideas, it is suggested that:

Hypothesis 8.1: Subsidiary autonomy will exhibit a triphasic (sinusoidal) association with subsidiary size.

Method

Measures

Subsidiary autonomy. This is the same variable that was used in Chapter 7.

Subsidiary size. This was measured by the respondent's estimation of the number of full-time employees. The natural logarithmic transformation was used.

Controls. The specific nature of this study and the consequent need to make every attempt to avoid misspecification demanded that all potentially relevant and available control variables be incorporated. The study included the industry sector (manufacturing, retail/distribution and finance/property/business services) as dummy variables; the nationality of the parent (UK, USA, Japan, and Western Europe) as dummy variables; corporate culture (Australian corporation and corporation from the parent home country) as dummy variables; parent's ownership stake (%); subsidiary tenure in Australia (years); the level of technology in primary operations; amount of R&D on behalf of rest of corporation; intensity of local competition; expatriate employees (number of employees); the speed of innovation in the industry; number of expatriates employed; and cultural distance. (See the survey instrument in the methodological appendix for further details.)

This study and the original Hedlund empirical work are both cross-sectional analyses. Hedlund's proposition, however, is dynamic in that it models the growth of a subsidiary over time. To truly test this model would require a research design that encompassed a considerable numbers of longitudinal studies. This problem can be mitigated, if not completely eliminated, by controlling for the size of the subsidiary relative to the size of the overall MNC size. Hence the relative size of the subsidiary *vis a vis* the parent corporation in terms of number of employees and turnover were also included as controls.

Table 8.1 shows the descriptive statistics (means and standard deviation) and inter-correlations for all the control variables operationalized in the study.

Results and analysis

It appears that the trigonometric (or sinusoidal) association between subsidiary size and the level of subsidiary autonomy has not been empirically investigated before. Following the procedure employed by Nygaard and Dahlstrom (2002), the study utilized the sine function of subsidiary size to estimate its triphasic effect on the level of subsidiary

Table 8.1 Descriptive statistics and intercorrelations

Variable	1	2	3	4	5	6	7	8	9	10	11	12	13	14	15	16	17	18	19
1. Parent: UK	—																		
2. Parent: US	-.37	—																	
3. Parent: Japan	-.11	-.19	—																
4. Parent: Western Europe	-.30	-.55	-.15	—															
5. Industry: manufacturing	.03	.00	.00	-.04	—														
6. Industry: retail/distribution	-.11	-.01	.04	.13	-.65	—													
7. Industry: finance/business services	.02	.02	-.00	-.11	-.26	-.38	—												
8. Level of technology	-.03	-.11	-.07	.20	-.09	.07	.07	—											
9. Amount of R&D for MNC	.09	-.04	-.04	-.06	.16	-.27	.12	.15	—										
10. Industry innovativeness	-.04	-.05	.05	.02	.00	-.04	.10	.18	.23	—									
11. Industry competitiveness	-.09	.04	.07	-.05	.03	-.05	.03	.08	.11	.23	—								
12. Tenure in Australia	.02	.12	-.07	-.13	.35	-.28	-.06	-.08	.15	.03	.13	—							
13. Number of expatriates	-.02	-.11	.16	.05	.03	-.11	.04	.20	.12	.08	.12	.07	—						
14. Parent's ownership stake	-.11	.05	-.11	.03	.06	-.17	.04	.09	.13	.06	.20	.31	.19	—					
15. Cultural distance	.08	-.83	.41	.70	-.03	.09	-.10	.13	-.07	.02	-.07	-.15	.16	.03	—				
16. Home country culture	-.06	.00	.18	-.06	-.06	.12	-.05	-.06	-.10	-.01	-.05	-.06	.00	.09	.03	—			
17. Australian culture	.13	-.13	.15	-.09	.10	-.17	.08	-.06	.04	.00	-.04	.08	-.07	-.14	.05	-.21	—		
18. Relative size (staff)	.14	.01	.08	-.12	.31	-.28	-.01	.00	.05	.09	.09	.19	.17	-.03	-.01	-.07	.11	—	
19. Relative size (turnover)	.12	-.01	-.01	-.05	.21	-.25	.05	.06	.07	.10	-.02	.15	.14	-.08	-.01	-.05	.09	.82	—
Mean or proportion	.17	.41	.05	.30	.31	.48	.13	3.82	1.99	2.94	4.33	30.29	2.07	98.48	.52	.15	.21	.02	.04
Standard deviation	—	—	—	—	—	—	—	.88	.90	.99	.77	24.19	5.57	7.67	.81	—	—	.06	.10

autonomy. The three phases in the triphasic perspective represent a cyclical behavior that is best modelled by a sine function ($-1 \le \sin \theta \le +1$). In addition, the direct and quadratic relationship between subsidiary size and the level of subsidiary autonomy were also examined. This is necessary for methodological rigor and to detect clearly whether an inverted-U relationship between subsidiary size and the level of subsidiary autonomy exists.

In line with Nygaard and Dahlstrom (2002), a two-stage data analysis was followed. Stage 1 was aimed at testing the direct and inverted-U relationship between subsidiary size and subsidiary autonomy. A three-model (hierarchical) regression analysis was employed. In Model 1, the control variables only were entered. Model 2 included control variables plus the main effect of subsidiary size (as a logarithmic transformation). Finally, Model 3 included control variables, the main effect of subsidiary size, and the squared term of subsidiary size (as a logarithmic transformation). Stage 2 was aimed at testing whether the level of subsidiary autonomy was a trigonometric (sine) function of subsidiary size.

The variance inflation factor (VIF) was calculated for each of the regression coefficients and used to test for collinearity among variables. Calculations of VIF ranged from a low of 1.15 to a high of 7.88. The higher values were for the categorical dummies and all were below the cut-off figure of 10 recommended by Neter, Wasserman and Kutner (1985).

The investigation first tested whether the level of subsidiary autonomy was highest at moderate level of subsidiary size (an inverted-U shape relationship). Methodologically, in order to detect a significant inverted-U association between subsidiary size (predictor variable) and subsidiary autonomy (dependent variable), two necessary and sufficient criteria must be satisfied: (1) the linear main effect of subsidiary size must be positively associated with the level of subsidiary autonomy and (2) the squared-term of subsidiary size must be negative and significantly associated with the level of subsidiary autonomy.

Table 8.2 (Linear Effect Model) indicated that the linear effect of subsidiary size was associated positively and significantly with the level of subsidiary autonomy ($t = 2.08$; $p < .05$). Hence the first criterion of an inverted-U relationship between the subsidiary size and subsidiary autonomy was satisfied. When the squared-term of subsidiary size was included in the equation (Quadratic Effect Model), the linear effect of subsidiary size still remained positively and significantly associated with subsidiary autonomy ($t = 2.51$; $p < .05$) but, more importantly, the squared-term was negatively and significantly associated with subsidiary autonomy (t = –2.01; p < .05). Hence, the second criterion was also satisfied. In addition, the inclusion of the squared term of subsidiary size had increased the R^2 of the model by 1.5 per cent over the Linear Effect Model. These findings indicated that as subsidiary size increased, the level of subsidiary autonomy also increased up to a

Table 8.2 Linear, quadratic and trigonometric effects of subsidiary size on subsidiary autonomy

Variable	Controls only model (t value) (t value)	Linear effect model (t value)	Quadratic effect model (t value)	Trigo-nometric effect model
Parent: UK[c]	1.78†	1.75†	1.51	1.73†
Parent: US[c]	.90	.78	.48	.88
Parent: Japan[c]	2.86**	2.86**	2.76**	2.88**
Parent: Western Europe[c]	2.04*	2.05*	1.87†	2.07*
Industry: manufacturing[b]	1.20	1.27	1.45	1.20
Industry: retail or distribution[b]	–.15	.65	.84	.33
Industry: finance or bus services[b]	–.55	–.32	–.30	–.58
Level of technology	–2.18*	–2.26*	–1.96†	–2.52*
Amount of R&D for MNC	–.10	.01	.17	–.22
Industry innovativeness	.15	–.23	–.43	.43
Industry competitiveness	–1.50	–1.82†	–2.04*	–1.61
Tenure in Australia	–.71	–1.44	–.93	–.94
Number of expatriates	–1.28	–1.85†	–1.58	–1.12
Parent's ownership stake	.98	1.11	1.08	1.08
Cultural distance	–1.09	–1.11	–1.13	–1.14
Parent's home country culture[d]	–2.40*	–2.29*	–2.30*	–2.42*
Australian culture[d]	.34	.32	.36	.19
Relative size (staff)	–.75	–1.04	–1.08	–.94
Relative size (turnover)	1.65	1.56	1.58	1.53
Ln (subsidiary size)		2.08*	2.51*	
Ln (subsidary size squared)			–2.01*	
Sine (subsidiary size)				–2.64**
R^2	.187	.204	.219	.214
ΔR^2		.017[a]	.032[a]	.027[a]
F	2.46**	2.60***	2.70***	2.76***

[a] Over controls only model
[b] Omitted group is other sectors than manufacturing, retail/distribution, and finance/property/business services.
[c] Omitted group is parents from other countries than UK, US, Japan, and Western Europe.
[d] Omitted group is global corporation culture.
*** p < .001; ** p < .01 ; * p < .05; † p < .10 (two-tailed test)

certain cut-off point. After this cut-off point, however, any increase in subsidiary size resulted in a diminishing level of autonomy. The association between subsidiary size and subsidiary autonomy was non-monotonic as revealed by a negative, significant quadratic effect.

The analysis next demonstrated the trigonometric effect of subsidiary size on the level of subsidiary autonomy. Table 8.2 (Trigonometric Effect Model) indicated that in addition to its linear and quadratic effects, subsidiary size (as a sine function) was significantly related to the level of subsidiary autonomy ($t = -2.64$, $p < .01$). Consequently, the hypothesis that posited a sinusoidal association between subsidiary size and the level of subsidiary autonomy was supported. This finding was important evidence to demonstrate that after a certain level of subsidiary size, subsidiary autonomy begins to increase again.

In terms of control variables (based on the Trigonometric Model), it was noted that Japanese ($t = 2.88$, $p < .01$) and Western European parents ($t = 2.07$; $p < .05$) were related positively and significantly to the level of subsidiary autonomy whereas the level of technology used in primary operations ($t = -2.58$, $p < .01$) and having a corporate culture that made the respondent feel that they worked for a firm from the parent's home country ($t = -2.42$; $p < .01$) were related negatively and significantly to the level of subsidiary autonomy. Despite a considerable number of control variables in the model, no other significant associations between control variables and subsidiary autonomy were detected. Overall, the trigonometric model explained just over 21 per cent of the variance in the level of subsidiary autonomy.

Discussion

The conclusions from the modeling were in obvious concordance with the inverted-U shape. In addition, however, in Figure 8.1 there was a discernible upwards movement in the curve at its tail. Hedlund did not comment on this but the analysis deduced that this was an indication of a second change in the sign of the curve slope. It appears that a number of the larger subsidiaries exhibit increasing levels of autonomy. This can be interpreted as a threshold point (or range) at which the subsidiary begins to establish greater decision-making autonomy and eventually loosens its dependence on HQ. A thorough literature search found considerable speculation on the optimal size of firms or plants but unearthed no theoretical or empirical evidence for the second threshold effect.

The present study investigated a wider range of home country MNCs than the Hedlund study. It is well-known in the international management literature that MNCs from differing home countries have varying predilections with regard to subsidiary autonomy and that Swedish MNCs have a tendency to decentralize decision-making more than others. In contrast to Hedlund's Swedish-only sample, the present study contained MNCs from 17 countries. Since most of the previous literature had examined US, UK, Japanese and various Western European MNCs, this sample was categorized broadly on that pattern. The totals in each category were US = 127, UK = 53, Japanese = 17, Western European = 95 and Others = 21. The category Western European contained subsidiaries of MNCs from 11 countries. These countries were spread over Hofstede's (1984) Germanic, Nordic and Latin European groups. The range engendered some confidence that any unique country partiality did not seriously affect the results. Overall, this helped to extend the universality of the Hedlund proposition.

While this study demonstrated considerable support for Hedlund's proposition, there were a number of reservations and issues to address. First, it was apparent from previous research and the analysis above that many factors other than size might affect the level of subsidiary autonomy in any given case. These other factors were no doubt contributors to the wide scatter found in the basic data. It is a testament to the robustness of Hedlund's fundamental logic that, despite these confounding influences, the quadratic/sinusoidal relationship was still evidenced. The curvilinear form can now act as a baseline relationship against which to measure these other effects.

A further point arises from Hedlund's (1981) contention that the overall shape of his initial curve should be understood as indicating the degree of autonomy given a certain size of parent company. For a smaller MNC, and hence greater size of the subsidiary relative to the size of the MNC, Hedlund proposed that the curve would be steeper and flatten out earlier. He stated 'a declining degree of autonomy is hypothesized for subsidiaries very large in relation to the parent company' (Hedlund, 1981: 55). These observations did not affect the basic hypothesis but they did emphasize that relative size of subsidiary to overall MNC may be an important consideration and relative size was controlled for in the models. In addition, it was noted that while subsidiary size ranged from 2 to 8000 employees, the overall MNC size was always very large in comparison. The relative size ranged only from near zero to 4 per cent. (The single outlier was one subsidiary that constituted 8 per cent of the MNC.) Thus, in this sample, the range of the relative size variable was so small that it precluded formal statistical testing of the conjecture. This small subsidiary relative size may simply have been a consequence of the relative size of the Australian market. Whether any markets have subsidiaries of relatively large enough size to test the relative size hypothesis must be the subject of future investigations.

A further issue lies in the measure of autonomy being somewhat at variance to that used by Hedlund. However, given the consistent use of autonomy measures very similar to that used here, this should not present insurmountable problems for acceptance of the results.

It is hoped that this study will stimulate future researchers to conduct more detailed studies on the size-autonomy relationship. In this line, future researchers should examine the causality between size and autonomy. Using longitudinal data, future studies might examine how a given level of autonomy at one point in time leads to subsidiaries' growth which will generate further claims for greater autonomy at other points in time. Given that subsidiary autonomy shows, or at least hints at, a cyclical association with size, the HQ-subsidiary relationship quality (in terms of communication effectiveness, mutual trust, relationship satisfaction, and commitment) may vary depending on level of subsidiary autonomy. Hence, future researchers might explore the role of subsidiary size on the HQ-subsidiary relationship quality in conjunction with the level of autonomy.

9
Control and Coordination

To continue the investigation of the HQ-subsidiary relationship, the next undertaking is to analyze the association between subsidiary task and control and coordination in the MNC. The types of control and coordination mechanisms imposed on the various subsidiaries are a central aspect of the HQ-subsidiary relationship. More specifically, this chapter investigates the use of the devices implemented by HQ to control and coordinate activities in the MNC's network of subsidiaries.

It was argued in the theoretical model in Chapter 5 that the nature of the control and coordination mechanisms was likely to be related to the nature of the knowledge asymmetries characteristic of the HQ-subsidiary relationships that were brought about by the MNC's advantage-generating strategy. A particularly aspect of this issue is whether this strategy brings about a structure in the MNC that is hierarchic or heterarchic. If these associations can be confirmed, then they act as further evidence for the external validity of the model.

The empirical work in this chapter investigates the relationship between the five subsidiary tasks derived from the model and a selection from the considerable range of control mechanisms used by the HQ in MNCs. In doing so this investigation performs two important undertakings. It brings evidence to bear upon the soundness of the original theoretical framework on HQ-subsidiary relations and it tests the relative validity of two competing explanations of control in MNCs. The early conceptual studies by Ouchi (1977), Baliga and Jaeger (1984) and Jaeger and Baliga (1985), reviewed in the next section, laid the foundation for much of the resultant work. More recent studies have challenged the basic implication of their work that the various control mechanisms available are used as alternatives. Two broad logics of control in MNCs have been suggested in the literature. The

Ouchi/Baliga/Jaeger (OBJ) model proposed that different control mechanisms will be used in different contexts. The more recent perspective proposed by Martinez and Jarillo (1991), Ferner, Edwards and Sisson (1995) and Ferner (2000) and others argued that different control mechanisms are not alternatives but are layered on top of each other and used in combination.

Literature and conceptual background

The control and coordination distinction

Control mechanisms are bureaucratic and normative tools, such as reporting systems, procedural or policy manuals and socialization devices, which ensure that performance, output and behavior in the subsidiary accord with HQ expectations. The argument presented in Chapter 5 was that the control measures instituted by HQ for each subsidiary task were specific to the different patterns of knowledge asymmetry that existed in different HQ-subsidiary relations. The mechanisms and their vigor of implementation are important factors in understanding the level of subsidiary autonomy that was investigated in the last two chapters.

Coordination mechanisms are systems designed to ensure that the necessary degree of integration is achieved between the activities of all subsidiaries. They focus upon the subsidiary's entrenchment within the processes and networks of the overall MNC. They are concerned with the subsidiary's multilateral relationships with other subsidiaries as well as with the subsidiary's specific dyadic relationship with HQ. They vary widely in detail but are usually related to flows of factor resources, intermediate products and/or knowledge and information.

While these explanations appear to clearly differentiate the two constructs, in practice, this is not so easily achieved. It is, for example, a fundamental premise of much of the critical management literature that socialization mechanisms are primary control tools in the modern corporation. They also act as coordination mechanisms by which the overall activities within the MNC are orchestrated. This control-coordination distinction has not been clearly elaborated in the literature and there are confusing interpretations of the terminology. Martinez and Jarillo (1989, 1991), for example, used control and coordination almost interchangeably. They stated (Martinez and Jarillo, 1991: 431) that formalization (the imposition of behavioral conformity via manuals, standard operating procedures and so on) was a mechanism of coordination and differentiated it from what they termed 'behavioral control' which they described as being based upon direct personal surveillance of the subordinate's behavior.

In addition, as Hoffman (1994) pointed out, the use of the term control has implications of a superior-subordinate relationship and terms such as 'parent company' or 'mother-daughter structure' (Hedlund, 1984) reinforced this notion of dependence. Many of the 'daughters', however, grew strong and influential in their own right, developing skills and knowledge that were valuable and transferable throughout the MNC. As the subsidiaries developed, interdependence became a more accurate representation of the nature of the bond and coordination a more accurate description of the process.

A further complication arises in that control and coordination issues are also clearly related to the issue of subsidiary autonomy examined in the previous two chapters. However, the nuances of the interactions in the relationship are not simple. For example, it might be that, in some instances, autonomy was conceded to a subsidiary only when systems had been set in place that ensured the subsidiary acted in accordance with HQ policies and plans. As Hennart pointed out, 'while the concept(s are) ... clear, the interpretation is more ambiguous. Decisions made by a perfectly socialized manager may be undistinguishable from those made at HQ. Autonomy measures the relative use of hierarchical control ... as opposed to socialization ... it does not necessarily reflect the subunit manager's ... responsiveness to local conditions' (Hennart, 1991: 91). While in reality Hennart's perfectly socialized manager may be an unlikely phenomenon, it does not detract from the complexity and contextual nature of the association between autonomy, control and coordination.

This distinction between control and coordination is a case of contextual interpretation and hence, for the purposes of clarity in this chapter, a single term will be used. Controls are the range of formal and informal, bureaucratic and cultural, mechanisms by which behavior and output are monitored and channeled in desired directions.

Control in organizations

It was argued in Chapter 2 that the accent on opportunism in the transaction costs approach provided insufficient depth of analysis to more fully understand the problem of control in the HQ-subsidiary relationship. Williamson (1975) extended the transaction cost analysis in several directions including, for example, a consideration of the trade-offs between monitoring and incentives but it is clear that control in modern MNCs is concerned with many more issues – capabilities, information, learning processes and so on – than simply attenuating the opportunistic behavior of individuals (or subsidiary firms) by various mechanisms. Nevertheless, the knowledge asymmetries (and the subsequent potential for opportunism) highlighted by the TCA are theoretically important with regard to HQ implementation of control mechanisms.

The centrality of control as a key managerial task can be traced back to the dawn of management theory. All of the major early theorists – Fayol, Taylor, Urwick, Follet – addressed the control issue. Control, as usually implemented in organizations, is essentially a cybernetic process. Planning sets a required standard of performance or behavior and actual performance or behavior is monitored and compared to this. Any deviation is assessed to ascertain whether action is required and if so the appropriate corrective action is taken. This basic process can be used to control operational processes, individuals, teams, departments, firms, divisions and so on as required. It can be an extremely powerful tool. McKinsey, for example, built the consultancy empire that bears his name on the principle of financial budgeting which derives directly from this process. The standard definition was given by Tannenbaum (1966: 84) 'control is any process in which a person or group of persons or organization of persons determines or intentionally affects what another person, group or organization will do'.

Since the 1960s there has been an extensive and varied literature dealing with control issues and systems in organizations and Egelhoff (1984) and Jaeger and Baliga (1985) presented reviews extracted from the international business literature. Much of the empirical work has been on domestic organizations but since the late 1970s an increasing body of literature on control in MNCs has accumulated. This chapter focuses primarily on literature from this domain. It remains, however, a diverse field with different studies tending to look at different aspects. Egelhoff's (1984) characterization of the field as having 'a wide base and little height' remains essentially true today. 'How to achieve the required 'control mix' ... remains a perennial MNE challenge' (Fenwick, De Cieri and Welch, 1999).

Theoretical developments

The first part of this research is primarily based upon the conceptual frameworks developed by Ouchi (1977) and Baliga and Jaeger (1984). The importance of Thompson's (1967) types of interdependence is also examined. The OBJ conceptual base for the practicalities of the control

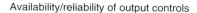

Availability/reliability of output controls

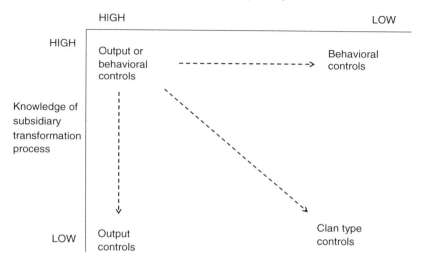

Figure 9.1 Ouchi's (1977) model of control mechanisms

process in MNCs can be traced, at least initially, back to Weber (1947) and his classic study on the bureaucratic organizational model. Ouchi (1977) argued that an understanding of control was driven by two criteria, that is whether reliable output measures were readily available and to what extent HQ's knowledge of the subsidiary's transformation process was inferior or superior to that of the subsidiary (see Figure 9.1). If reliable measures of output were available then the subsidiary would be monitored on the basis of formal performance reports such as indicators of production volumes, market share, revenues, sales, profit, return on investment (ROI) and so on. If these measures were not available or did not regulate effort effectively, then HQ would tend towards the use of behavior controls whereby subsidiary managers' decisions were guided by centrally developed manuals on company policies and standard operating procedures. Hence when efficient output measures were available and HQ knowledge of the transformation process was high, then either output or behavioral controls were equally appropriate. As the reliability or existence of suitable output measures decreased, the MNC needed to shift its focus to behavioral controls. However, as HQ's knowledge of the transformation process in the subsidiary declined (Hennart, 1982), the preference for objective measures of output control increased. Finally, as the presence of both mechanisms diminished, the need for what Ouchi called clan-type (normative or cultural) controls arose.

A pure bureaucratic system relied upon explicit formal rules and regulations. This stood in contrast to what Ouchi, Baliga and Jaeger termed cultural control – a formal and informal, explicit and implicit, organization-wide system of accepted norms and values on how things should be done. Under cultural control, conformance was established by socialization mechanisms that developed commitment to the organization, ensuring that managers could be trusted to act in accordance with the shared philosophy and expectations. Baliga and Jaeger (1984) and Jaeger and Baliga (1985) both present the following table (Table 9.1) to demonstrate the mechanisms used to monitor behavior and output under bureaucratic and cultural control systems.

Analytically, under firm rather than market governance, there are only two phenomena that can be controlled – output and behavior – and these can be controlled either by bureaucratic or normative (labeled cultural by Baliga and Jaeger) mechanisms. Controlling output by bureaucratic means gives rise to extensive formal reporting in a range of manifestations. Policies of controlling behavior by bureaucratic means are accompanied by a plethora of policy and instructional manuals, standard operating procedures and the like. Successful normative control lies in encouraging, disseminating and inculcating shared values and norms of behavior. Normative control of output is evidenced by shared beliefs of what is appropriate performance and normative control of behavior is achieved by embedding a joint philosophy of 'how things are done around here'. All these control mechanisms appear to be found in the modern MNC but the extensive dispersion of communications, knowledge management and decision-making distinctive of the heterarchic/transnational MNC means that normative controls are particularly vital to the successful implementation of this organizational form and strategy.

Table 9.1   The Baliga/Jaeger typology of control mechanisms

Object of control	Type of control	
	Bureaucratic	Cultural
Output	Performance reports	Shared norms of performance
Behavior	Company manuals	Shared philosophy of management

There is, however, no clear concordance in the literature as to what exactly constitutes or how to operationalize output, behavioral and cultural controls or the nature of the relationship between them. Various authors used alternative conceptualizations. Hamilton and Kashlak (1999), for example, began from the basic Ouchi (1977) model but then differentiated input controls – selection and induction training – from behavioral controls although both can be classified under Baliga and Jaeger's (1984) cultural control category. Eisenhardt (1985) also adapted the Ouchi model focusing on the ties between task programmability and outcome measurability. Weaving agency issues into the mix (see also O'Donnell, 2000), Govindarajan and Fisher (1990) modified Eisenhardt's (1985) model by introducing outcome and behavior observability. Gupta and Govindarajan (1991) made a distinction between formal organizational structures and control systems (design of decision processes and control systems) and informal coordination mechanisms (emergent patterns of communication and socialization). This distinction largely paralleled Baliga and Jaeger's bureaucratic-cultural differentiation. In contrast, Harzing (1999) differentiated controls on the basis of two dimensions. One dimension was based upon social interactions (personal or cultural) vs instruments (impersonal or bureaucratic) and the other direct (explicit) vs indirect (implicit). Marginson (2002) followed Simons (1995, 1999) and clustered controls into value systems, administrative systems and performance measurement systems.

Baliga and Jaeger (1984) extended their model to demonstrate the relationship between control and delegation and then offered a framework which managers could use to select the most efficacious control or autonomy mix (they used the term delegation rather than autonomy). The key variables were type of interdependence between units (pooled, sequential or reciprocal), level of environmental uncertainty and degree of cultural proximity. Type of interdependence was based upon the Thompson (1967) categories (see Figure 9.2).

Pooled interdependence was, in effect, dependence rather than interdependence. Essentially it was exhibited when subunits were obliged to depend upon a central pool of resources, knowledge or expertise held at HQ. Sequential interdependence was exhibited when a subunit was dependent upon the unit one step further up the value chain and was the source unit for the next unit one step further down the value chain. Reciprocal interdependence was evidenced when many units were reciprocally dependent upon each other.

In practice it is clear that most large MNCs have available, and usually employ, a wide range of control mechanisms. As well as

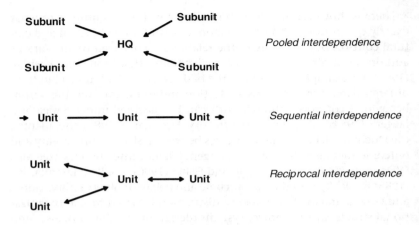

Direction of arrows shows direction of dependence

Figure 9.2   Types of interdependence (after Thompson, 1967)

bureaucratic controls, they are also likely to use feed-forward (input) controls such as sophisticated selection procedures as well as various training and socialization schemes. Ouchi and Jaeger's (1978) well known typology of Type A (the US 'ideal' type), Type J (the Japanese 'ideal' type) and Type Z (the modified US type exhibiting Type J characteristics) organizations was largely derived from the frequency of use of these various control systems. The distinctive phenomenon of cultural control in Type Z organizations was manifest in the presence of what Ouchi and Jaeger (1978) call 'clans'. Hence, as presented in Figure 9.1, cultural control was termed clan control. There is a wide range of alternative terminology in the literature. While some authors are at pains to define terms as precisely as possible and there are some subtleties of meaning, there is a general flexibility and interchangeability. Administrative, formal and explicit are usually synonyms or descriptors for bureaucratic controls while normative, clan and implicit are the same for cultural controls.

The nature of the local host environment is another issue of importance in the literature on control. Ghoshal and Nohria (1989) proposed that host country operating environments impose demands for internally differentiating HQ-subsidiary relationships. The results of a number of studies have highlighted aspects of this need for 'differentiated fit' (Nohria and Ghoshal, 1994). Muralidharan and Hamilton stated 'managers must define differential control systems for multiple foreign subsidiaries' (1999: 352). Kobrin (1988) demonstrated a dramatic replacement of expatriate managers by local managers in US MNCs in the early 1980s. He argued that this came about in order to align the MNC more effectively with the local environment. Chang and Taylor (1999) argued that type of control exerted was a product of HQ-host cultural distance. Nobel and Birkinshaw (1998) showed that different types of international R&D unit were managed through different control mechanisms (see also Chiesa, 1999).

Closely linked to this subject there are only two studies that have attempted to address the impact of cultural differences on strategy and control. Horng (1993) sketched a model using trust built from managerial transfers as the intervening variable. There were limitations, however, and if a MNC became too culturally diversified the adoption of clan type control presented considerable problems and needed to be replaced by a return to more formal, often financial, control systems.

Sohn (1994) built upon the concept of clans to introduce the value of social knowledge – defined as the ability to understand and predict others' behavior – as a control mechanism. A series of hypotheses were tested with Japanese FDI data in the US, Singapore, Taiwan and Korea and the results offered broad support for the proposition that MNCs with social knowledge have less need to resort to ownership (and presumably other mechanisms) for control purposes.

In order to hold many of these factors constant and thus produce more consistent and interpretable results while exploring the different subsidiary tasks, the present study is looking at a single host country, Australia. Hence, the varying context issue was not likely to affect the investigations substantially.

Despite these developments, the fundamentals of the OBJ conceptualization have generally remained as the most useful starting point for understanding control in practice. A major exception was Hennart's (1991, 1993) additional proposal of the use of the price mechanism in the guise of transfer pricing and profit centers. These mechanisms are, in practice, important control tools, especially in globally integrated MNCs. There are, however, two reasons why internal transfer pricing and profit centers are not an appropriate concern for this research. First, the confidential nature of the information necessary to pursue this line of research implies that it could only be obtained via detailed case study work after an extensive period of trust building with appropriate firms. Second, with regard to transfer pricing specifically, the infrequency (or absence) of the contributor subsidiary task provides some evidence that subsidiaries in Australia are not much used as intermediate product suppliers within their MNC. Australia tends to be either a final product market or a distribution center for the smaller economies of the region. Hence, an examination of transfer pricing issues is both beyond the scope of this research and probably not of great relevance in this context. The focus here will be primarily upon the OBJ mechanisms since there have been few direct theoretical alternatives.

An alternative perspective

In the use of the OBJ model, it had been an implicit assumption of the research that the various control systems were alternatives. Martinez and Jarillo (1991) proposed, however, that:

> these mechanisms go from relatively simple (formal mechanisms) to more sophisticated and expensive tools (subtle): these latter mechanisms are added, not substituted for, the formal ones (Edstrom and Galbraith, 1977; Galbraith and Kazanjian, 1986). Thus, although all organizations have some sort of informal structure, the conscious development and use of subtle mechanisms of coordination would appear only when the demands for coordination exceed that afforded by the purely formal (and cheaper) mechanisms. Ghoshal (1984) and Jarillo and Martinez (1990) have analyzed these mechanisms of coordination within the international context, finding that they indeed can be found in MNCs (Martinez and Jarillo, 1991: 432).

In contrast to the common OBJ perspect Ferner et al. (1995) and Ferner (2000) began from the perspective of HQ's power to manipulate the corporate culture of the organization and, thus, shape the perceptions and values of its employees. They considered the relationship between the many control mechanisms and argued that formal bureaucratic controls depend for their effectiveness upon informal systems and power relations. In particular, they suggested that bureaucratic controls were underpinned by the 'deployment of social control mechanisms relating to the creation of common value systems, understandings, and expectations about the rules of the game' (Ferner, 2000: 521). Ferner et al. (1995) were arguing that in modern MNCs the various control mechanisms were not simply alternatives, as presented in the various Ouchi and co-workers models, but were cumulative and were mutually supportive. Each control mechanism performed a different function but they were used in combination as a control system. This was the argument that lay behind Pucik and Katz's (1986) assertion that the effectiveness of any control system depended upon the human resource management structures behind it. They argued, specifically, for the importance of the management of technical and social information systems in the areas of selection, development, appraisal and rewards. The implication of these alternative analyzes is that investigators are unlikely to find distinguishing types of control mechanisms in different types of subsidiary since all HQs will probably be utilizing the entire range of mechanisms.

Thus there are two broadly competing models for the use of controls. The OBJ conceptualization suggested that reports acted as bureaucratic output monitors, formalization was used for bureaucratic behavior control and formal and informal socialization tools for cultural control but all of these were implemented in specific contexts. The second suggestion was that these mechanisms were imposed concurrently in the manner of Martinez, Jarillo, Ferner et al. above. Both of these interpretations are congruent with the theoretical framework derived in Chapter 5.

Research propositions

For the purposes of these empirical investigations, the earliest control formulation, the OBJ conceptualization, was used as the starting point. The large number of dependent and predictor variables precluded the use of detailed formal hypothesis testing of all dependent to predictor associations and, in consequence, the investigation is structured around a series of more general research propositions. Basing the analysis on the expected outcomes of differing knowledge asymmetries, the types of control mechanisms likely to be associated with the different subsidiary tasks are proposed.

Distributor and implementer subsidiaries

Most knowledge relevant to the effective operation of the distributor subsidiary is held at HQ. Their primary output is easily measurable sales volume and HQ will probably impose detailed operating procedures to ensure the subsidiary conforms to global administrative and marketing protocols.

For the implementer subsidiary task, all the significant knowledge is held at HQ, with the subsidiary's role restricted to implementing HQ's ownership advantage. Knowledge of the local environment is of little concern at HQ since the MNC's basic products are unopposed in the market. Again, bureaucratic/hierarchical controls are appropriate and both output and behavioral controls are likely to be available. Overall it is proposed that:

> **Proposition 9.1:** Relative to the other subsidiary tasks, control of distributor and implementer subsidiaries will be more likely to be associated with bureaucratic mechanisms.

Adapter subsidiaries

For these subsidiaries, basic knowledge of the transformation process lies at HQ since it was probably developed there. However, the detailed knowledge of the host environment that enables suitable adaptation, integration into the host market and brings some of the advantage from the strategy resides with the subsidiary. Some bureaucratic control of output and/or behavior is possible but it is likely to be augmented by cultural controls. Overall, the type of bureaucratic control will depend upon the context especially the availability of suitable output measures. If they are available, HQ control of the adapter subsidiary is likely to be based upon bureaucratic output reports and if not, the element of bureaucratic control will be based upon bureaucratic behavioral controls. On balance it is proposed that:

> **Proposition 9.2:** Control of adapter subsidiaries will be likely to be associated with a combination of bureaucratic and cultural controls.

Innovator subsidiaries

The theoretical link between the OBJ control model and the hierarchy/heterarchy distinction is very straightforward. Hierarchy is generally congruent with bureaucratic control and heterarchy with cultural control. The non-hierarchical nature of the HQ's relationship with the innovator subsidiaries theoretically rules out the likely use of hierarchical control mechanisms of any kind. Hence it is proposed that:

> **Proposition 9.3:** Relative to the other subsidiary tasks, control of innovator subsidiaries will be more likely to be associated with cultural control mechanisms.

Independent subsidiaries

With inferior knowledge of the transformation process, the host environment and most other factors, the literature suggests that HQ should utilize cultural controls. However, shared norms and values are likely to be difficult to inculcate in subsidiaries performing diverse tasks in differing industries. It is even possible that attempts to impose such corporate conformity might be counterproductive. The theoretical models from the literature above do not make specific predictions for this context. If the output of a subsidiary is easily measured then Hennart's proposition of making the subsidiary a profit center with performance-based subsidiary management remuneration might be appropriate. If the output is not easily measured then HQ can only impose broadly-based performance requirements such as return on assets (ROA). Generally, however, it is proposed that

> **Proposition 9.4:** Relative to the other subsidiary tasks, independent subsidiaries will be the least tightly controlled with the major tool likely to be output reporting.

Method

Dependent variables

The individual control mechanisms, the dependent variables in the study, are now considered in more detail.

Bureaucratic controls. There were two mechanisms of bureaucratic control investigated. First, the single measure of bureaucratic output reporting was the variable labeled reports. This was derived from a question asking respondents the frequency with which they communicated with HQ via reports. The scale was 1 = never through 5 = very frequently. Descriptive statistics for this and all the other dependent variables are given in Table 9.2 and further details on the questions

Table 9.2   Descriptive statistics for dependent variables

Variable	n	Range	Mean/ proportion	s.d.	Reliability (α)
Reports	306	1–5	3.97	0.91	–
Formalization	308	0–6	2.89	1.69	0.69
Contact HQ	307	1–5	3.27	1.34	–
Contact other group firms	305	1–5	2.67	1.47	–
Expatriate density	299	0–0.6	0.0256	0.0757	–
Induction	303	1–5	3.79	1.17	–
Training	307	0–4	2.54	1.40	0.76
Expatriates – yes/no	313	1/0	48.9	–	–
Mentor – yes/no	308	1/0	36.0	–	–

and the necessary factor analysis can be found in the methodological appendix in Chapter 12.

Second, the bureaucratic behavioral control variable, formalization, was calculated as the sum of six dichotomous variables in which 1 indicated the presence and 0 the absence of the use of a range of types of manual. The respondent was asked whether they had manuals for procedures in the following areas: technical design/manufacture; accounting; marketing; company philosophy; supplier relations; and customer relations.

Cultural controls. Baliga and Jaeger (1984) differentiated cultural control into two analytical types – 'shared norms of performance' and 'shared philosophy of management'. In practice, it is very difficult to differentiate these two types. Instruments such as career development systems, the use of expatriate employees and induction courses can all be expected to inculcate the company's 'norms of performance' and the 'philosophy of management'. It is suggested, therefore, that cultural controls are more logically and usefully divided into informal and formal mechanisms. Informal systems are usually longer-term or ongoing such as regular interpersonal contacts or the use of expatriate managers. Formal systems include goal-focused short-term events such as training courses, induction courses and the like.

There were five informal interpersonal cultural control variables. Bartlett and Ghoshal (1987) suggested that mentoring is a technique finding increasing use as a socialization tool for subsidiary managers. The variable was obtained from a question asking whether the respondent ever had a mentor at HQ and was coded 1 for Yes and 0 for No. Thus the variable, mentor, indicated the frequency of use by HQ of a mentoring scheme. The frequency of contacts between the subsidiary and HQ and between the subsidiary and other group companies was likely to be influenced by the nature of the subsidiary task and the hierarchical or heterarchical structure of the MNC. Respondents were asked the frequency of contact, by any available means, with HQ (contact HQ) and with other group companies (contact others). The data were coded as 1 = monthly or less often through 5 = several times daily. The mean for contact with HQ was a little less frequent than daily and for other group companies was approximately every three days.

The use of expatriate managers is a commonly employed control device in MNCs. Respondents were requested to give the number of positions in their firm that were filled by expatriate employees. No specific information on the positions filled by the expatriates was collected. The 308 responses included 160 subsidiaries (52%) that had no expatriate employees, 52 (17%) had one, 36 had two, 19 had three continuing to one subsidiary that had 75. Because the number of expatriate managers was highly correlated with size of the subsidiary based upon number of employees ($r = 0.286$, $p < .001$), for the purpose of this investigation two separate expatriate measures were set up. These were a simple dichotomous 1/0 variable based upon use/no use of some expatriates and density of expatriates which was calculated as the number of expatriates divided by the total number of employees in the subsidiary.

There were two formal cultural control variables in the investigation. Induction courses are often the initial step in the socialization process of new employees into the values and culture of the company. Respondents were asked how important the induction course was in introducing new management level employees to the subsidiary (induction). This was scaled from 1 = unimportant through 5 = very important.

Once inducted into the company, training of various types is a common tool to further the socialization process. Respondents were asked for a simple yes/no response to the question of whether suitable employees were encouraged and enabled to attend *non-vocational* training courses. Seventy per cent (219 from 312) replied in the affirmative for in-house training, 152 of 312 (49%) for training at HQ, 156 of 312 (50%) for training in other parts of the corporation and 261 of 312 (84%) for training at external venues. The training variable was derived from the factor analysis procedure (see Chapter 12) and was the sum of the four variables in which 1 indicated the availability and 0 indicated the lack of availability of access to the four types of non-vocational training.

The data from the survey presented in Table 9.2 suggest a widespread application of many of these tools. The formal bureaucratic mechanisms of regular reporting and the presence of at least one procedural manual were almost universal while the formal and informal cultural controls were only slightly less common.

Predictor and control variables

Predictor variable. This was the categorical variable subsidiary task.

Control variables. The investigation controlled for a range of other variables: MNC size (natural logarithm of number of employees – continuous variable); subsidiary size (natural logarithm of number of employees – continuous variable); industry: manufacturing, retail/distribution,

Table 9.3 Descriptive statistics and intercorrelations for control variables

Variable	(1)	(2)	(3)	(4)	(5)	(6)	(7)	(8)	(9)	(10)	(11)
1. Subsidiary size (ln)	—										
2. MNC size (ln)	.42	—									
3. Industry: manufacturing.	.27	.06	—								
4. Industry: retail, wholesale and distribution	-.38	-.16	-.64	—							
5. Industry: finance, property and bus. services	.05	.04	-.26	-.37	—						
6. Corporate culture	-.10	-.04	-.06	.12	-.05	—					
7. Technology level	.03	.08	.08	.06	.07	-.06	—				
8. Industry competitiveness	.26	.21	.04	-.04	.04	-.05	.08	—			
9. Industry innovativeness	.18	.07	-.00	-.03	.10	-.01	.16	.23	—		
10. Years in Australia	.43	.30	.35	-.29	-.06	-.06	-.07	.11	.02	—	
11. Parent nationality	-.06	.06	-.06	.13	-.06	.00	.12	.05	.05	-.10	—
Mean or proportion	4.47	9.84	—	—	—	.15	3.82	4.31	2.94	30.32	—
s.d.	1.59	1.60	—	—	—	—	.89	.79	1.00	24.04	—
n	303	268	313	313	313	312	309	312	305	312	313

Correlation coefficients of > .11 are significant at $p < .05$ level.

finance and business services (three dichotomous variables each coded 1/0); corporate culture (whether the firm had a culture that made the respondent feel that they worked for a corporation from the parent's home country – dichotomous variable coded 1/0); level of technology of primary process; innovativeness of the industry; competitiveness of the industry (all three scale variables 1–5); years operating in Australia (continuous); and parent nationality (categorical variable -11 countries or groups). Details of all of these are found in the Appendix and/or have been described in detail in earlier chapters. The means (or proportions), standard deviations (as appropriate) and intercorrelations are shown in Table 9.3.

Analysis

Two methods were chosen for hypothesis testing in this investigation. The continuous variables – reports, formalization, contact HQ, contact others, expatriate density, induction, training – were investigated using ANCOVA since this method delivers estimated marginal means for the subsidiary tasks and least significant difference (LSD) pairwise comparisons of these. The two dichotomous variables, mentor and expatriates (dichotomous), were examined using logistic regression.

Results and discussion

The uncontrolled means and standard deviations for the seven continuous variables and the yes/no response proportions for the two dichotomous variables for each of the five subsidiary tasks are presented in Table 9.4. Significant differences between subsidiary tasks are shown below the table. The results of independent sample two-tailed tests between subsidiary tasks from this basic analysis suggested that the independent subsidiary was subject to less control effort via formalization, density of expatriates and the induction course. This was in line with expectations but more detailed examination, controlling for exogenous factors, is necessary.

A series of ANCOVA procedures was performed on the seven continuous dependent variables to establish any associations with the predictor and control variables. The results are shown in Table 9.5. Subsidiary task was only significantly associated ($F[4,225] = 2.73$, $p < .05$) with contact with other group companies (4.6 per cent of the variance explained) while there was a weak association with formalization ($F[4,226]$; $p < .1$) and training ($F[4,226]$; $p < .1$). Both cases had 3.8 per cent of the variance explained.

Table 9.4 Uncontrolled means and standard deviations for control mechanisms for each subsidiary task

Control mechanisms utilized		Distrib	Adapt	Imple	Innov	Indep
Use of reports	mean	3.87	4.02	3.93	4.02	4.04
	s.d.	0.96	0.82	1.06	0.87	0.79
	n	94	65	46	53	52
Use of manuals	mean	3.06	2.98	2.93	2.98	2.21
	s.d.	1.57	1.65	1.82	1.83	1.59
	n	95	65	46	54	53
Contact with HQ	mean	3.34	3.46	3.35	3.20	2.85
	s.d.	1.33	1.35	1.21	1.41	1.32
	n	94	65	46	54	53
Contact with other group firms	mean	2.82	2.77	2.51	2.79	2.26
	s.d.	1.44	1.45	1.56	1.48	1.42
	n	94	65	45	53	53
Density of expatriates	mean	0.037	0.034	0.021	0.012	0.008
	s.d.	0.089	0.103	0.069	0.026	0.020
	n	95	63	44	51	51
Induction course	mean	3.89	3.89	3.67	3.62	3.79
	s.d.	1.13	1.30	1.21	1.21	0.97
	n	92	64	46	53	53
Training courses	mean	2.64	2.37	2.74	2.80	2.08
	s.d.	1.49	1.45	1.27	1.31	1.28
	n	94	65	46	54	3
Expatriates (dichotomous)	yes/no	46/49	34/31	20/26	26/28	27/26
	% yes	48.4	52.3	43.5	48.1	50.9
	n	95	65	46	54	53
Mentor	yes/no	34/59	27/37	13/32	23/30	14/39
	% yes	36.6	42.2	28.9	43.4	26.4
	n	93	64	45	54	53

Significant differences:
Formalization: Indep < all others, $p < .05$
Density of expats: Indep < Distr, $p < .05$
Induction: Indep < Innov, $p < .01$; Indep < Distr, Imple, $p < .05$
Mentor: Indep < Innov, $p < .10$.

Table 9.6 contains the estimated marginal means for each subsidiary task for each control mechanism and any significant LSD pairwise comparisons.

The ANCOVA results for the seven mechanisms bear some similarity to the uncontrolled variables results. A brief summary of the overall

Table 9.5 Analysis of covariance summary for all control mechanisms

Variable	df	Use of reports	Use of manuals	Contact HQ	Contact others	Expat density	Induction course	Training courses
Subsidiary size (ln)	1	.01	3.30† (.014)[a]	.22	.16	10.50** (.045)	10.12** (.044)	13.39*** (.056)
MNC size (ln)	1	.06	.15	.23	1.06	.28	4.56* (.020)	1.56
Industry: Manufacturing	1	1.32	2.55	.04	.99	.13	.67	.05
Industry: Retail/wholesale	1	.11	.87	.00	.37	.37	.01	.11
Industry: Fin./bus. serv.	1	1.19	1.03	.02	.80	.25	1.81	.44
Corporate culture	1	.11	.15	1.21	1.14	1.26	.23	3.32† (.014)
Technology level	1	.33	15.47*** (.064)	.82	.01	3.22† (.014)	2.58	.14
Industry competitiveness	1	1.58	.01	.22	3.42† (.015)	.00	.03	.12
Industry innovativeness	1	.86	.37	.45	.90	.09	.39	.04
Years in Australia	1	.01	.25	.27	.69	.45	.37	.29
Parent nationality	10	1.09	2.26* (.091)	2.22* (.089)	1.11	2.10* (.086)	.60	1.06
Subsidiary task	4	.66	2.21† (.038)	1.16	2.73* (.046)	.58	.12	2.24† (.038)
Intercept	1	38.66** (.147)	.11	10.57** (.045)	5.58* (.024)	1.69	17.27*** (.072)	6.72* (.029)
Model	24	1.18	2.65***	1.24	1.27	2.43***	1.26	1.54†
R²		.11	.22	.12	.12	.21	.12	.14
Mean square error df		225	226	226	225	222	222	226

*** $p < .001$; ** $p < .01$; * $p < .05$; † $p < .10$ (two-tailed test)

[a] Partial eta shown in brackets

Table 9.6 Estimated marginal means and significant pairwise comparison for all subsidiary tasks and control mechanisms

Subsidiary task	Use of reports	Use of manuals	Contact HQ	Contact others	Expat density	Induction course	Training courses
1. Distributor	3.72	3.49	3.29	3.36	.041	3.73	2.53
2. Adapter	3.91	3.09	3.15	3.04	.034	3.73	2.31
3. Implementer	3.71	3.05	3.43	2.54	.032	3.64	2.72
4. Innovator	3.88	3.15	3.10	2.74	.021	3.58	2.88
5. Independent	3.96	2.30	2.75	2.14	.018	3.59	2.00
Significant pairwise comparisons	None	1>5** 2>5† 3>5† 4>5*	3>5*	1>5** 1>3* 1>4† 2>5* 4>5†	None	None	4>2† 4>5* 3>5*

** $p < .01$; * $p < .05$; $p < .10$ (two-tailed test)

picture is now presented. The bureaucratic output variable, reports, indicated that formal reporting was used equally frequently to control all types of subsidiary. There were no significant differences between any of the subsidiary tasks for this variable.

For the bureaucratic behavioral controls variable, formalization, the independent subsidiary was significantly lower than all of the other subsidiaries (distr > indep, $p < .01$; innov > indep, $p < .05$; adapt/imple > indep, $p < .10$).

Contact with HQ was significantly greater for implementer subsidiaries than for independent subsidiaries ($p < .05$), otherwise there were no significant differences.

Contact with other group companies presented the most inconsistent pattern among the subsidiaries. The distributor subsidiaries had notably the highest mean and the independent subsidiaries the lowest. The significant differences were distr > indep, $p < .01$; distr > adapt, $p < .05$; distr > innov, $p < .10$; adapt > indep, $p < .05$; innov > indep, $p < .10$.

The expatriate density and importance of the induction course had no significant differences between subsidiary tasks.

The training availability variable showed the innov/imple > indep, $p < .05$ and innov > adapt, $p < .10$.

The Wald statistic based results for the two dichotomous dependent variables – mentor and expatriates (dichotomous) – are shown in the logistic regression equations in Table 9.7. For both of these variables the subsidiary task was not a significant predictor. Logistic regression can be used to assess the contribution of individual categories in a categorical variable predictor and the innovator subsidiary was weakly associated ($p < .10$) with the use of mentoring.

Proposition 9.1 was concerned with the distributor and implementer subsidiaries suggesting they would be controlled primarily by bureaucratic mechanisms. Examining the estimated marginal mean scores, for the two bureaucratic mechanisms both subsidiary tasks were not significantly lower than other subsidiaries. However, for the cultural control variables, contrary to the proposition, the distributor subsidiaries scored the highest for contact with other group companies, expatriate density and importance of the induction course. Similarly contrary, the implementer subsidiaries scored the highest for contact with HQ and second highest for use of training courses. With one exception (imple < distr, $p < .05$, for contact with other group companies) neither subsidiary task was significantly lower than the rest on any of the cultural control variables. Proposition 9.1 was not supported.

Table 9.7   Logistic regression results for the two dichotomous dependent variables

Variable	df	Expats	Mentor
Subsidiary size (ln)	1	21.20***	1.02
MNC size (ln)	1	.01	.00
Industry: Manufacturing	1	.18	.83
Industry: Retail/wholesale	1	1.73	.03
Industry: Fin./bus. serv.	1	.06	.00
Corporate culture	1	.04	.00
Technology level	1	5.51*	.00
Industry competitiveness	1	1.13	2.79†
Industry innovativeness	1	2.33	.00
Years in Australia	1	2.63	1.78
Parent nationality	10	12.40	4.28
Subsidiary task	4	4.67	4.20
-2LL		287.01	295.65
Hosmer/Lemeshow		5.73	3.71
Model Chi^2		65.75***	26.06
Cox and Snell R^2		.21	.10
Nagelkerke R^2		.29	.14
n		251	247

*** $p < .001$; * $p < .05$; † $p < .10$ (two-tailed test)

With regard to Proposition 9.2, the adapter subsidiaries scored second and third highest on the two bureaucratic controls but the differences were not significant except for adapt > indep, $p < .10$ on the formalization variable. Examining the cultural controls, the adapter was between highest and third on four of these but fourth and weakly significantly lower ($p < .10$) than the innovator subsidiaries with regard to training courses. On balance the proposition of the use of a combination of mechanisms (Proposition 9.2) seemed to have some support.

Proposition 9.3 related to the innovator subsidiaries. These subsidiaries did not score significantly lower than the other subsidiaries on the two bureaucratic variables. In addition and contrary to the prediction, they scored between third and last on the first four cultural controls but most differences were not significant. The exceptions were innov < distr, $p < .10$ and innov > indep, $p < .10$ for contact with other group companies. Only on the training variable did the innovator subsidiaries score the highest (innov > indep, $p < .05$ and innov > adapt, $p < .10$). Hence Proposition 9.3 that innovator subsidiaries were more likely to be associated with cultural controls was not supported.

Proposition 9.4 suggested that the independent subsidiaries were subject to the least amount of control effort by HQ and the primary control mechanism would be reporting. These subsidiaries scored lowest on five of the seven variables with many of the differences being significant. For the reports variable the independent subsidiaries had the highest (although non-significant) score. The support for Proposition 9.4 was quite strong.

The overwhelming conclusion from the results above is a rejection of the argument, implicit in the Ouch/Baliga/Jaeger models of control, that different types of control mechanisms are applied to different types of subsidiary. It was clear that the perspectives of Jarillo and Martinez (1990), Pucik and Katz (1986) and Ferner (2000) offered a closer reflection of reality. This conclusion does not take account, however, of the distinctively weaker control efforts directed at the independent subsidiary

Further, with regard to the hierarchy vs heterarchy distinction there were no significant differences in the types of mechanisms used to control subsidiaries in hierarchic and heterarchic MNCs.

If these results are accepted then two questions immediately arise that merit further investigation. First, are all control mechanisms applied with equal rigor and vigor at all times or are they applied selectively to suit the needs of the situation? Second, Heide (2001) suggested that applying a range of governance mechanisms simultaneously might lead to either synergistic or disruptive interaction effects. For example, is the simultaneous implementation of performance monitoring or behavioral controls likely to affect whether there are positive or negative responses to socialization and cultural conformity initiatives?

The results for some of the control variables associations were also of interest. Subsidiary size was a positive predictor of training opportunities ($F[1,226] = 13.39$; $p < .001$), induction courses ($F[1,222] = 10.12$; $p < .01$) and weakly of formalization ($F[1,226] = 3.30$; $p < .10$) while being negatively associated with expatriate density ($F[1,222] = 10.50$; $p < .01$). MNC size was negatively associated with induction courses ($F[1,222] = 4.56$; $p < .05$). Level of technology is positively associated with formalization ($F[1,226] = 15.47$; $p < .001$). Most of these appear uncontroversial with the exception of the unexpected MNC size-induction course link.

For parent nationality there were several interesting results. Table 9.8 presents the estimated marginal means for each parent nationality for the control mechanisms that were significantly associated with parent nationality plus any significant LSD pairwise comparisons.

Table 9.8   Estimated marginal means and significant pairwise comparisons for parent nationality and significantly associated control mechanisms

Parent nationality	Use of manuals	Contact HQ	Expat density
1. UK	3.16	3.63	.018
2. US/Canada	3.51	3.09	.012
3. Japan	1.78	3.73	.057
4. Sweden	2.73	2.72	.034
5. Germany	3.48	3.40	.021
6. Italy	2.74	2.09	.016
7. Switzerland	2.50	3.05	.003
8. Netherlands/Belgium	2.66	2.67	.070
9. France	2.93	3.16	.017
10. Denmark/Norway	3.62	2.53	.087
11. Other[a]	4.10	4.49	.014
	1>3**	1>6**; 3>6**	10>1**; 10>2**
	2>3**	1>2*; 1>10*	10>7**
	5>3**	2>6*; 3>10*	3>2*; 8>2*
	10>3**	5>6*	8>7*; 10>5*
			10>6*

** $p < .01$; * $p < .05$ (two-tailed test)
[a] Other category excluded from pairwise comparisons.

The language difference probably explains the Japanese significantly lower use of formalization *vis a vis* UK, US/Canada, Germany and Denmark/Norway. For frequency of contact with HQ, Italy was significantly lower than UK, US/Canada and Japan. Expatriate density demonstrated the greatest scatter with a number of significant differences ($p < .05$ or less). Denmark/Norway was notably the highest with US/Canada and Switzerland the lowest.

Conclusions

The OBJ framework presented a rationale underlying the use of different control systems. First, it tied specific control mechanisms to types of subsidiary and, second, to the nature of the knowledge asymmetries between the subsidiary and HQ. Certain types of control practice were only likely to be found with certain types of subsidiary. For example, output measurement would be found only when HQ to subsidiary knowledge flows were the dominant form and output monitoring would be unsuitable when the subsidiary was extensively involved in innovation. In addition, it set a basic pattern into which cultural and other influences could be dovetailed. This perspective has been quite convincingly refuted by the investigations above.

It appears that the source of the problem with the framework lies in the processes of the MNC's development and transformation. The knowledge asymmetries between HQ and subsidiaries changed and the concept of 'control' became insufficient to explain the new relationship. The OBJ framework largely assumed that HQ was in charge and HQ dominated the knowledge flows. This outlook was arguably only valid at earlier stages of the MNC's development and is less directly applicable to modern learning and innovating subsidiaries.

Despite Collis and Montgomery's (1995) efforts, the integration of the knowledge and resource-based literatures with the control literature remains undeveloped and there was no clear underpinning for the socialization and 'shared norms of performance and behavior' constructs. Delegation might be a more accurate term when the subsidiary is a local adapter or encouragement of entrepreneurship when the subsidiary is involved in innovation. As the interdependence between the subsidiary and the rest of the MNC shifted from pooled interdependence (Thompson, 1967) between subsidiary and HQ to reciprocal interdependence between the subsidiary all other MNC units, the distinction between control and coordination became even less clear. This accorded with Bartlett and Ghoshal's (1987) thesis of the relationship moving from control to coordination to cooption, although the present data and results do not offer any evidence of the last phase. There is a need, therefore, for a more complete understanding of control, coordination, socialization and so on that fully integrates the recent developments in the knowledge-based view and organizational learning.

10
Knowledge Management and Innovation

Theories of the firm have usually emerged to explain why firms differ in their performance (Chandler, 1962; Donaldson, 1995; Coase, 1937; Williamson, 1975; Wernerfelt, 1984; Barney, 1991) and these performance differentials emerge essentially as a result of a firms ability to create a sustained competitive advantage that generates, sustains and appropriates rents (Coff, 2003b: 245). Today, knowledge, learning and innovation are at the heart of our understanding of competitive advantage and firm performance. For the purposes of this chapter the two most important theoretical perspectives to have been applied to understand these issues are organizational learning and the RBV. Building upon Kogut and Zander (1992) and Tsai and Ghoshal (1998), Tsai (2001: 996) stated that 'inside a multiunit organization ... knowledge transfer among organizational units provide opportunities for mutual learning and interunit cooperation that stimulate the creation of new knowledge and, at the same time, contributes to the organizational units' ability to innovate'. The intricate web of relationships that links these themes is currently the dominant paradigm in the strategy and international business academic literatures.

There are many examples that demonstrate the immense complexity of these conceptual links. For example, at the core of the RBV is the argument that sustainable competitive advantage arises only if the firm has the capability to safeguard its valuable, rare, not easily imitable and not substitutable resources (Barney, 1991; Collis and Montgomery, 1995). This argument also underpins internalization theory that sees the rise of the MNC as a product of innovating firms protecting their knowledge from appropriation by competitors by retaining that knowledge within firm boundaries. However, from the opposite perspective, others argue that sustained competitive advantages can arise from knowledge sharing via spillovers from such things as extra-firm networks (Uzzi and Gillespie, 2002; Spencer, 2003) or industrial or regional clusters (Birkinshaw and Hood, 2000). Feinberg and Gupta (2004) found that MNCs appeared to anticipate spillover opportunities in these contexts and made R&D subsidiary location decisions on the basis of them. To add to the complexity, the entire domain is constrained by issues such as stickiness, individual vs organizational learning, knowledge tacitness, path dependence, absorptive capacity and so on.

It is a basic tenet of the international business literature that the internalization of its knowledge-based, firm specific advantage is the defining characteristic of the MNC. In particular, in many MNCs, the management of the knowledge resources of the firm is the primary means of generating and disseminating innovations (Bartlett and Ghoshal, 1989). It was argued in Chapter 5 that the distinguishing characteristic of the heterarchic MNC form is the management of the knowledge resources of the firm as a means of generating and disseminating innovations. Thus this chapter makes a contribution to the literature by investigating the place of various types of subsidiaries, in particular the innovator subsidiary, in the knowledge management and innovation networks of MNC. While Von Krogh, Ichijo and Nonaka (2000: vii) stated 'the creation of knowledge cannot be managed, only enabled', this study will use the term knowledge management to include the enabling process.

The contribution of this chapter is to extend the understanding of knowledge and innovation in MNCs by investigating the characteristics of subsidiaries that are involved in knowledge management and innovation processes and some of the enabling mechanisms that are being used. The task is approached by presenting some basic associations between a range of predictive variables and the embeddedness of subsidiaries in the knowledge management systems and innovation networks of the MNC. The chapter deals predominantly with the understanding of outbound as opposed to inbound knowledge. More specifically, outbound knowledge is primarily concerned with how organizations deploy and leverage collective knowledge to improve responsiveness and gain an advantage in the market place (Hult, 2003).

The chapter is structured in the following manner. First it provides a brief overview of the commonalities of the organizational learning and RBV approaches in understanding and managing knowledge. These well-established literatures ground the conceptual apparatus and underpin the hypotheses. The next section covers the variable construction and methodology. The third section presents the results and, finally, the research is set in context.

Conceptual and empirical background

Introduction

As market turbulence continues to increase, firms wishing to succeed must be able to respond to market opportunities and threats in innovative and timely ways (Chakravarthy, 1997; Grover and Davenport, 2001). They must focus upon the effective use of the knowledge (intellectual capital) that resides within the firm and its employees to increase their effectiveness in tackling this increasingly competitive external environment (Janz and Prasarnphanich, 2003). As Teece (1998: 56) asserted, the 'essence of the firm is its ability to create, transfer, assemble, integrate and exploit knowledge assets'. From the mainstream management domain, Stewart (1997: 6) broadened the rhetoric by stating 'knowledge has become the single most important factor of production, and managing intellectual assets the single most important task of business'. Drucker (1999: 92) has further extended the argument by suggesting that 'knowledge workers own the means of production ... That knowledge between their ears is a totally portable and enormous capital asset ... they are mobile ... management's job is to preserve the assets of the institution in its care'. He maintained that these knowledge workers must be treated as assets rather than as costs. He further argued that although the last two decades have seen furious debate on the governance of the corporation, the near future would see a resurgence of that debate from a new perspective. 'We will have to redefine the purpose of the employing organization and of its management as both satisfying the legal owners (such as shareholders) and satisfying the owners of the human capital that gives the organization its wealth-producing power' (Drucker, 1999: 92). A major question for management academics now, and in the future, is how can we understand, analyze and measure the value of knowledge in some useful way? Thus the last decade has seen the management of knowledge, learning and innovation take center stage in the academic and professional management literature.

Much of the literature has been theoretical and the concepts and frameworks of organizational learning and the RBV of the firm have developed as the most appropriate and viable means of expression by which to examine and understand knowledge and to derive learning and knowledge management techniques that can be implemented by a firm.

There is, in addition, a prolific practitioner literature with the earlier exhortations to be aware of the need to manage knowledge (see Davenport and Prusak, 1998: 179 for a sample list) being replaced by more pragmatic output, often appearing in the major practitioner journals. These include extensive use of examples of successful and unsuccessful projects.

The empirical and hypothesis testing literature is more limited and, until recently, it is probably true to say that the majority of empirical work on knowledge management has been in the information technology domain (Grover and Davenport, 2001; Nonaka and Reinmoeller, 2003). In particular, large dataset-based studies have not been much in evidence. Coff (2003a), Gupta and Govindarajan (2000), Moorman and Miner (1997) and Poppo and Zenger (1998) are among a small but increasing number of examples. Hence, despite conceptual variety and perhaps richness, there remains a continuing need for studies that map the domain and establish some basic associations between variables within the various ambits of knowledge management.

Understanding knowledge management using the RBV and organizational learning

The precise boundaries between the RBV, organizational learning, knowledge management and innovation are elusive and there is considerable overlap. For example, the major conceptual studies on organizational learning (Argyris and Schon, 1996; Nonaka and Takeuchi, 1995; Senge, 1990) have centered upon the processes whereby individual knowledge is transformed into organizational knowledge. This transformation can be important in many organization functions but is particularly vital to the sustaining and reinvigoration of competitive advantage that is the rationale for innovation. Gupta and Govindarajan (1991), for example, argued that flows of tacit and explicit knowledge are the lifeblood of innovation.

To be effective, learning is dependent on the acquisition, processing, storage and retrieval of critical knowledge (Helleloid and Simonin, 1994: 214). As a result, knowledge generation and sharing has a direct effect on the learning process enabling a firm to add to existing knowledge and enhance its competencies to innovate and achieve a sustained competitive advantage (Helleloid and Simonin, 1994; Hurley and Hult, 1998; Morgan, Zou, Vorhies and Katsikeas, 2003). Janz and Prasarnphanich (2003) argued that this route to knowledge acquisition and management was consistent with the RBV and evolutionary economics.

The organizational learning literature has been the progenitor of much theoretical and practical guidance but the conceptual basis of knowledge management and innovation receives considerable further enrichment from the RBV of the firm and its more recent focus on knowledge as a key resource. The RBV was described in detail in Chapter 3 but the key issues are the uniqueness, appropriability and value of the knowledge that is to be generated and shared.

Knowledge is incorporated in many facets of the firm including (but not limited to) processes, structures and technology and all of these lie within the context of a firm's culture, values and competences. According to Grover and Davenport (2001), knowledge has the highest value to a firm and is the most difficult to manage because it resides in the minds of the organizational members: 'Knowledge management can be framed as the problem of creating an efficient and effective knowledge marketplace in the organization' (Grover and Davenport, 2001: 15). When described in this manner, the objectives of knowledge management are analogous to those of organizational learning and the RBV in that they bring about innovation and sustained competitive advantage. Structures must be implemented that encourage and support the creation of new knowledge and innovation within the firm (Nonaka and Reinmoeller, 2002).

Information technology systems have received the main thrust of attention as effective mechanisms through which to trigger such actions. The emphasis on IT is reflected in the literature (see for example Nonaka, 1994; Nonaka and Reinmoeller, 2003; Sabherwal and Becerra-Fernandez, 2003; Tippins and Sohi, 2003). For example, Coff (2003b: 247) asserts 'real advances in productivity often arise from new technologies that enhance or assist knowledge creation and management'.

IT alone however does not take into account the context of knowledge and its embeddedness in social relationships. Human intervention is necessary to create and promote knowledge creation. Hence, while knowledge management initiatives should encompass IT systems and technological levels, they should be complemented by other 'human' initiatives (Chiesa and Barbeschi, 1994; Nonaka and Reinmoeller, 2002). For example, Hansen and Lovas (2004), studying technological competence transfers, found that teams preferred to approach people they knew rather than people who knew related technologies well.

Knowledge management espouses the notion that the development of knowledge commences with the individual and emanates throughout the firm through a combination of mechanisms and technology, recognized as information gaps (Sabherwal and Becerra-Fernandez, 2003). This is largely consistent with the themes of organizational learning. In addition, collaborative arrangements between MNCs can allow a firm to maximize the use of knowledge within the organization, increasing firm efficiencies and the value of these resources (Kearns and Lederer, 2003; Hunt, 2000). Consistent with the RBV, these stocks of knowledge must be constantly replenished to ensure that the resource remains valuable and does not erode over time (Barney, 1991; Garcia, Calantone and Levine, 2003; Hult, 2003). Indeed, as Foss and Pederson (2004) pointed out, the research has tended to focus primarily on knowledge flows with consequently less concern for knowledge stocks.

This study complements the extant research by integrating technological with non-technological variables to empirically analyze their effect on knowledge management techniques. Research shows that an integration of business knowledge and IT knowledge would be most beneficial to the firm and assist it in defending against competitive threats (Kearns and Lederer, 2003).

The knowledge management system

Following on from the discussion of knowledge management in the heterarchic MNC in Chapter 3, the conception of the knowledge management system of the MNC used in this chapter is that it consists of three sets of tools: groupware technologies; organizational memory systems and valuation of the firm's intellectual capital. Investigation of these three processes provides, in combination, a representative guide for assessing a company's commitment to the knowledge management process. As this conception of the knowledge management system is a new construct and central to the investigation, each of the components are described and analyzed in some detail.

Groupware technology. The first of the three tools is the system for facilitating and enabling the dissemination of organizational knowledge among the relevant communities of users, in particular groupware technologies such as intranets, video-conferencing and so on (Orlikowski and Hofman, 1997; Muammer, 1999; Ramarapu, Simkin and Raisinghani, 1999). Collaborative teams are usually geographically dispersed in MNCs. Hence, groupware enables these teams to rapidly facilitate communication between these members hence assisting in idea generation and coordination (Coman, 2000).

Groupware technology is a general label for a range of group support systems that enable and enhance the efficacy of collaborative work group communications. Enright (1997) stated that groupware was anything that facilitated communication and coordination among people. The difference between the Internet and groupware was that groupware required some facilitation and management by the organization. Orlikowski and Hofman (1997) advocated the use of groupware technologies in an improvizational model for managing change initiatives. They stated:

> Groupware technologies provide electronic networks that support communication, coordination, and collaboration through facilities such as information exchange, shared repositories, discussion forums, and messaging. Such technologies are typically designed with an open architecture that is adaptable by end users, allowing them to customize existing features and create new applications. Rather than automating a predefined sequence of operations and transactions, these technologies tend to be general-purpose tools that are used in different ways across various organizational activities and contexts. Organizations need the experience of using groupware technologies in particular ways and in particular contexts to better understand how they may be most useful in practice. (Orlikowski and Hofman, 1997: 12)

The research on computer support of cooperative work dates back to the 1960s (Greif, 1988; Licklider and Taylor, 1968) but the application of these concepts began in earnest during the 1970s with the development of several systems for threaded discussions (Hiltz and Turoff, 1978). At first, these tools were used primarily in research and education but, with the spread of LANs (local area networks) in the 1980s, commercial application accelerated, and the term 'groupware' came to describe software intended to enhance group productivity. The first commercial software platforms for developing and deploying groupware applications – for example, Group Systems (Nunamaker, Dennis, Valacich, Vogel and George, 1991) and Lotus Notes – were developed in the late 1980s. E-mail, listserv, and early manifestations such as USENET News, thrived on these precursors of the Internet and ultimately on the Internet itself. For a while, full-feature groupware with various tools and information structuring was only available on private internal corporate networks that were often LAN-based and required expensive proprietary software. By the late 1990s, however, the field had witnessed a rapid extension into Internet and Web applications (Wheeler, Dennis and Press, 1999; Muammer, 1999; Dennis, Quek and Pootheri, 1996).

Coman (2000) explained that collaborative teams in MNCs were usually geographically dispersed, on tight time schedules and brought together people from a broad range of cultures and disciplines. The value of groupware technologies lay in their ability to facilitate communication between these team members rapidly and in the use of shared or common facilities that made all participants feel comfortable. Ramarapu et al. (1999) and Wong and Lee (1998) argued that the theoretical underpinnings of the functioning of groupware technologies were still not clear. Coman (2000), Shirani, Tafti and Affisco (1999) and Tan, Wei and Lee-Partridge (1999), however, concluded that evidence was mounting to indicate the expected gains in idea generation and coordination were forthcoming. To date, however, these developments have largely been reported on the basis of case studies of corporate use (Downing and Clark, 1999; Tabor, Pryor and Gutierrez, 1997).

Organizational memory systems. The second mechanism is the development of repositories whereby knowledge can be collected, stored, accessed and retrieved at need. This is essentially the building of organization memory systems (Ackerman, 1994; Walsh and Ungson, 1991). Any organization should be able to store and retrieve information and knowledge of its past activities (Ackerman and Halverson, 2000). Organizational memories, in the form of collections of skills, knowledge and information have been found to be vital sources of competitive advantage in the RBV and core competencies literatures (Hamel and Prahalad, 1994; Hurley and Hult, 1998).

According to Walsh and Ungson (1991) the key elements for understanding organizational memory were the structure of the retention facility, the information contained in that facility and the processes of acquisition, storage and retrieval.

There are three main types of memory that we are usually concerned with. The first is the role of historical experience that allows individuals to coordinate their tasks within the firm. This is analogous to what is referred to as 'common knowledge' or 'organizational code' (David, 1994: 209 and 213) within the organization. The second type is the technical knowledge of firms reflected in routines and procedures and is comprised of explicit and tacit knowledge. If this knowledge is to be retrieved by an individual, the explicit knowledge may reside in the manuals but the tacit aspect must be learned from experienced co-workers. The third type of memory is the set of consciously designed and installed systems, instituted to more efficiently access the types of knowledge mentioned. This is often stored and retrieved from hard copy manuals, IT databases or interpersonal contacts.

The organization memory construct was examined in detail in Chapter 3. Wijnhoven (1999) pointed out that, in some instances (see, for example, Weick, 1979), organizational memories were recognized as sources of inertia but that is clearly not the case today (Moorman and Miner, 1997, 1998; Sveiby, 1997). Organizational memories, in the form of collections of skills, knowledge and information (resources and capabilities in the sense used by Teece, 1998 and Teece et al., 1997), were viewed much more positively. They have, for example, been interpreted as vital sources of competitive advantage in the core competencies literature (Hamel and Prahalad, 1994; Hamel and Heene, 1994).

Almost every study to date has acknowledged the need for more empirical work but, given the evident diaspora of meanings and interpretations, it is understandable that little empirical examination of organizational memory has taken place. Ackerman and Halverson (2000) commented that when empirical examination has taken place, it has either focused upon the technological systems designed to replace human and paper-based memory or concerned itself with single case studies (often prototypical) in action.

Auditing of intellectual capital. The third process is the task of putting a value on the corporate knowledge asset stock – the auditing of a company's intellectual capital (Nahapiet and Ghoshal, 1998; Dzinkowski, 2000). Traditionally, economists have examined physical and human capital as the key resources of the firm that facilitated economic activity and have only recently acknowledged the central role of knowledge as a critical resource (Quinn, 1992).

Nahapiet and Ghoshal (1998) defined intellectual capital as the knowledge and knowing capability of a social collectivity such as an organization, an intellectual community or a professional practice. That this type of capital has considerable value to a business is an issue receiving attention in several academic literatures. Traditionally, economists have examined both physical and human capital as the key resources of the firm that facilitated economic activity. They have not, however, totally ignored knowledge as a valuable resource. Johnson (1970) focused on the failure of the market for know-how as central to the internalization process. Marshall (1965: 115) stated 'knowledge is our most powerful engine of production' and this perspective was shared by Arrow (1974), among others. More recently, Quinn (1992) suggested 'with rare exceptions, the economic and producing power of the firm lies more in its intellectual and service capabilities than its hard assets ... most successful corporations are becoming dominantly repositories and coordinators of intellect' (Quinn, 1992: 241).

This investigation is concerned primarily with auditing of the firm's intellectual capital. A number of the approaches that have appeared include this particular task within more general intellectual asset management practices (Bontis, Dragonetti, Jacobsen and Roos, 1999; Bontis and Girardi, 2000; Marti, 2000; Martin, 2000) although King and Zeithami (2003) suggest a managerial perceptual approach to measuring organizational knowledge. Measuring intellectual capital is a complex assignment and Dzinkowski (2000) noted that Skandia, a pioneer in this field, had no less than 164 separate measures. Skandia's measures were largely internal but the best-known methods available (for example, market-to-book value and Tobin's q) are dependent upon an essentially external valuation – market value. These methods are variations on the theme of differences between the market value of a firm and the value of its hard assets.

There is an obvious need for more data and research in this area and the present study is a step in that direction. In this investigation, no attempt was made to ascertain which particular metric had been used, respondents were simply requested to assess the frequency of their organization's use of auditing of intellectual capital techniques.

Innovation

As stated in Chapter 3, the broad purpose of knowledge management, as conceived in this research, is to access the organizational knowledge stored in these types of organizational memories in order to develop the organization's capabilities, and generate innovations, thus creating and sustaining the firm's competences and competitive advantage. The construct of the subsidiary's place in MNC's innovation network does not require the detailed description that was given above for the knowledge management system. It is simply conceived as the subsidiary's contribution to R&D in the MNC combined with an assessment of the subsidiary's propensity to (1) generate product or process innovations; (2) be involved in using and sharing these with the rest of the MNC; and (3) adopting innovations from elsewhere in the MNC.

Hypotheses

Subsidiary task

Following from the above discussion, it is expected that the differing tasks of subsidiaries will determine the extent to which they are involved in knowledge management and innovation. Hence it is hypothesized that:

Hypothesis 10.1a: Subsidiary task will be positively associated with the frequency of use of knowledge management techniques.

Hypothesis 10.1b: Subsidiary task will be positively associated with the level of involvement in the innovation network of the MNC.

The innovator subsidiary is the archetypal subsidiary associated with the global innovation strategy that typifies the heterarchic MNC. Hence it is hypothesized that:

Hypothesis 10.2a: Among all the subsidiary tasks, the subsidiary task typical of the heterarchic MNC – the innovator – will exhibit the highest value for frequency of use of knowledge management techniques.

Hypothesis 10.2b: Among all the subsidiary tasks, the subsidiary task typical of the heterarchic MNC – the innovator – will exhibit the highest value for level of involvement in the innovation network of the MNC.

In addition to these hypotheses relating to subsidiary task the investigation expands our understanding of these processes by examining a number of potential predictors and/or enablers of the use of knowledge management techniques and involvement in the innovation network of the MNC.

Communications

An important consideration for a MNC that deals with a number of subsidiaries each having specialized or complementary knowledge is how to link the dispersed parts of the firm so that they may learn from each other. Information technology is one of the most useful available tools. The IT system has three vital capabilities. First, it allows the MNC to tap into the abundance of data and information that has accumulated within the firm in order to determine which of this information provides competitive utility (Grover and Davenport, 2001). Second, it is the primary horizontal mechanisms by which firms link and leverage the dispersed capabilities of their often global network to generate innovations (Bartlett and Ghoshal, 1989). Third, it is one of several tools that can be used to facilitate the acquisition, storage and retrieval of knowledge in the organizational memory system (Walsh and Ungson, 1991). The IT system is clearly an important knowledge asset for the firm.

From a multinational perspective, Bartlett and Ghoshal's (1989) transnational and its descendants, the differentiated network (Nohria and Ghoshal, 1997) and the individualized corporation (Ghoshal and

Bartlett, 1997) are the forms most involved in innovation. Bartlett and Ghoshal (1989) labeled the two mechanisms of innovation typical of this form as locally leveraged and globally linked and argued that the cross-unit integrating devices are central to successful innovation. These integrating devices are largely IT-based. To use these integrating devices most employees require direct access to the firm's electronic communications network.

For open learning to be effective between organizational members firms must have mechanisms to assist the management of knowledge acquisition. Communication channel usage must therefore be frequent and clear to assist knowledge acquisition to take place and encourage continuous information exchange and learning (Helleloid and Simonin, 1994). This information exchange assists a firm in all of Nonaka's (1994) knowledge creating processes and also contributes to the development of organizational memory (Sabherwal and Becerra-Fernandez, 2003). Bartlett and Ghoshal's integrating devices mentioned earlier require an extensive communications structure. Clearly in firms concerned with knowledge management and global innovations, we would expect to find a wide range and richness of channels. For example, Bresman, Birkinshaw and Nobel (1999) demonstrated that know-how transfer was facilitated by interpersonal communication and Gupta and Govindarajan (2000) revealed that the richness of communication channels aided knowledge transfer. In addition, many other authors (for example Anand, Manz and Glick, 1998; Cross and Baird, 2000; Davenport, De Long and Beers, 1998; Davenport and Prusak, 1998; Moorman and Miner, 1997, 1998; Nielsen and Ciabuschi, 2003; Orlikowski and Hofman, 1997; Zack, 1998, 1999b) have, in various guises, asserted the importance of supportive and enabling aspects of corporate culture, social networks, socialization processes or the need to replace the command and control culture with something more trust-based. These are all linked to the communication networks of the organizations. The communication channels are separated into two types: electronic and hard copy.

Hypothesis 10.3a: Frequency of use of electronic communication channels will be positively associated with the frequency of use of knowledge management techniques.

Hypothesis 10.3b: Frequency of use of electronic communication channels will be positively associated with the level of involvement in the innovation network of the MNC.

Hypothesis 10.4a. Frequency of use of hard copy communication channels will be positively associated with the frequency of use of knowledge management techniques.

Hypothesis 10.4b. Frequency of use of hard copy communication channels will be positively associated with the level of involvement in the innovation network of the MNC.

Level of technology

The link between technology, innovation and knowledge management has been mentioned earlier in this and many other studies (Davenport, De Long and Beers, 1998; Fruin, 1997; Nielsen and Ciabuschi, 2003; Storck and Hill, 2000; Zack, 1999a). Almeida and Phene (2004), for example, showed that the technological richness of the MNC had a positive impact in innovation in subsidiaries. This association suggests that it might be the companies in the fast-moving, innovative high technology industries that are leading the way in innovation and knowledge management projects. In addition, Cross and Baird (2000) suggested that a developed level of technology is a necessary (but not sufficient) central resource for effective knowledge management.

Hypothesis 10.5a: Level of technology will be positively associated with the frequency of use of knowledge management techniques.

Hypothesis 10.5b: Level of technology will be positively associated with the level of involvement in the innovation network of the MNC.

Local knowledge

It is well established in the literature that internal knowledge development must be externally assisted. Firms need to look to and use external sources to benefit internal knowledge (Helleloid and Simonin, 1994; Andersson, Forsgren and Holm, 2002). Almeida and Phene (2004) demonstrated that the subsidiary's knowledge links to host country firms and the technological diversity within the host country both affected subsidiary innovation. Schmid and Schung (2003) illustrated that the role of different internal and external network partners varied for different functional activities in the subsidiary and hence presumably for different subsidiary tasks as specified here. These are a particularly significant consideration for the MNC that deals with local and global issues when managing knowledge. As a result, involvement with local organizations is fundamental to a MNC's strategy, as this specialist knowledge will assist a firm to acquire new information from the market place and various networks and disseminate this throughout the firm.

Hypothesis 10.6a: Involvement with local organizations will be positively associated with the frequency of use of knowledge management technique.

Hypothesis 10.6b: Involvement with local organizations will be positively associated with the level of involvement in the innovation network of the MNC.

Thus this inquiry has several purposes. First, the relationships between subsidiary task and the knowledge management system and the innovation network of the MNC are investigated. Second, hypotheses regarding the characteristics of subsidiaries involved in these processes are examined.

Method

Dependent variables

There are no accepted extant measures of a firm's level of involvement in knowledge management. The broad purpose of knowledge management is to construct mechanisms to create, store, access and utilize organizational knowledge in order to develop the firm's capabilities, and generate innovations, thus creating and sustaining the firm's competences and competitive advantage. Therefore, for the purposes of this analysis, the knowledge management system was suggested to consist of three sets of tools, as detailed above: the use of groupware technologies such as intranets and video-conferencing; the building of organization memory systems whereby knowledge can be collected, stored, accessed and retrieved at need; the auditing of a company's intellectual capital by placing a value on the corporate knowledge asset stock.

The dependent variable, knowledge management, was arrived at by summing the answers to questions asking respondents to assess the frequency of their company's use of these three techniques. Groupware technology was described in the survey as 'facilitating global teams via electronic means e.g. screen-sharing, video-conferencing etc', the organization memory systems was explained as 'electronic storage of knowledge or information' and auditing of intellectual capital was 'putting a value on the company's knowledge capital'.

The scales for these three variables (and for the subsequent dependent variables) were 1 = never, 2 = rarely, 3 = sometimes, 4 = often and 5 = very frequent giving a minimum score of 3 and maximum of 15. The knowledge management variable had n = 312, mean = 7.54 and s.d. = 2.82. Principal components factor analysis of the three variables (without rotation as only one factor was expected and found) gave highly significant factor scores of 0.79, 0.76 and 0.77 (see Chapter 12) and reliability analysis gave a satisfactory standardized item reliability (for exploratory work such as this) of $\alpha = 0.66$ (Hair, Anderson and Tatham, 2002).

The next dependent variable is the extent to which a subsidiary is involved in the network of innovation generation and dissemination. Several questions on the survey focused on this issue. First, the respondent was asked to assess how much R&D the subsidiary performed on behalf of the rest of the corporation. Then a series of questions were asked requesting the frequency of the following innovation outcomes and practices:

Creation of significant product or process innovations within your company;
Adoption of these innovations by your company;
Adoption of these innovations by other parts of the corporation;
Your company adopting innovations from elsewhere in the corporation.

After factor analysis (see Chapter 12), the first four of these variables (amount of R&D on behalf of the corporation plus the first three above) were combined into an aggregated variable labeled innovations (mean = 9.99; s.d. = 3.18; range 4–20; n = 310; $\alpha = 0.78$). The last variable, innovations from elsewhere (mean = 3.18, s.d. = 0.99; range 1–5; n = 310), persistently loaded independently and was consequently examined separately.

Predictor variables

The primary predictor variable was the categorical variable that indicated each of the five subsidiary tasks being investigated. There were an additional four predictor variables presented in Hypotheses 3a through 6b.

Communications. An assessment of the use of two types of communication channels by the firm was calculated by first obtaining the sum of responses to three questions asking the frequency of use of various hard copy media – newsletters, magazines and reports (scale variable; range = 3–15; n = 310; mean = 9.65; s.d. = 2.48; factors scores 0.83, 0.82 and 0.63; α = 0.65). The second was obtained by summing the responses to five questions asking the frequency of use of various electronic media – TV/video, email, intranet, edi, electronic commerce (scale variable; range 5–25; n = 301; mean = 14.84; s.d. = 3.92; factor scores 0.58, 0.55, 0.67, 0.68 and 0.71; α = 0.63).

Level of technology. Respondents were asked to assess the level of technology of their primary operations on a scale from 1 to 5 (scale variable; range 1–5; n = 309; mean = 3.82; s.d. = 0.89).

Local involvement. This was calculated by summing the responses to five questions asking the extent to which the company was actively involved with several types of local organizations (scale variable; range 5–25; n = 312; mean = 12.58; s.d. = 3.28; factor scores 0.64, 0.56, 0.74, 0.67, 0.59; α = 0.64).

Control variables

Several control variables were included to allow for the influence of factors such as industry characteristics, MNC and subsidiary size and any factors that might arise as a result of subsidiaries having parent corporations from differing home countries.

Industry. Using the Australian Standard Industrial Classification system, firms were allocated to four industrial types – manufacturing; marketing/wholesale/distribution; finance, property and business services; and other. Firms in the 'other' category were used as the reference category for this variable. Three dichotomous 1/0 variables were included: (1) industry: manufacturing, proportion = 0.31; (2) industry: retail/distribution, proportion = 0.48; (3) industry: finance/business services, proportion = 0.13).

Industry innovativeness. Respondents were asked to assess the rate of generation of product and process innovations that was characteristic of the local market for their most important products (scale variable; range 1–5; n = 305; mean = 2.94; s.d. = 1.00).

Subsidiary size. Bjorkman, Barner-Rasmussen and Li (2004) found subsidiary size not significant as a control variable in an examination of factors affecting knowledge outflows. It was included here nevertheless. Non-normal distribution of the subsidiary size variable required that the natural logarithmic transformation of number of employees be used (continuous variable; n = 303; mean = 4.47; s.d. = 1.59).

MNC size. Again the natural logarithmic transformation of number of employees was used (continuous variable; n = 268; mean = 9.84; s.d. = 1.60).

Parent nationality. Nationality was based upon a specific home country or two countries closely related on Hofstede's (1984) indices. There were 53 MNCs from the UK, 135 from US/Canada, 17 from Japan, 11 from Sweden, 32 from Germany, 12 from Italy, 11 from Switzerland, 12 from Netherlands/Belgium (N/B), 9 from France, 14 from Denmark/Norway and 6 from other countries..

Table 10.1 presents the intercorrelations for the predictor and control variables. Because of the dichotomous variables, the matrix

Table 10.1 Descriptive statistics and intercorrelations for predictor and control variables[a]

Control variables	(1)	(2)	(3)	(4)	(5)	(6)	(7)	(8)	(9)	(10)
(1) Industry innovativeness	—									
(2) Industry: manufacturing	–.00	—								
(3) Industry: retail/distr	–.03	–.64	—							
(4) Industry: fin/bus serv	.01	–.26	–.37	—						
(5) Subsidiary size	.18	.27	–.38	.05	—					
(6) MNC size	.07	.06	–.16	.04	.42	—				
(7) Level of technology	.16	–.08	.06	.07	.03	.08	—			
(8) Electronic communications	.15	–.01	–.09	.07	.36	.30	.25	—		
(9) Hard copy communications	.03	–.02	.07	–.08	.10	.21	.13	.29	—	
(10) Local involvement	.15	.12	–.13	–.03	.36	.20	.13	.23	.24	—
Mean or proportion	2.94	.31	.48	.13	4.47	9.84	3.82	12.78	9.65	12.58
s.d.	1.00	—	—	—	1.59	1.60	.89	3.50	2.48	3.28
n	305	313	313	313	303	268	309	313	310	312

Correlation coefficients of > .11 are significant at the $p < .05$ level
[a] The categorical variables parent nationality and subsidiary task are not included.

uses Spearman's rho. Other than the correlations between the dichoto-mous industry variables, the correlation of 0.42 between subsidiary size and MNC size is the highest in the matrix. This is not, however, a value that will generate major concern for problems of collinearity (Hutcheson and Sofroniou, 1999).

Results

Table 10.2 shows the uncontrolled means of the five subsidiary tasks for the three predictor variables and significant differences are shown below the table. It is immediately clear that for both knowledge management and innovation the innovator subsidiary exhibited, as expected, the highest mean score. In five of the eight comparisons with other subsidiary tasks the differences were significant at $p < .05$ and two at the marginally significant $p < .10$. In addition, the innovator subsidiary was the highest score for the innovations from elsewhere dependent variable and the independent subsidiary, unsurprisingly, was significantly the lowest. These, however, are uncontrolled mea-sures and to investigate these relationships more accurately and to

Table 10.2   Uncontrolled means for the three dependent variables and five subsidiary tasks

Dependent variables		Distrib (1)	Adapt (2)	Imple (3)	Innov (4)	Indep (5)
Knowledge management	Mean	7.18	7.82	7.33	8.30	7.23
	s.d.	2.91	2.89	2.97	2.54	2.58
	n	94	65	46	54	53
Innovations	Mean	8.34	10.40	10.07	11.44	10.49
	s.d.	3.58	3.08	3.06	2.43	2.60
	n	95	65	46	54	53
Innovations from elsewhere	Mean	3.15	3.27	3.24	3.48	2.79
	s.d.	1.08	1.04	.90	.88	.85
	n	94	64	46	54	52

Pairwise comparisons
Knowledge management:
$4 > 3\ p < .10$; $4 > 5$ and $4 > 1\ p < .05$.
Innovations:
$4 > 5\ p < .10$: $4 > 2$ and $4 > 3\ p < .05$; $4 > 1\ p < .001$.
Innovations from elsewhere:
$1 > 5$ and $3 > 5\ p < .05$; $2 > 5\ p < .01$; $4 > 5\ p < .001$

assess the dependent variables' associations with the other predictor and control variables, the ANCOVA method of analysis was again used.

Table 10.3 shows analysis of covariance summary and Table 10.4 the estimated marginal means and pairwise comparisons for the three

Table 10.3   Analysis of covariance summary for the three dependent variables

Variable	df	Knowledge management	Innovations	Innovations from elsewhere
Subsidiary size (ln)	1	.98	.00	.63
MNC size (ln)	1	3.56† (.016)	1.68	.03
Industry: manufacturing	1	.43	1.19	3.94* (.018)
Industry: retail, wholesale and distribution	1	1.09	.06	.73
Industry: finance, property and business services	1	2.18	.47	.02
Industry innovativeness	1	3.39† (.015)	17.87*** (.075)	17.25*** (.073)
Parent nationality	10	1.13	1.33	2.23* (.092)
Technology level	1	9.74** (.042)	3.76† (.017)	5.31* (.024)
Electronic communications	1	18.13*** (.076)	2.09	5.31* (.024)
Hard copy communications	1	2.77† (.012)	.07	.32
Local involvement	1	1.95	4.43* (.020)	.22
Subsidiary task	4	1.14	2.33† (.041)	1.04
Intercept	1	4.48* (.020)	9.67** (.042)	7.62** (.033)
R^2	–	.377	.315	.271
Mean square error df	–	220	220	220

*** $p < .001$; ** $p < .01$; * $p < .05$; † $p < .10$ (two-tailed test)

Table 10.4   Estimated marginal means for subsidiary task and parent
nationality for each dependent variable

Variable	Knowledge management	Innovations	Innovations from elsewhere	
(1) Distributor	7.75	9.56	3.31	
(2) Adapter	7.86	10.54	3.33	
(3) Implementer	8.04	10.41	3.47	
(4) Innovator	8.76	11.37	3.54	
(5) Independent	8.06	10.58	3.13	
Significant pairwise comparisons	4>1* 4>2†	4>1** 2>1†	4>5†	
(1) UK	8.62	11.03	3.52	
(2) US/Canada	8.00	10.61	3.37	
(3) Japan	7.56	9.33	2.61	
(4) Sweden	6.59	11.29	3.24	
(5) Germany	8.21	11.24	3.49	
(6) Italy	8.13	11.85	2.67	
(7) Switzerland	7.22	9.20	3.67	
(8) Netherlands/Belgium	9.56	10.57	3.65	
(9) France	9.16	10.02	3.80	
(10) Denmark/Norway	7.99	9.20	3.59	
(11) Other	7.96	11.08	3.33	
Significant pairwise comparisons $p > .05$ or higher only	8>4* 8>7* 9>4* 1>4*	6>3* 5>3* 6>10* 5>10* 6>7*	10>3** 9>3** 8>3** 7>3** 5>3** 2>3** 1>3**	10>6* 9>6* 8>6* 7>6* 5>6* 2>6*

*** $p < .001$; ** $p < .01$; * $p < .05$; † $p < .10$ (two-tailed test)

dependent variables and five subsidiary tasks. The figures in brackets in Table 10.3 are the partial eta values (the proportion of variance explained) for the significant variables.

Knowledge management

After controlling for a range of other variables, the subsidiary task variable was not a significant predictor of the use of knowledge management techniques (F[4,220] = 1.14; p = ns). Hypothesis 10.1a was not supported. The innovator subsidiary had the highest score for the use of knowledge management techniques. In addition there were significant differences between the innovator and the distributor ($p < .05$) and between the innovator and adapter ($p < .10$). While this provided some evidence in support of H10.2a it was not significantly supported. These were somewhat in contrast to the uncontrolled results. There was, however, support for H10.3a (frequency of use of electronic communications; $F[1,220] = 18.13$; $p < .001$) and H10.5a (level of technology; $F[1,220] = 9.74$; $p < .01$). Use of hard copy communications (H10.4a) was marginally significantly supported ($F[1,220] = 2.77$; $p < .10$) and local involvement (H10.6a) was not supported ($F[1,220] = 1.95$; $p = ns$).

Among the control variables there were weak associations for both MNC size ($F[1,220] = 3.56$; $p < .10$) and innovativeness of the industry ($F[1,220] = 3.39$; $p < .10$). The parent nationality variable was not significantly associated ($F[10,220] = 1.13$; $p < .10$) but there were several interesting significant pairwise comparisons among the marginal mean scores. Netherlands/Belgium was notably the highest of the 11 categories and significantly higher than Sweden and Switzerland ($p < .05$). France and the UK were also significantly higher than Sweden (both $p < .05$).

Innovations

The results of this analysis stand in considerable contrast to those above. The subsidiary task was a marginally significant ($F[4,220] = 2.33$; $p < .10$) predictor of involvement in the innovation network of the MNC. Hypothesis 10.1b was supported. The innovator subsidiary had the highest score for involvement with the innovation network of the MNC but it had only a single significant pairwise comparison ($p < .01$). Again this was between the estimated marginal means of the innovator and the distributor subsidiaries and while some support for H10.2b was indicated it was not significant. Equally noticeable was the low score of the distributor subsidiary. It was marginally significantly lower than the adapter ($p < .10$) and independent ($p < .10$). The effects of the other predictor variables were not strong. Only H10.6b was supported (local involvement; $F[1,220] = 4.43$; $p < .05$) with marginal support for H10.5b (level of technology; $F[1,220] = 3.76$; $p < .10$) and no support for H10.3b (electronic communications; $F[1,220] = 2.09$; $p = ns$) and H10.4b (hard copy communications; $F[1,220] = .07$; $p = ns$).

Among the control variables, the major association with involvement in the MNC's innovation network was very clearly the degree of innovativeness of the industry ($F[1,220] = 17.87$; $p < .001$) which accounted for 7.5 per cent of the variance. Parent nationality was not significantly associated (F[10,220] = 1.13; p = ns) but there were several significant inter-country pairwise comparisons. Germany and Italy both scored higher than Japan and Denmark/Norway (all at $p < .05$) while Italy > Switzerland ($p < .05$).

Innovations from elsewhere

The results for this variable show some noteworthy differences from the other innovation dependent variable above. Subsidiary task was not a significant predictor of adoption of innovations from elsewhere in the MNC (F[4,220] = 1.04; p = ns) hence this result did not support H10.1b. While the innovator subsidiary task had the highest estimated marginal mean the differences were not significant except marginally so in comparison with the independent subsidiary ($p < .10$). Hypothesis 10.2c was not supported. Given the focus upon links with other parts of the MNC, the most obvious and expected feature is the low score for the independent subsidiary. In addition, two of the four other predictors were significant: level of technology (F[1,220] = 5.31; $p < .05$) and use of electronic communications (F[1,220] = 5.31; $p < .05$) offering support for H10.3b and H10.5b. H10.4b (hard copy communications; F[1,220] = .32; p = ns) and H10.6b (local involvement; F[1,220] = .22; p = ns) were not supported.

Once again the industry innovativeness control demonstrated the strongest association (F[1,220] = 17.25; $p < .001$) and parent nationality was also significant (F[10,220] = 2.23; $p < .05$). The pairwise comparisons of the latter indicated many differences at the $p < .01$ and $p < .05$ levels. They are listed in Table 10.4.

Discussion

This chapter set out to analyze some of the basic links between firm and industry characteristics and the propensity of firms to be involved in innovation networks and the use of knowledge management techniques in Australian subsidiaries of MNCs. The most recent literature on the organizational strategy and form of modern MNCs has stressed the importance of knowledge management and innovation as the driving force of competitive advantage for these firms. The need to develop organizational capabilities that encourage and enhance innovation has led to the growth of an organizational configuration variously labeled the transnational (Bartlett and Ghoshal, 1989), the differentiated network (Nohria and Ghoshal, 1997), the heterarchy (Hedlund, 1986) or the individualized corporation (Ghoshal and

Bartlett, 1997). The structure of these firms is characterized by network form, differentiated roles and responsibilities and multiple organizational processes. Thus, the evidence that firms working with advanced technologies and placing considerable emphasis upon R&D were significantly associated with the use of knowledge management techniques is in line with expectations. This was also the case with the significant associations found between knowledge management techniques and the use of internal and external communication networks. The range of significant variables enhances Hansen and Lovas's (2004) contention that there are usually multiple determinants in these cases.

Despite the extensive literature linking knowledge management and innovation, the most striking result from these investigations is the difference between the significant variables associated with frequency of use of knowledge management techniques and those associated with involvement in the innovation processes. Broadly interpreted the use of knowledge management is primarily associated with the internal firm characteristics of level of technology, internal communication intensity and MNC size. Involvement in innovation is, to a much greater extent, associated with external and industry variables such as industry innovativeness, manufacturing and involvement with local organizations.

To further examine this differentiation an additional ANCOVA was run with use of knowledge management as the dependent variable and the two innovation variables among the associative variables. The results are shown in Table 10.5. Neither of the innovation variables was a significant predictor of use of knowledge management techniques (innovation; $F[1,218] = 2.51$; p = ns; innovations from elsewhere; $F[1,218] = .76$; p = ns) and, between them, they accounted for only 1.4 per cent of the variance in the dependent variable. The logical conclusion is that knowledge management is an internal initiative of large MNCs while innovation networks are responses to external business environment pressures.

The pairwise comparisons between subsidiary tasks indicated that, in contrast to the results of Chapter 9 regarding control mechanisms, there is some supporting evidence for the assertion that knowledge management and innovation processes used by MNCs are linked to the hierarchy/heterarchy distinction. The literature on the heterarchic form (see, for example, Hedlund, 1986; Bartlett and Ghoshal, 1989; Nohria and Ghoshal, 1997) has argued that the MNC needed to implement much greater levels of horizontal coordination. The results for the innovator subsidiaries (scoring significantly higher than some

Table 10.5   Analysis of covariance summary for use of knowledge management techniques including the two innovation variables

Variable	df	F	Partial eta
Subsidiary size (ln)	1	1.09	
MNC size (ln)	1	4.08*	.018
Industry: manufacturing	1	.17	
Industry: retail, wholesale and distribution	1	1.05	
Industry: finance, property and business services	1	1.95	
Industry innovativeness	1	1.14	
Parent nationality	10	1.01	
Technology level	1	7.50**	.033
Electronic communications	1	15.41***	.066
Hard copy communications	1	2.59	
Local involvement	1	1.41	
Subsidiary task	4	.78	
Innovation	1	2.51	.011
Innovations from elsewhere	1	.76	.003
Intercept	1	6.53*	.029
R^2	–	.389	
Mean square error	218	–	–

*** $p < .001$; ** $p < .01$; * $p < .05$ (two-tailed test)

other subsidiary tasks) suggested that, for the mechanisms examined in this investigation, these had eventuated.

Two other results merit particular comment. First, in line with their simple distribution and sales roles, the distributor subsidiaries made somewhat lesser contributions to the knowledge management and innovation processes in the MNC than other subsidiaries. Second, the low score for the independent subsidiaries on the innovations from elsewhere variable emphasized the extent of the alienation of those subsidiaries from any part of the MNC other than HQ.

Among the control variables parent nationality posed some intriguing questions. Japanese MNCs scored relatively low on three variables and this might be surprising given that Japanese firms have been at the forefront of the knowledge management and innovation literature as demonstrated by Fruin's *Knowledge Works* (1997) and the many examples given by Nonaka and his co-workers (1995, 2003). These examples are primarily within Japan and the cultural and linguistic problems associated with extensive communications may be the reason why subsidiaries of Japanese MNCS demonstrated such a low mean score. Explicit knowledge, by definition, is more easily stored and transferred than tacit knowledge and it is probable that these knowledge management techniques are most valuable for the enabling of tacit knowledge. It therefore seems likely that linguistic and/or cultural similarity of the home country to Australia will be a factor in enhancing the ease of the transfer process for communicating subtle tacit knowledge. JIT, TQM and other techniques have not generally transplanted readily so it is unsurprising that 'ba' – a shared mental space for knowledge creation (Nonaka and Konno, 1998) – and other distinctive Japanese concepts have also lacked easy transferability.

This same logic results in the outcome for Swedish MNCs being surprising. They were the second highest for the two innovation variables but the lowest and significantly less than Netherlands/Belgium, France and the UK for use of knowledge management techniques. Swedish MNCs such as Volvo, Skandia and so on have generally been noted for their innovativeness. There appears to be no obvious explanation for their dissociation from the use of knowledge management techniques other than to mention the rather small sample and the subsequent risk.

The industry innovativeness variable was in line with the results for the technology and innovation results above. The size association was also in line with expectations since the development of these knowledge management techniques is not likely to be financially viable for small firms. The marginally significant negative association with cultural distance was perhaps expected and explicable on the basis of the discussion above.

Limitations and future research

The major limitations in this study arise from the undeveloped nature of the field of enquiry and the absence of accepted constructs with which to examine any proposed relationships. The particular difficulty in this study was the nature of one of the dependent variables, knowledge management.

The fundamental weakness of cross-sectional research is that it is unable to determine the development of relationships and thus impedes any assumption of causality, thereby limiting the investigation to a static model. In this study the R^2 values were strong for cross-sectional research and there were some powerful statistical inferences but the above interpretations must still be weighed carefully. Only the use of longitudinal data would enable better assertions regarding causality and to assess the robustness and generality of the model.

11
Conclusions, Limitations and Future Directions

Summary of theoretical and empirical outcomes

In the development of the HQ-subsidiary model, this research further clarified the nature of the HQ-subsidiary relationship in the MNC by providing a detailed theoretical underpinning for a series of HQ-subsidiary connections. Based upon Chandler's development of strategic contingency theory, the transaction cost approach and the knowledge-oriented variant of the resource-based view, a new model was presented. This model posited that the choice of advantage generating strategy employed by the MNC, the knowledge asymmetries that this strategy engendered, the subsidiary tasks, subsidiary autonomy, how the subsidiaries were controlled by HQ and the place of the subsidiaries in the knowledge management and innovation networks of the MNC were intimately and reciprocally interrelated features of the HQ-subsidiary relationship. While some of the links in this interplay had been addressed previously in the literature, this model was an important step forward because, for the first time, it synthesized, integrated and extended, often disparate, conceptual and empirical knowledge, to produce a new model of an important organizational phenomenon.

The research created the new model by integrating the established IB and IM literatures with recent work on the knowledge-based view of the firm. The strategies adopted by the MNC at the corporate and business levels were related to the tasks needed at the subsidiary level. Six distinct subsidiary strategies were identified (contributor, implementer, distributor, adapter, innovator and independent) and each was proposed to be congruent with a corporate or business level strategy (vertical integration, geographical first move, cost minimization, differentiation/focus, innovation and portfolio diversification, respectively). The model also built upon previous conceptualizations in that it focused upon the hierarchy-heterarchy distinction in MNC form.

Up to this point, only two other studies have derived subsidiary task from an examination of higher-level strategies in the MNC. Jarillo and Martinez (1990) and the extension of that study by Taggart (1997b) both utilized the Integration-Responsiveness grid as their lens for examining the subsidiary. Both paper explicitly recognized that they were, in effect, correlating subsidiary tasks with the Bartlett and Ghoshal (1987) MNC strategies. Jarillo and Martinez's (1990) active subsidiary accorded with the Bartlett and Ghoshal's transnational strategy, the receptive subsidiary strategy with the global strategy and the autonomous subsidiary strategy with the multinational (multidomestic) strategy. Taggart's (1997b) study found the fourth subsidiary strategy. His quiescent subsidiary was consistent with Bartlett and Ghoshal's international strategy. The model developed in this thesis can be seen to be substantially different from these studies for three reasons. First, two additional subsidiary types were hypothesized based upon subsidiary tasks directly derived from the HQ-subsidiary model. In addition, since the model was not simply a high-low 2×2 matrix of dimensions, it left scope for further subsidiary tasks to be developed on the basis of different MNC level strategies. Second, the existence of five of the six subsidiary tasks was demonstrated and validated via several investigations on the basis of specific data regarding the subsidiary's task within the MNC, rather than on indirect assessments of degree of integration and local responsiveness. Third, the present study relied upon a larger sample size and data from MNCs in a wider range of industries, rather than the specific manufacturing data of the Jarillo and Martinez (1990) and Taggart (1997b) studies.

This new HQ-subsidiary model was created using a new, distinctive and partly theoretically driven restructuring and fusion of the several literatures that pertain to this topic. To date only Birkinshaw (1994) had attempted this task. His review of MNC strategy and structure imposed a useful and more or less chronological structure on this dispersed literature and he drew two important conclusions that influenced the present study. First, Birkinshaw argued that hierarchy was the dominant organizing principle in the pre-1980 MNC but heterarchy was steadily emerging and supplanting hierarchy. This important and well-founded conclusion underlies much of the research presented here. As in this study, Birkinshaw set up an idealized description of heterarchy, based upon Hedlund's (1986) formative work. Birkinshaw's second conclusion was that, at the time of his review, research in the IM field was focusing increasingly upon the position and role of the subsidiary within this new MNC form. While a major stimulus for this study, the structuring of his review was essentially normative and limited to the IM literature.

The next contribution of this research was to collect the first large-scale dataset on subsidiaries in Australia across most industries and most major MNC home countries while focusing on many aspects of the relationship between HQ and the subsidiary. The size of the sample (313 firms), the excellent response rate of 34 per cent, encompassing nearly 8 per cent of the estimated total population of subsidiaries and its good representativeness, enabled the use of all major statistical tools and gave considerable confidence in the results of these analyses. In addition, the single host country research design acted a consistent baseline to measure effects.

The research used the dataset obtained to legitimate the model. This was accomplished in the first investigation by employing k-means cluster analysis. By analyzing the responses of CEOs to questions regarding their perception of the subsidiary's role within the MNC, five of the six hypothesized subsidiary tasks were identified. The internal and external validity of the solution was then verified using appropriate statistical and analytical procedures. While neglected in the past, cluster analysis is an increasingly used technique in management probably because of its obvious value in mapping new domains of inquiry.

The next outcome was a new, theoretically grounded, empirical analysis of the determinants of subsidiary autonomy. A central dimension of the HQ-subsidiary relationship is the extent and forms of the knowledge asymmetries that exist between the two parties. These knowledge asymmetries have implications for the amount of autonomy of decision-making conceded to the subsidiary by HQ or appropriated by the subsidiary, by virtue of its knowledge, resources and capabilities. In the research's second investigation, hypotheses were tested that linked level of autonomy of decision-making in the subsidiary to subsidiary task and a range of control variables relating to the MNC, the subsidiary and the local environment. These hypotheses were examined using ANCOVA and post hoc pairwise comparison of marginal means for each task. The chapter first examined related vs unrelated diversification and then the four related diversification subsidiary tasks. The levels of autonomy for related vs unrelated diversification and the distributor, innovator and independent subsidiary tasks were generally as predicted. The predictions for the adapter and implementer subsidiaries tasks were the reverse of the levels expected. In these cases, contextual explanations for the non-significances were readily available. In addition, some interesting new and confirmatory results were obtained regarding the MNC home country and subsidiary size control variables employed in the analysis.

The research then investigated Hedlund's (1981) suggestion of the existence of a curvilinear relationship between subsidiary autonomy and subsidiary size. The investigation confirmed that, as small subsidiaries grew, they acquired more autonomy but, at some stage, it appeared that their importance to the MNC reached a point where HQ exerted further influence on decision-making and autonomy declined. In a new extension of the Hedlund hypothesis, the results of this study suggested that as the subsidiary grew further in size, and presumably in resources and capabilities, a further slope change point was reached. At this point, it was suggested that the subsidiary attained enough ascendancy in the relationship to throw off the shackles of HQ control and autonomy suddenly increased again. Thus a three phase sinusoidal model was suggested and confirmed.

The conceptual scenarios of Ouchi (1977) and Baliga and Jaeger (1984) were used as the framework to set up hypotheses predicting the types of control mechanisms implemented by HQ in differing types of subsidiary. The results indicated that, with the exception of the independent subsidiary task and contrary to the hypotheses, subsidiary tasks were generally equally subject to the influence of each of the separate control mechanisms. This direct refutation of the Ouchi/Baliga/Jaeger formulation was in line with observations from several studies (see Martinez and Jarillo, 1991 for details) that MNCs commonly equip themselves with the entire range of mechanisms at their disposal.

The final contribution of the research emanated from a study that examined the frequency of use of knowledge management techniques by subsidiaries and their embeddedness in the innovation network of the MNC. This investigation highlighted the hierarchy-heterarchy contrast in MNC form and the implications this contrast has for knowledge and innovation mechanisms in the MNC. The study examined hypotheses proposing that subsidiaries of heterarchic MNCs (the innovator subsidiaries) would be more frequently involved in knowledge management relationships and more embedded in the innovation network of the MNC than subsidiaries of hierarchic MNCs. The results offered some support for these propositions. However, in addition, the use of knowledge management seemed to be primarily associated with the internal firm characteristics of level of technology, internal communications intensity and MNC size while involvement in innovation was, to a much greater extent, associated with external and industry variables such as industry innovativeness, manufacturing and involvement with local organizations

There are some important links between these contributions and several important studies in the extant literature and these will be examined in the following discussion.

Discussion

While this study has provided a number of useful theoretical and empirical advances, it remains only the first step in a potentially productive research stream. In the following section, the relationship of the conceptual aspects of the thesis with Bartlett and Ghoshal's (1989) framework is explored and then several potential extensions of the work are examined.

Comparison with Bartlett and Ghoshal's model

It was noted above that the Jarillo and Martinez (1990) and Taggart (1997b) studies on subsidiary classifications were constructed from an extension of the Integration-Responsiveness framework. At first glance, it appears that four of the five MNC level strategies that brought about particular subsidiary tasks in this research are very similar to those in the Bartlett and Ghoshal variation on this framework. The cost minimization, focus plus differentiation, geographic first mover and innovation strategies of this study have elements in common with Bartlett and Ghoshal's global, multinational, international and transnational strategies, respectively. Further, Bartlett and Ghoshal brought attention to the nature of the HQ-subsidiary knowledge asymmetries typical of their MNC types. A continuation of the Bartlett and Ghoshal analysis in the direction of subsidiary tasks would probably arrive at five of the six typical subsidiary tasks hypothesized in this study – the distributors, adapters, implementers, contributors and innovators.

While the results appear similar, this is not surprising since they are examining the same phenomenon albeit from alternative directions. The congruence is, in an analytical and theoretical sense, only superficial. The subsidiary task in this study were arrived at from a direct logic evolving from a consideration of Porter's corporate and business level strategies. Bartlett and Ghoshal taxonomy was derived from two postulated contingent characteristics of the business environment that have often proved difficult to define and hence operationalize. The 'need for integration' and 'need for responsiveness' dimensions of the I-R grid are useful lenses through which to view MNC strategy but they have been difficult constructs to measure. In general, the 'need for responsiveness' has been more easily measured, primarily by the use of managerial opinion. The 'need for integration' has usually been proxied by actual (or perceptions of actual) amount of integration in the form of inter-unit product flows in manufacturing MNCs. Given that this measure is based upon the assumption that the current configuration reflects some theoretically ideal 'need for integration', this is by no means, necessarily, a good proxy.

Possible theoretical developments

The features of subsidiary tasks in the present study were, *vis a vis* most earlier studies, analyzed from a very different viewpoint. The major difference is that the perspective in this research is subsidiary-centric. From the subsidiary's view, there are two orthogonal dimensions of concern. First, the subsidiary is interested in its specific relationship with HQ and, second, its relationship with the other units and its overall embeddedness in the MNC. As shown in Figure 11.1, the subsidiary-HQ dimension has been the focus of the autonomy and control influences and the subsidiary-other units dimension has been the focus of the hierarchy/heterarchy and co-ordination issues.

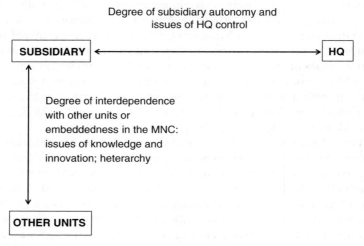

Figure 11.1   Subsidiary-HQ and subsidiary-other units relationships

This perspective has some advantages over the I-R grid. First, the dimensions are based upon more specific characteristics of the subsidiary and its relationships and these are much more amenable to quantification than the 'need for integration' and 'need for responsiveness' of the I-R grid. Subsidiary autonomy has been successfully operationalized in this and many other studies and the knowledge management and innovation variables used in Chapter 10 are partial measures of the subsidiary's organizational embeddedness.

Second, using these measures of interdependence, it was possible to offer evidence for the orthogonality of the two dimensions. The Pearson product moment coefficients of correlation between the variable subsidiary autonomy and the three variables: knowledge management, innovation and innovations from elsewhere were very low (–0.097, 0.053 and –0.061, respectively, all insignificant) suggesting minimal collinearity and hence appropriateness as orthogonal dimensions.

Third, if the autonomy and embeddedness dimensions are set up as the axes of a two dimensional matrix, it becomes possible to conjecture the likely positions for the six tasks derived in this research. These are shown in Figure 11.2. The independent subsidiary is expected to be very high on autonomy (low on contact HQ) and very low on interdependence or embeddedness. The distributor should be low on autonomy (high on contact HQ) but having a role that involves selling product from elsewhere in the MNC should have considerable interdependence with other units. The innovator should be high on autonomy (low on contact HQ) and relatively high on embeddedness.

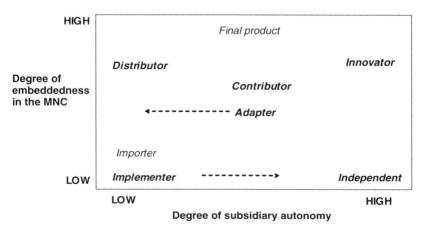

Figure 11.2   A suggested autonomy vs. embeddedness matrix

Table 11.1   **Autonomy and contact data for five subsidiary tasks**

	Distributor	Adapter	Implementer	Innovator	Independent
Autonomy	31.59	31.97	34.34	35.14	35.82
Contact other firms	3.36	3.04	2.54	2.74	2.14
Contact HQ	3.29	3.15	3.43	3.10	2.75

Analysis from first principles suggests the adapter is expected to have some degree of autonomy (moderate contact HQ) and embeddedness depending upon the amount of adaptation involved. The implementer's simple role of executing HQ's firm specific advantage in another location should indicate low on autonomy (high contact HQ) and embeddedness. However, in these cases, the evidence in Chapter 7 indicated greater than expected autonomy for the implementer and less for the adapter. Table 11.1 presents the autonomy and contact data from Chapters 7 and 9 and these are generally in line with these comments. The contributor subsidiary would be expected to show moderate amounts of autonomy and embeddedness.

Further subsidiary strategies

Equally importantly, Figure 11.2 also allows room for other potential strategies to be located and analyzed. Two additional subsidiary types had been proposed in earlier research. A marketing subsidiary had been proposed by both D'Cruz (1986) and White and Poynter (1984) as a precursor to the implementer task. As a simple importer of HQ produced goods and not linked to the overall MNC, this would be expected to be very low on both dimensions.

D'Cruz (1986) and White and Poynter (1984) also confirmed the presence of at least two types of production units. These subsidiaries performed roles in the manufacture of items to be sent to the distributor subsidiaries. The two subsidiary types acted either as single function units in the vertically integrated production chain or as complete producers of the final product.

The first of the two types of production unit found by D'Cruz (1986) and White and Poynter (1984) – the single function units – are likely to have their primary links with the units before and after them in the value chain. These are the contributor subsidiary task addressed above. Meanwhile, the latter type – the final product producers – are likely to be linked to many parts of the MNC for distribution purposes but somewhat constrained in autonomy of action because of the import-ance of their production role to the overall MNC and dependence on HQ for key knowledge. Thus the six subsidiary types from the theory and the two additional types conjectured above might be categorized as shown in Figure 11.2.

The six strategies of the present research are presented in bold type and the two other proposed types are in italic. This is clearly a tentative analysis and a subject for further examination but a framework very similar to this had been presented previously by Johnston (2000) although the theoretical underpinning had not been so well developed.

Subsidiary autonomy

In the research subsidiary autonomy was conceived as a product of subsidiary task and characteristics of the MNC, the local environment and individual characteristics of any particular subsidiary. While an adequate starting point, there was a need for a more formal theoretical derivation of subsidiary autonomy before the subsequent empirical investigation. As discussed in Chapter 7, the influences examined in the study provided an initial analysis but a more complex and nuanced analysis is necessary.

The research indicated that the subsidiary size variable is also of concern for at least two reasons. First, if its relationship to subsidiary autonomy is curvilinear (sinusoidal) in the manner suggested in Chapter 8, then the complexity must be must be taken into account. Second, and a more basic concern, is the question of whether absolute subsidiary size is the appropriate measure? While in this study an attempt was made to allow for relative size, it is arguable that a sub-sidiary of any given size will be allowed or take more autonomy (or have its autonomy constrained) in a smaller MNC than in a larger one. It may be that size relative to the overall MNC is the more important construct.

A further aspect of the autonomy issue that the investigations in the research suggested was the extent to which autonomy is a product of the characteristics of the host country. *A priori,* a broad-based argument can be made that, since the Australian business environment is low risk, economically well-developed and relatively small (and therefore not of major importance to HQ) and the subsidiaries are likely to be staffed by personnel exhibiting considerable levels of expertise, the HQ would be prepared to accept and encourage high levels of autonomy, as long as the subsidiaries results fulfilled expectations. Comments to this effect were common in a final open-ended question in the survey

Table 11.2   HQ's rationale for managing the subsidiary

Expressed reason	n	%
Profitability/performance	37	14.4
Lack of local knowledge	37	14.4
Corporate philosophy of local autonomy	99	38.5
Specifically 'think global, act local'	24	9.3
Needs of global integration	27	10.5
Other	33	12.8
Total	257	100

that asked the respondent to give their opinion as to why HQ managed the subsidiary in the manner it did. Many (257 out of 313) gave suggestions and they exhibited a wide range of levels of comprehension and empathy. An analysis of the focus of the content of the responses is shown in Table 11.2. The data tentatively support the validity of the argument above.

Control and coordination

HQ generally sets up a range of control mechanisms to monitor and direct output and behavior in the subsidiary. The results obtained in Chapter 9 indicated the concurrent use of many such control mechanisms. These results require further confirmation if the postulates of Ferner (2000), Pucik and Katz (1986) and others are to be allowed to overtake the OBJ approach that hypothesized the use of controls related specifically to context.

The first question that arises from the results is to what extent the range of control mechanisms, despite all being in place, are actually used concurrently. Second, are there any interaction effects between the mechanisms and if there are, do they generate disruptive or synergistic outcomes? For example, does the implementation of tight performance monitoring or behavioral controls affect the likelihood of positive or negative responses to socialization and cultural conformity initiatives?

Despite the indications produced in the research, the nature of coordination processes in the MNC requires much further illumination. A convincing definition would be a good start. Theoretically, the first need is to amalgamate the conflicting conceptions on integration. These arise from the differences between Kobrin's work on integration that focused on flows of intermediate products, the cultural construct evoked by the term 'normative integration' and the more mundane practicalities of coordination in firms that appear in phenomena such as cross-functional teams, boundary spanning roles and interdepartmental committees.

Knowledge and innovation

The mapping efforts in the investigations here have barely scratched the surface of a huge domain. We are only at the beginnings of our understanding but the apparent absence of a relationship between the use of knowledge management techniques and involvement in innovations provides an intriguing starting point.

Limitations

Many researchers have also acknowledged the problems associated with the key informant approach, primarily random and systematic measurement error and common method variance (Bagozzi, Yi and Phillips, 1991). Despite this, senior executives were targeted, as they were the most capable of answering corporate-level decision making issues, as compared to a middle-level manager. Bowman and Ambrosini (1997) pointed out that use of a single respondent was common in strategy research. The comparison with the 1995 Australian Workplace Industrial Relations Survey (AWIRS 95) detailed in Chapter 12 also helped to counter these problems and allowed greater confidence to be placed in the results. Future research should take these issues into account and include additional informants. Obtaining this broader sample of respondents will help reduce the likelihood of any bias in the data that may result from the use of a specific level of respondent (Jaworski and Kohli, 1993).

These studies allow the researcher to determine the development of relationships and make powerful inferences regarding the causation of relationships being estimated. While being associated with limitations including informant membership, this does suggest that a replicated study would be beneficial to increase our confidence in both measures and models assessed throughout this research.

Another issue is the question of a perception gap between headquarters and the subsidiary. There is limited research but Birkinshaw, Holm, Thilenius and Arvidsson (2000) have offered some evidence of its existence although Asakawa (2001b) argues that they appear to be more salient in information-sharing than in autonomy-control issues.

While it is essential to recognize the limitations of the research methods and techniques employed, it is equally important to recognize the robustness of the variables employed. All methods applied, ranging from data collection techniques, managing data and data analysis are derived from widely applied and accepted psychometric theory. In addition, the statistical techniques provide strong analytical power. Hence, the results and conclusions drawn from these analyses are all reported with confidence.

12
Methodological Appendix

In order to preserve the logic and development of the research, the details of the data collection procedure, the survey instrument and some technical issues regarding factor analysis and validation of the cluster analysis have been subsumed into this appendix.

Data collection

Multinational corporations operate within and across widely varying markets, industries and cultures. The response of MNCs in their continuing quest for survival and growth has been an array of strategies, structures, systems, tools and organizational designs. This variety and the constant development and change have imposed on academic students of MNCs a pressing need to constantly refine and redesign their analytical tools. This requirement has generated a large and diverse literature on how and why MNCs are managed in the way they are. As a general criticism, however, Doz and Prahalad (1993) pointed out that scholars had been more concerned with illuminating the phenomenon than providing a theoretical explanation and subsequent testing and 'Most deemed the testing of hypotheses premature or too difficult given the complexity of MNCs and the large number of control variables' (Doz and Prahalad, 1993: 49). The excellent case study access to MNCs that enabled Ghoshal and Bartlett's pioneering research was, nevertheless, balanced by their acknowledgement that 'Collecting objective level measures for the relatively large number of variables for meaningful statistical analysis represented enormous and, for us, insurmountable practical problems' (Ghoshal and Bartlett, 1988: 382). The lack of a substantial and well-grounded theoretical base and the considerable practical difficulties of obtaining a sufficiently large amount of data on the internal operations of a large number of MNCs made this a powerful argument.

Bearing these constraints in mind, Nohria and Ghoshal's (1994) recommended that, in addressing the control problem in MNCs, future researchers should work with small samples of companies and go into greater depth. This penetrating case study approach has been extremely productive, reflecting the rationale behind the Harvard School of MNC research that shares the case study approach typical of the Harvard research on domestic companies. The Harvard MNC data project that generated Stopford and Wells' major studies (1968, 1972) was a notable exception but most authors, particularly recently, in this school have, in these case studies, described and defined mechanisms, systems and constructs to the extent that data can now begin to be assembled to enable theory development and hypothesis testing. Depending, of course, upon the precise topic of research into MNC practice, larger scale data collection and analysis have become viable.

There have been no large-scale studies of how MNCs managed their Australian subsidiaries. This research remedied that deficiency. In the process this study achieved two broad objectives. The first was central to the design and implementation of the research and the second was essentially a by-product. The major intent was to open up the 'black box' of the HQ-subsidiary relationship, derive a model of it and then test that model empirically, adding to the corpus of knowledge in the HQ-subsidiary field. The second was to provide a benchmark understanding of the management techniques of foreign MNCs operating subsidiaries in Australia. These purposes might have been achieved in several ways but the need for data from a wide range of firms imposed a survey methodology. Several other factors were relevant also. First, the resources available for the research were quite limited. Second, while most of the firms in any sample were likely to be in the major cities others would be distributed throughout Australia. Third, the nature of the research questions developed ensured that the questions could easily be constructed in a closed-ended manner and the number required would not be prohibitive to potential respondents. The use of a postal questionnaire for data collection was indicated.

Sample selection

No previous study of MNCs in Australia could be found that described the sampling frame. Initially, the aim of the sampling frame design procedure in this investigation was 100 per cent coverage. This was to be achieved by the admirable if optimistic goal of submitting a questionnaire to one subsidiary of every MNC operating in Australia. However, in order to reduce redundancy and to increase the comparability in the later analysis, MNCs were only selected from US, Canada, UK, Japan and the major European nations, largely because virtually all past research had focused on these countries. This placed only minimal constraints on the sampling frame, as there were only relatively limited numbers of African, other Asian or South American companies that have Australian subsidiaries. Even allowing for some shrinkage in the sample frame, this meant that the research drew on a relatively large proportion of the whole population and this, to a considerable extent, limited the sampling error. Thus, sampling a large proportion of the population acted as a statistical counterbalance to the expected modest response rate.

Collecting data on MNCs operating in Australia presented some difficulties since many of the compendia that were accessible to researchers in the US, Japan, UK and Europe did not present suitable data for Australia. After some searching, the most recently available volume of *Who Owns Whom* (Anon, 1994) was selected as the best convenient source for the purpose. The data for this volume was collected in 1992 and there was an obvious deficiency in the timeliness of the information. The major result of using a 1992 list in 1999 was an apparent lowered response rate caused by inaccurate information regarding the name of the firm or changes in ownership. Fortunately, this was to some extent rectified when a more recent edition (Anon, 1999) of the reference source was published while the first round of surveys was being returned. It was thus possible to ameliorate many of the time-based deficiencies of the initial sample frame.

Who Owns Whom (Anon, 1994, 1999) catalogued companies by MNC home country and then listed the names of their subsidiaries and the subsidiary's country of business. No attempt was made to classify companies as multinationals on the basis of any specific quantitative definition of a multinational. In accordance with Dunning's (1993: 3) definition that a MNC owns or controls value-adding activities in more than one country, when a company had a unit operating in Australia, it was categorized as a multinational. In the final selection only firms with three or more overseas units were included, so that all companies in the sample frame had enough foreign subsidiaries to require some consideration of HQ-subsidiary relations. In the case of MNCs having a number of Australian subsidiaries, the most senior (based on the reference source categorization) was selected on the basis that this would probably head the Australian operations and thus be in direct contact with HQ. Using this method the names of 1692 subsidiaries and their parent corporations were obtained.

The task of obtaining addresses, telephone numbers and fax numbers for these subsidiaries was accomplished using the Australian Yellow Pages site on the Internet. This was reasonably successful for the majority of firms that were based in and around Sydney and Melbourne but somewhat less so for those based elsewhere. It is possible that this metropolitan predisposition generated some sampling bias against state or rurally oriented firms in industries such as mining or agriculture. The data collected did, however, suggest that many of these types of firms had their headquarters in the major centers.

The information to be collected required a deep and wide knowledge of a firm's activities to the extent that the respondent would necessarily be a senior executive of the firm. It was concluded that the survey needed to be directed to the Chief Executive Officer. This had major implications regarding methodology since survey responses rates from CEOs have been notoriously poor relative to other employees (see, for example, Baruch, 1999). The decision then had to be made as to whether or not to personalize the mail-out. Mangione (1995) had generally been used as the guideline for data collection and his review of the personalization literature suggested that there was no consistent benefit to response rates. However, informal information from colleagues who were experienced in survey work in Australia suggested otherwise and the decision was made to personalize the survey as far as possible. This was achieved by addressing the mail and covering letter to the CEO of each firm although each letter was not signed individually. To obtain the name of the CEO every firm was telephoned. It was explained to whoever answered that we would like to send a questionnaire to the CEO and the name was requested. This process further reduced the sampling frame as some firms were no longer at that address or telephone number or requested not to be included. Where it was impossible to obtain a response to the telephone call, for whatever reason, the survey was simply addressed to the CEO at the address obtained earlier.

The parent name, company name, chief executive name (where known), address, telephone number and fax number were set up on a spreadsheet to facilitate letter writing and envelope addressing. Finally, useable information was procured from 917 companies. In the midst of the mailing and follow-up procedures, a more recent edition of the reference source was obtained. Time, resource and financial constraints precluded a detailed replication of the previous information gathering process but, following approximately the same procedure, it was possible to relatively quickly acquire details of an additional 104 suitable subsidiaries. From the initial sample of 917 companies 746 CEO names had been obtained. The additional 104 companies were simply addressed to the CEO. Thus, in total, the sampling frame contained 1021 firms.

Questionnaire design

The survey instrument is presented at the end of this chapter. Simplicity, brevity and clarity were the guiding principles of the design of the questionnaire. The research questions had been clarified in advance from theory and the empirical literature and the questions were designed to elicit the necessary information to generate the data variables. All the questions were closed-ended except for six that requested numerical information, two that required statements of parent company nationality and the firm's primary products and a single, final, open-ended exploratory question.

The closed-ended questions were either of the yes-no type or required circling an option based upon the semantic differential five-point Likert-type format. There was a mixture of unipolar and bipolar scales and care was taken, as far as possible, to equalize the 'psychological distance' (Mangione, 1995: 12) between points on scales. The guidelines on question construction concerning brevity, avoidance of unclear pronoun referents, jargon, unidimensionality, category exhaustiveness, 'loading' and so on were carefully adhered to. The survey was also divided into 5 sections with separate short titles to improve the 'flow' and 'look'. A clean balanced professional looking document was aimed for by choice of typeface and overall format.

The questions covered five pages and an eight-page booklet was designed around the questions. Some professional graphic design with appropriate two-color printing was solicited to enhance the visual presentation of the booklet. Mangione (1995) recommended prestigious sponsorship to enhance response rates. While it is debatable whether they constituted prestigious sponsorship in the sense meant by Mangione, the University of Melbourne and Australian Centre for International Business crests were prominently displayed on the front cover to indicate the provenance of the survey. The survey title was also prominent. The inside front cover gave simple completion instructions, contact information, an assurance of confidentiality, return instructions and a prominent 'Thank You'. The outside back cover contained further thanks, return instructions and a text box offering a summary Business Report derived from the data collected. The literature on inducements generally supports the efficacy of their use with the proviso that the inducement should be perceived as valuable by the respondent. It was hoped that the inducement of summary information from the research would assist response rates.

Several rounds of pre-testing of the questionnaire took place via colleagues and questions were reworded and adapted until they appeared satisfactory. Ideally, the final survey booklet should have been piloted with a small number of actual respondents. However, had changes been required that would have entailed fully reprinting the survey, an option not available given the resource-base of the project. Many of the questions, or minor variations on them, had been used previously in the literature and given the pre-testing efforts, the risks involved in not piloting were considered relatively small.

The overall project was presented to and approved by the University of Melbourne Ethics Committee.

Mail-out

The spreadsheet was used to generate name and address labels of the sample firms. The covering letter was also produced containing this information. The covering letter was prepared in accordance with the recommended style. The letter was printed on University of Melbourne headed paper, was one page in length, explained the purpose, importance and likely distribution of the research, gave assurances of data aggregation and confidentiality, explained the value of Business Report inducement to the addressee and gave queries and information contact details, via telephone and email. A prepaid reply envelope addressed to the project coordinator was placed inside the questionnaire. The covering letter, questionnaire and reply envelope were collated and placed into the external envelope that was sealed and then stamped with the Department of Management return address. All of the first 917 envelopes were posted simultaneously.

The pattern of returns unfolded as expected. There was nothing for several days, a small number of returns around days 5 to 7 then the bulk of returns between days 7 and 10. The rate of responses declined rapidly thereafter although it was several months before the last return was received. Completed returns, letters declining cooperation and 'return to senders' (RTS) were each recorded separately.

Mangione's (1995) survey of the literature on follow-up mail-outs concluded that the evidence is universally in favor of their use. He claimed that the single most important technique for improving response rates was to send out reminders. The literature was unanimous on this point. Whatever the initial response rate, the reminder can be expected to generate approximately half that amount in the second wave. After 3 weeks, the follow-up procedure was instituted. An attempt was made to establish correct addresses for the RTS cases. When unsuccessful these were included with the no response cases. A further mailing was sent out to all firms that had not returned a completed survey. The second mailing contained a further questionnaire, reply-paid envelope and a new follow-up letter. The letter, as well as reassuring aggregation and confidentiality, reported an encouraging response to the first round to emphasize the potential value of the business report.

Data on the additional 104 companies were obtained during the first round mail-out and reminder period and these additional cases were mailed and followed-up in a similar manner to the first round.

Response rate and patterns

A total of 1021 questionnaires were sent out. To assess the likely proportion of the MNC population that this total constituted, it was necessary to understand what was meant by the term MNC in the context of this research. The sample firms were only chosen if the parent had three or more subsidiaries worldwide and, at the time of mail-out, it was not possible to be very accurate in estimating the number of MNCs of this type operating in Australia. On the basis of the data available, the total number of MNCs that might fall into this sampling frame was probably around 3000 to 4000. (This issue is considered in more detail in the section on the representativeness of the study and later data enabled a more accurate assessment to be made.) This suggested that the sample frame had captured a considerable proportion of the possible target companies. It was not possible to calculate the sampling error since there was no method of calculating the population variance on any criteria. However, not drawing from an infinite population and drawing on perhaps a third of the possible population undeniably had beneficial effects upon the sampling error.

From the 1021 potential responses, 11 notifications of unwillingness to be involved were received. These were treated as non-responders. There were 111 returned as not known or RTS. Hence, it was assumed that 910 firms received a questionnaire at least once. 313 useable completed surveys were returned. This was an effective response rate of 34.2 per cent. There has been considerable debate as to what might be considered a good response rate in surveys of this type. Baruch (1999) reviewed the literature and found no agreed norm of acceptability. Many variables intervene and Denison and Mishra (1995), for example, were able to justify a 21 per cent response rate for a CEO level survey and have it published in a leading journal. There was general acceptance that rates for high-level company representatives were lower than for populations of individuals. Baruch's (1999) study examined response rates in studies published in five leading management journals. Clearly, this study suffered considerable sampling bias since it was extremely unlikely that low response rate studies would have been published in leading journals. Despite this caveat, some interesting results were presented. First, response rates appeared to have declined over time. For employees, they had fallen from 64 per cent in 1975 to 48 per cent in 1995. An alternative explanation is that the journals were accepting lower rates. As these leading journals publish only the best studies, it seems reasonable to accept the declining rates hypothesis. Second, for top management, the overall rate was around 36 per cent with a standard deviation of 13 per cent. Since this figure was from an extended time period, the current rate is likely to be somewhat lower, if the declining rates hypothesis is accepted. Response rates for studies in the *Journal of International Business Studies,* which mostly surveyed top managers, were only 32.1 per cent. Baruch (1999) concluded that, if it was accepted that the norm should be within 1 standard deviation of the mean, then a norm of 36 per cent +/– 13 per cent was reasonable for reputable academic studies. There were other influences including country of study (the norms were based largely upon US data) and the design of the study but in general the response rate of 34.2 per cent for this study appears very acceptable.

The response rate for the personalized mailings was 245 acceptable responses from 645 mailings or 35.8 per cent. For those surveys addressed to the CEO, Head Office or Managing Director, 69 were received out of 225 effective mailings. This response rate was 30.7 per cent. The difference, while in the expected direction, was not significant using a one-tailed independent sample t-test.

The offer of a copy of a summary business report based upon the survey findings had a take-up rate of 71 per cent. Whether the report acted as an inducement or was simply requested after completing the questionnaire cannot be ascertained but the rate can be presumed to indicate an interest in the results of the study.

The returns to the second mail-out conformed more or less to the 50 per cent improvement pattern (Mangione, 1995) mentioned earlier but detailed analysis was difficult since responses from the first mail-out were still coming in, albeit quite slowly, when responses from the second began. In general, the responses continued to come in for a considerable period after the mail-outs and the tail of the response pattern was much longer than the accepted model.

Data entry and coding

When it appeared that no more returns were expected, the data were entered into an SPSS 10.0 data editor spreadsheet for analysis. Each company entry had an identification number based upon the original sampling frame. The majority of the data were very simple. Yes-No questions were coded as 1 and 0. Scale questions were coded from 1 to the limit of the scale, always from small values to large regardless of the characteristics of the variable being measured by the scale. Numerical responses on size, age and so on were entered as the numerical value. The parent nationality variable was answered by the name of a country and these were coded 1, 2, 3, and so on with a number for each different country. Two variables – company's primary product or service and company's primary role in the MNC – required further consideration. The company's primary product was categorized on the basis of the four digit Australian Standard Industrial Classification. The company's primary role in the MNC was determined on the basis of a series of questions asking about the basic tasks of the subsidiary. This topic is examined in detail in Chapter 6. Frequencies were then run for all the variables and these were inspected to find and correct any obvious data entry errors.

Details of the formal name for every variable, the questions used in the survey to elicit the data or the variable's method of derivation and the descriptive data for each are presented as the variable appears in the series of empirical investigations that are presented in Chapters 6 through 10.

Representativeness

A major question in any survey is the reliability of using the sample as a representative of the overall population. This can clearly affect the validity of any interpretations from the data obtained. There have been no large-scale MNC focused investigations of Australian firms. However, the Australian Workplace Industrial Relations Survey 1995 (AWIRS 95) provides some useful comparative data. This survey is conducted periodically by the Australian Government Department of Industrial Relations. It aims to provide a statistically reliable database on workplaces in Australia. The AWIRS 95 survey was carried out between September 1995 and January 1996. It sampled 2001 workplaces with 20 or more employees (finally 19 or more employees) covering all major industrial divisions. The 2001 workplaces represented 5.4 per cent of an estimated population of 37,200. A full description of the data is available in Moorhead, Steele, Alexander, Stephen and Duffin (1997).

Of the 2001 firms in the AWIRS 95 survey, 192 (9.6 %) were wholly foreign owned. If this proportion is an accurate representation of the overall sample (AWIRS is based upon an industrially stratified random sample) then there are 3571 wholly foreign owned subsidiaries in Australia with 19 or more employees. If all the 313 firms in this survey with > 98 per cent foreign ownership had 19 or more employees this would represent 8.5 per cent of the total population. However, 16.5 per cent of firms in this survey were less than 19 employees so, assuming this was a representative proportion, the present sample represented a very satisfactory 7.3 per cent of the total population of Australian subsidiaries of MNCs.

The remaining representativeness issues were size, MNC home country and industry. The median size of workplace in the AWIRS 95 survey was 100 employees compared to a median firm size of 84 employees in this study. Given the inclusion of 16.5 per cent of smaller firms in this study, the two samples were closely comparable. With regard to percentage of MNCs from differing home countries, a comparison is presented in Table 12.1. The overrepresentation of European vs UK MNCs in this study led to a $\chi^2 < .05$.

Both studies used the Australian Standard Industrial Classification to categorize industry. In terms of industry comparability, the imbalance regarding rural industries such as agriculture and mining that had been suspected earlier was not evident. Both surveys had representation in all industry groups but there were some differences. The present study had more firms in wholesale and retail and in finance, property, insurance and business services while AWIRS 95 had proportionately more in construction and transport and transport services. The differences,

Table 12.1   Comparison of MNC home countries between AWIRS 95 and the present study

Studies	US	UK	Japan	European	Other
AWIRS 95	42.1	25.8	6.8	–	25.3
This study	40.6	17.0	5.4	30.3	6.7

Notes: All figures in percentages. The 'Other' category in AWIRS 95 includes the European category in this study.

however, were not sufficient to cause concern over the representativeness of the present study. Thus, the analysis above suggests that the balance of firm characteristics obtained in the final sample of the present study demonstrated a satisfactory level of representativeness.

The data collection procedure produced a very satisfactory database. A sample large enough to sanction the use of most common statistical techniques was obtained. In addition, on the basis of comparison with a large-scale government conducted survey, AWIRS 95, and with some minor deviations, the sample proved to be a good representation of MNC subsidiaries in Australia. Further, the factor analysis procedure described in detail later in this appendix demonstrated that multi-collinearity issues were not likely to seriously affect the results of the data analysis.

Factor analysis of the data collected

In several of the empirical investigations, it became necessary to derive aggregated variables based upon the responses to a series of related questions. Five were required in all. First, an overall measure of subsidiary autonomy had to be derived from a series of ten individual questions regarding the relative influence of HQ and the subsidiary on decision-making. Second, an overall measure of degree of formalization in the behavioral control process was required from a series of seven questions asking whether the subsidiary used any of several types of procedural manuals. Third, the commitment of the MNC to non-vocational training came from four questions asking about opportunities for training at various venues. Fourth, a measure of the subsidiary's involvement in knowledge management processes had to be derived from questions requesting the frequency of use of three knowledge management oriented techniques. Finally, the subsidiary's embeddedness in the innovation network of the MNC had to be assessed on the basis of five questions.

This required the use of factor analysis – a technique that identifies underlying variables, or factors, that explain the pattern of correlations within a set of observed variables. It is often used in data reduction to identify a small number of factors that explain most of the variance observed in a much larger number of manifest variables. In addition, it can also be used to generate hypotheses regarding causal mechanisms or to screen variables for subsequent analysis (for example, to identify collinearity prior to performing a linear regression analysis or similar techniques).

The particular statistical procedure employed for these processes was principal components factor analysis. This is a technique that transforms an original set of variables into a substantially smaller set of uncorrelated variables that still retain most of the information in the original set (Dunteman, 1994). It works by describing 'the variation of the n individuals in p-dimensional space in terms of a set of uncorrelated variables which are linear combinations of the original variable' (Everitt and Dunn, 1983: 39).

The variables to be analyzed should be quantitative at the interval or ratio level. Categorical data (such as religion or country of origin) are not suitable for factor analysis. Generally, data for which Pearsonian product-moment correlation coefficients can sensibly be calculated should be suitable for factor analysis.

The statistical assumptions are that the data has a bivariate normal distribution for each pair of variables, and that all observations are independent. The factor analysis model specifies that variables are determined by common factors (the factors estimated by the model) and unique factors (which do not overlap between observed variables). The computed estimates are based on the assumption that all unique factors are uncorrelated with each other and with the common factors. All of these assumptions are reasonable for the present data.

Several methods are available to extract the basic factors – principal components, unweighted least squares, generalized least squares, maximum likelihood, principal axis factoring, alpha factoring, and image factoring. The first listed, principal components analysis, is the most common in practice. The principal components method is derived from the overall correlation matrix of all the variables under consideration. The matrix is decomposed hierarchically. The principal factors are the ones that sequentially give the best least-squares fit to the entire correlation matrix. Each succeeding factor accounts for the maximum amount of the correlation matrix obtainable (Gorsuch, 1983).

The specific method used was principal components analysis with direct oblimin rotation. Principal components factor analysis was chosen as the most appropriate technique. First, because it was assumed that the error variance represented a relatively small proportion of the total variance and, second, because the purpose of the procedure was to determine the minimum number of factors needed to account for as much of the variance as possible in the original variables.

If the variables are not appropriately sampled, the initial solution axes may not produce the best solution. They need to be rotated.

Factor rotation is the process of rotating the principal factor axes until the best solution is obtained (Kim and Mueller, 1994). Again several methods are available – varimax, direct oblimin, quartimax, equamax, or promax. It was not possible to assume that the factors were uncorrelated therefore no orthogonal rotation method was applicable. Since an oblique rotation method was required, direct oblimin was chosen because it produces the simplest pattern matrix (Kim and Mueller, 1994).

In this study factor analysis was used to collapse those collinear variables that appeared to be indicators of the same underlying concept into a single composite variable (Hutcheson and Sofroniou, 1999). For example, the four variables concerning the availability of non-vocational training courses for suitable employees at various venues were collapsed into a single aggregated variable (training) that reflected the overall use of training as a control and socialization tool.

The analysis was set for a maximum of 25 iterations for convergence of the solution and factors were extracted with an Eigenvalue of >1. In all, ten decision-making variables, seven formalization variables, four training variables, three knowledge management variables and five R&D and innovation variables were subject to the analysis. The number of variables in the analysis combined with a degree of multi-collinearity between some variables presented several problems. After some experimentation, it was apparent that the decision-making variable based upon 'Borrowings from a local bank' persistently loaded independently. It was concluded that a level of confusion existed in the minds of the respondents over the meaning of this question. This may have arisen since the amount of the loan was not stipulated and it is clearly possible that HQ influence upon a large loan would be much greater than on a small one. The variable was eventually eliminated from the analysis. Thus the composite decision-making autonomy variable was actually derived from the responses to nine questions. The variable based upon the question asking the frequency of 'Your company adopting innovations from elsewhere in the MNC' similarly persistently loaded independently. There does not appear to be much potential for misinterpretation of meaning and this variable was important in that it captured the subsidiary's links with and responsiveness to other units. Issues such as the 'Not invented here syndrome' (Katz and Allen, 1982; Ghoshal and Bartlett, 1988) and the subsidiary's absorptive capacity are incorporated in this construct so it was retained as a separate variable 'innovations from elsewhere'. The variable from the question 'Do you have manuals on any other topics' also presented persistent erratic loading. It was evident in the responses to this question that a considerable number and range of other types of manuals were being described. This variable clearly did not capture a single phenomenon and the loading problems were unsurprising. This variable was also dropped from the analysis resulting in the overall degree of formalization of behavioral controls variable being calculated using the remaining six variables.

Finally, the decision-making variable relating to influence over the setting of ROI criteria loaded with the other decision-making variables and with the formalization variable derived from 'Do you have manuals on accounting'. There was a clear logic in these two loadings and no simple resolution was possible. The problem was overcome by splitting of the sets of variables. Once the ROI setting variable was removed from the analysis, the 'Do you have manuals on accounting' variable loaded with other variables concerned with manuals. The result of this procedure, however, was that a significant degree of collinearity ($r = -0.181$, $p < .01$) was merely hidden by the data and not resolved. This must be considered in any interpretation involving these variables.

The results of the factor analysis are shown in Table 12.2. In an orthogonal solution the factor loading is the correlation coefficient between the factor and the variable. This analysis was not orthogonal and sample size is an intervening issue but, nevertheless, factor loadings of > 0.4 are considered significant and > 0.5 and above are very significant (Hair et al., 2002).

The decision-making variables loaded into Factors 1 and 2. One related to decision-making regarding day-to-day operational issues and the other to decision-making regarding the setting of objectives. Ghoshal and Bartlett (1988) discuss the possible need for two autonomy variables relating to strategic vs operational subsidiary autonomy but conclude that a single measure is adequate. For the purposes of the ANCOVA analyses in Chapter 7 and the regressions in Chapter 8, the two factors were combined into a single aggregated variable 'subsidiary autonomy'. This was an acceptable aggregation given that the final aggregated variable had a very robust reliability of $\alpha = 0.81$. Factor 3 loaded the three variables relating to knowledge management and was labeled 'knowledge management'. The four training variables loaded on Factor 4 (training). Factor 5 loaded the first six variables concerned with the use of manuals. This was the 'formalization' variable. The R&D variable and the first three innovation variables loaded as Factor 6, the 'innovations' variable. The remaining single innovation variable was 'innovations from elsewhere'. The descriptive statistics for all the variables derived from the factor analysis above are shown in Table 12.3.

Table 12.2 Rotated factor matrix for aggregated variables used in study

Variable	Factor loadings					
	F 1	F 2	F 3	F 4	F 5	F 6
Subsidiary/HQ influence on:						
Extension of credit	0.774					
Product introduction to local market	0.472					
Training programs	0.781					
Choice of advertising agency	0.710					
Setting production schedule	0.408					
Hiring operational personnel	0.793					
Quality control norms	0.445					
Setting sales targets		0.579				
ROI criteria		0.901				
Use of groupware technology			0.756			
Use of organizational memory systems			0.736			
Use of auditing of intellectual capital			0.744			
Training in house				0.767		
Training at HQ				0.772		
Training elsewhere in corporation				0.791		
Training at external venues				0.706		
Manuals on design/manufacture					0.526	
Manuals on accounting					0.465	
Manuals on marketing					0.677	
Manuals on company philosophy					0.561	
Manuals on supplier relations					0.779	
Manuals on customer relations					0.776	
R&D on behalf of rest of MNC						0.594
Innovations created by your company						0.833
Innovations adopted by your company						0.883
Innovations adopted by rest of MNC						0.774

Table 12.3 Descriptive statistics for variables derived from factor analysis

Variable	n	Range	Mean	s.d.	α
Subsidiary autonomy	310	5–45	34.56	6.73	0.81
Knowledge management	312	3–15	7.54	2.82	0.66
Training	312	0–4	2.53	1.40	0.76
Formalization	313	0–6	2.87	1.69	0.69
Innovation	313	4–20	9.92	3.25	0.78
Innovations from elsewhere	310	1–5	3.18	0.99	n/a

The validation procedure for the cluster analysis

Since cluster analysis is a data classification technique that requires careful theoretical and empirical validation, the validation of the results is discussed below.

External validation

External validation requires that the clusters are useful in some larger sense. The ultimate test of a set of clusters is its usefulness (Everitt, 1980: 5 and 96). The cluster analysis should provide a demonstration that clusters are related to variables other than those used to generate the solution. The clusters in this case have already been theoretically argued to relate to MNC strategy variables and the several empirical investigations demonstrated their relationships to variables concerned with autonomy, control, knowledge management and innovation in the MNC.

Internal validation

Following on from the analyses of the clusters obtained in Chapter 6, the results of the one-way analysis of variance of the differences between groups are shown in Table 12.4.

All between group differences are significant ($p < .001$). It should be noted, however, that while clear group differences are present, the F tests should be used only for descriptive purposes because the clusters have been chosen to maximize the differences among cases in different clusters. The observed significance levels are not corrected for this and thus, while the clusters appear distinctive, the significance levels cannot be interpreted as a rejection of the null hypothesis that the cluster means are equal. To offer greater support than that provided by simple inspection, there is a requirement to demonstrate that 5 clusters is the best available solution. To do that it is necessary to examine the differences between the means for each variable in each cluster for the 4, 5 and 6 clusters' solutions.

To assess distinctiveness of the clusters, one-way analysis of variance was performed using Duncan's Multiple Range test. This test makes pair-wise comparisons using a stepwise order of comparisons and sets a protection level for the error rate for the collection of tests, rather than an error rate for individual tests. This is considered the least conservat-

Table 12.4   One way analysis of variance between groups

	Cluster Mean square	df	Error Mean square	df	F	Significance
S1	153.4	4	0.8	308	192.3	<.001
S2	108.7	4	1.1	308	95.4	<.001
S3	66.0	4	1.1	308	58.2	<.001
S4	41.3	4	1.2	308	35.0	<.001
S5	85.6	4	1.2	308	72.7	<.001

ive ANOVA test when the basic unit of analysis is the pair-wise comparison between variables (Winer, 1971; Thomas, 1974). Using this test, consistent patterns of non-significance between means suggest that the clusters are not distinctive. Since the purpose of the study was to explore differences, and since one wrong inference would not make other inferences in the study meaningless, Duncan's Multiple Range test was appropriate.

The Duncan Multiple Range tests for the 4 clusters solution indicated only 4 of the possible 30 pair-wise comparisons were not significantly different (using $p < .05$ criterion) and there was no consistent pattern among these 4 cases. This suggested that 4 clusters was a satisfactory solution but not necessarily the best available.

For the 6 clusters solution the situation was very different. Thirteen of the possible 75 pair-wise comparisons were not significant ($p < .05$) but, more importantly, for all five of the variables, the sixth cluster was not significantly different in at least one case. This persistent non-significance of the sixth cluster indicated that the 6 clusters solution was probably unsatisfactory.

For the 5 clusters solution, of the possible 50 comparisons between cluster means for each variable only 8 did not demonstrate significant difference ($p < .05$). Table 12.5 lists both the 42 significant and the 8 insignificant contrasts. These eight insignificant comparisons were reasonably spread throughout the variables and clusters and display no consistent pattern that might nullify the overall conclusion of distinctiveness. The 5 clusters solution was satisfactory while the 6 clusters solution was not.

Table 12.5   Contrasts between cluster means ($p < .05$)

	Significant
S1	1,2; 1,3; 1,4; 1,5; 2,4; 2,5; 3,4; 3,5; 4,5
S2	1,3; 1,4; 1,5; 2,3; 2,4; 2,5; 3,4; 4,5
S3	1,2; 1,3; 1,4; 2,3; 2,4; 2,5; 3,5; 4,5
S4	1,3; 1,4; 1,5; 2,4; 2,5; 3,4; 3,5; 4,5
S5	1,2; 1,4; 1,5; 2,3; 2,4; 2,5; 3,4; 3,5; 4,5
	Insignificant
S1	2,3
S2	1,2; 3,5
S3	1,5; 3,4
S4	1,2; 2,3
S5	1,3

Survey instrument

Section A. Some basic data about your company

1. **What is the nationality of your Parent Corporation?**
    ....

2. **What is the Parent Corporation's ownership stake in your company?** ....%

3. **How many years has your company operated in Australia?**
    ....years

4. **In your company, how many positions are filled by expatriate employees?** ....

5. **Have you ever worked at Head Office?**
    (Please circle answer)
                   No   Yes   No of years ....

6. **Did you at any stage have a mentor at Head Office?**
    (Please circle answer)
                   Yes   No

7. **What are your company's primary product(s)/service(s)?**
    (Please list a maximum of three in order of percentage contribution to sales)
    1. ....%
    2. ....%
    3. ....%

8. **What is your company's PRIMARY role in the overall corporation?**

    Please consider that question and then rank the following statements as to how well they describe that role. Please select from a scale where:

    1 = not accurate/important   through
    5 = very accurate/important

    sales/distribution of goods produced elsewhere   1 2 3 4 5
    in the group

    generation and marketing of similar products   1 2 3 4 5
    to Head Office

adapting product or its delivery for the local market	1	2	3	4	5
performing a single value-adding activity in the production process of the corporation's leading product	1	2	3	4	5
product and/or process innovation	1	2	3	4	5
generation of a range of products/services largely from our own resources	1	2	3	4	5
we have a particular connection with one major company within the corporate network, despite being linked with and contributing to many other parts	1	2	3	4	5

9. **Please circle the level of technology your company utilises in its primary operations.**

   1 = very basic   2 = quite basic   3 = intermediate
                4 = advanced   5 = leading edge

10. **We need to categorise companies on the basis of size, can you please give approximate figures for the following?**

   Annual Sales (Aus$) ....

   Number of employees ....

Section B. Communications

---

1. **Please rank, in terms of frequency, the use of the following means of communication between Head Office and staff in your company.**

	Never	Rare	Sometimes	Often	Very frequent
Video or TV broadcasts	1	2	3	4	5
Electronic mail	1	2	3	4	5
Intranet	1	2	3	4	5
Newsletters	1	2	3	4	5
Magazines	1	2	3	4	5
Reports	1	2	3	4	5

2.   **Please rank the frequency of your company's use of the following techniques.**

	Never	Rare	Sometimes	Often	Very frequent
Electronic data interchange (linking the computer systems of buyers and sellers)	1	2	3	4	5
Electronic commerce (buying or selling electronically)	1	2	3	4	5
Groupware technology (facilitating global teams via electronic means e.g. screen-sharing, video-conferencing, etc)	1	2	3	4	5
Organisational memory systems (electronic storage of knowledge or information)	1	2	3	4	5
Auditing of intellectual capital (putting a value on the company's knowledge capital)	1	2	3	4	5

3.   **Please circle the frequency of your contacts with managers at Head Office or other group companies via mail, telephone, fax, electronic mail or any other means.**

	Several times daily	Daily	Every other day	Weekly	Monthly or less
Contact with Head Office	1	2	3	4	5
Contact with other group companies	1	2	3	4	5

4.   **Please circle which of the statements is most accurate.**

(a)   Most of our communications are with Head Office and we have relatively little contact with other group companies.

(b) Most of our communications are with Head Office or with one or two other group companies who are closely linked to us in the generation of the company's products/services.

(c) We communicate, on an ongoing basis, with many companies within our corporate network.

5. **Typically, in your company, is there a networked PC with standardised support software on every desk or in every briefcase?**
(Please circle answer)   Yes   No

6. **Please circle to what extent your company is <u>actively involved</u> with the following organisations (e.g. as sources of information, knowledge, new recruits or as platforms for campaigns, lobbying, publicity, etc).**

	<u>Never</u>	<u>Rare</u>	<u>Sometimes</u>	<u>Often</u>	Very <u>frequent</u>
Local industry associations	1	2	3	4	5
Local Chamber of Commerce	1	2	3	4	5
Local schools	1	2	3	4	5
Local universities/ colleges	1	2	3	4	5
Local charitable organizations	1	2	3	4	5
Local government agencies	1	2	3	4	5
State government agencies	1	2	3	4	5
Federal government agencies	1	2	3	4	5

7. **Please circle the frequency of meetings between a member of your management team and the following:**

	<u>Never</u>	Once/twice <u>per year</u>	<u>Quarterly</u>	<u>Monthly</u>	Weekly <u>or more</u>
Major suppliers	1	2	3	4	5
Major customers	1	2	3	4	5
Major competitors	1	2	3	4	5

Section C. Head Office influence on decision-making in your company

---

1. **Typically, how much influence would Head Office have on the sample decisions given below?**

   After each decision please circle a number on a scale of 1 to 5 where:

   1 = subsidiary decision
   2 = subsidiary decides – Head Office influences
   3 = equal influence on decision
   4 = Head Office decides – subsidiary influences
   5 = Head Office decision

Borrowings from a local bank	1	2	3	4	5
Extension of credit to a major customer	1	2	3	4	5
Product introduction to your local market	1	2	3	4	5
Training programmes in your company	1	2	3	4	5
Choice of advertising agency	1	2	3	4	5
Setting aggregate production schedule	1	2	3	4	5
Hiring of operational personnel	1	2	3	4	5
Setting sales targets	1	2	3	4	5
Return on investment criteria	1	2	3	4	5
Quality control norms	1	2	3	4	5

2. **Do you have manuals from Head Office for procedures in the following areas?**

Technical design/manufacture	Yes	No
Accounting	Yes	No
Marketing	Yes	No
Company philosophy	Yes	No
Supplier relations	Yes	No
Customer relations	Yes	No
Any others	Yes	No

   (Please specify)

   ....

Section D. Innovation and competition

---

1. **Please circle how much R&D your company performs on behalf of the rest of the corporation.**

   1 = none   2 = a little   3 = some   4 = a lot   5 = virtually all

2.   **Please rank the frequency of the following events over the last two years.**

	Never	Rare	Sometimes	Often	Very frequent
Creation of significant product or process innovations within your company	1	2	3	4	5
Adoption of these innovations by your Company	1	2	3	4	5
Adoption of these innovations by other parts of the corporation	1	2	3	4	5
Your company adopting innovations from elsewhere in the corporation	1	2	3	4	5

3.   **Please circle the rate of generation of product and process innovations that is characteristic of the local market for your most important products.**

1 = very slow   2 = quite slow   3 = moderate
4 = quite rapid   5 = very rapid

4.   **Please circle the intensity of competition that your company faces locally.**

1 = none   2 = a little   3 = moderate   4 = considerable
5 = very intense

Section E. Working for your company
---

1.   **Please circle the importance of the formal Induction Course in introducing new management level employees to your company.**

1 = unimportant   2 = a little important
3 = somewhat important   4 = quite important
5 = very important

2.   **Are suitable employees encouraged and enabled to attend further <u>non-vocational</u> courses?**

In house	Yes	No
At Head Office	Yes	No
At other venues in the Corporation	Yes	No
At external venues	Yes	No

3.   **Does the corporate culture of your firm make you feel that you work for:**

   (a)   a Global Corporation
   (b)   an Australian Company
   (c)   a Corporation from the Parent's home country

4.   **In your opinion, why does Headquarters manage its relationship with your subsidiary in the way it does?**

....
....
....
....
....
....
....

References

Ackerman, M. S. 1994. Augmenting the organizational memory: A field study of Answer Garden. Paper presented at the Proceedings of CSCW'94.

Ackerman, M. S. and Halverson, C. A. 2000. Reexamining organizational memory. *Communications of the ACM*, 41(1): 59–64.

Albaum, G. and Murphy, B. D. 1989. Extreme response on a Likert scale. *Psychological Reports*, 63(2): 501–2.

Albaum, G. 1997. The Likert scale revisited: An alternative version. *Journal of the Market Research Society*, 39(2): 331–48.

Aldenderfer, M. S. and Blashfield, R. K. 1984. *Cluster analysis*. Beverly Hills, Calif.: Sage.

Almeida, P. and Phene, A. 2004. Subsidiaries and knowledge creation: The influence of the MNC and host country on innovation. *Strategic Management Journal*, 25(8–9): 847–64.

Amit, R. and Schoemaker, R. J. H 1993. Strategic assets and organizational rent. *Strategic Management Journal*, 14, 33–46.

Anand, V., Manz, C. C. and Glick, W. H. 1998. An organizational memory approach to information management. *Academy of Management Review*, 23(4): 796–809.

Andersson, U., Forsgren, M. and Holm, U. 2002. The strategic impact of external networks: Subsidiary performance and competence development in the multinational corporation. *Strategic Management Journal*, 23(11): 979–96.

Anon. 1989. *A survey of Japanese business activity in Australia* (3rd ed.). Sydney: Australia-Japan Economic Institute.

Anon. 1992. *A directory of Japanese business activity in Australia 1992*. Sydney: Australia-Japan Economic Institute.

Anon. 1994. *Who owns whom* (North American, Australasia and the Far East, Continental Europe and United Kingdom and Republic of Ireland editions ed.). London: Who Owns Whom Ltd.

Anon. 1999. *Who owns whom* (Australia and the Far East, North America, United Kingdom and Republic of Ireland and Continental Europe editions ed.). High Wycombe, Bucks, UK: Dun and Bradstreet.

Anon. 2001. Why do businesses choose to invest in Australia. Canberra: Austrade.

Aoki, M., Gustafsson, B. and Williamson, O. E. 1990. *The firm as a nexus of treaties*. London: Sage.

Argyris, C. and Schon, D. 1978. *Organizational learning*. Reading, MA: Addison-Wesley.

Argyris, C. and Schon, D. A. 1996. *Organizational learning II: Theory, method, and practice*. Reading, MA: Addison-Wesley.

Armstrong, R. L. 1988. The mid-point on a five-point Likert-type scale. *Perceptual and Motor Skills*, 64(2): 359–62.

Arrow, K. 1974. *The limits of organization*. New York: Norton.

Arthur, J. B. 1994. Effects of human resource systems in manufacturing performance and turnover. *Academy of Management Journal*, 37(3): 670–87.

Asakawa, K. 2001a. Evolving headquarters-subsidiary dynamics in international R&D: The case of Japanese multinationals. *R&D Management*, 31(1): 1–14.

Asakawa, K. 2001b. Organizational tension in international R&D management: The case of Japanese firms. *Research Policy*, 30(5): 735–57.

Aylmer, R. J. 1970. Who makes marketing decisions in the multinational firm. *Journal of Marketing*, (October): 25–39.

Bacharach, S. B. 1989. Organizational theories: Some criteria for evaluation. *Academy of Management Review*, 14(4): 496–515.

Bagozzi, R. P; Yi, Y. and Phillips, L. W. 1991. Assessing construct validity in organizational research. *Administrative Science Quarterly*, 36, 421–58.

Baliga, B. R. and Jaeger, A. M. 1984. Multinational corporations: control systems and delegation issues. *Journal of International Business Studies*, 15(Fall): 25–40.

Bambrick, S. (ed.) 1974. *The multinational corporation and international investment in Australia*. Sydney, NSW: Sydney University Extension Board.

Barney, J. B. 1986. Strategic factor markets: expectations, luck and business strategy. *Management Science*, 32 (10): 1231–41.

Barney, J. B. 1990. The debate between traditional management theory and organizational economics: Substantial differences or intergroup conflict. *Academy of Management Review*, 15(3): 382–93.

Barney, J. B. 1991. Firm resources and sustained competitive advantage. *Journal of Management*, 17: 99–120.

Barney, J. B. 1996. The resource-based theory of the firm. *Organization Science*, 7(5): 469.

Barney, J. B. 1997. *Gaining and sustaining competitive advantage*. Reading Mass.: Addison-Wesley.

Barney, J. B. 2001. Resource-based theories of competitive advantage: A ten-year retrospective on the resource-based view. *Journal of Management*, 27(6): 643–50.

Bartlett, C. A. 1981. Multinational structural change: Evolution versus reorganization. In L. Otterbeck (ed.), *The management of headquarters-subsidiary relationships in multinational corporations*: 121–46. Aldershot: Gower.

Bartlett, C. A. 1983. MNCs: Get off the reorganization merry-go-round. *Harvard Business Review*, 61(March–April): 138–46.

Bartlett, C. A. and Ghoshal, S. 1986. Tap your subsidiaries global reach. *Harvard Business Review*, 64(November–December): 87–94.

Bartlett, C. A. and Ghoshal, S. 1987. Managing across borders: New organizational responses. *Sloan Management Review*, 29(1) (Fall): 43–53.

Bartlett, C. A. and Ghoshal, S. 1989. *Managing across borders: The transnational solution*. Boston, Mass.: Harvard Business School Press.

Baruch, Y. 1999. Response rates in academic studies – a comparative analysis. *Human Relations*, 52(4): 421–38.

Bell, D. 1973. *The coming of post-industrial society*. New York: Basic Books.

Benito, G. R. G., Grogaard, B. and Narula, R. 2003. Environmental influences on MNE subsidiary roles: economic integration and the Nordic countries. *Journal of International Business Studies*, 34(5): 443–56

Bettis, R. A. 1981. Performance differences in related and unrelated diversified firms. *Strategic Management Journal*, 2: 379–83.

Birkinshaw, J. M. 1994. Approaching heterarchy: A review of the literature on multinational strategy and structure. *Advances in International Comparative Management*, 9: 111–144.

Birkinshaw, J., Holm, U., Thilenius, P. and Arvidsson, N. 2000. Consequences of perception gaps in the headquarters-subsidiary relationship. *International Business Review*, 9(3): 321–44.

Birkinshaw, J. and Hood, N. 1998. Introduction and overview. In J. Birkinshaw and N. Hood (eds) *Multinational corporate evolution and subsidiary development*: 1–19. Houndsmills, Basingstoke: Macmillan.

Birkinshaw, J. and Hood, N. 2000. Characteristics of foreign subsidiaries in industry clusters. *Journal of International Business Studies*, 31(1): 141–54.

Birkinshaw, J., Hood, N. and Jonsson, S. 1998. Building firm-specific advantages in multinational corporations: The role of subsidiary initiative. *Strategic Management Journal*, 19: 221–41.

Birkinshaw, J. M. and Morrison, A. J. 1995. Configurations of strategy and structure in subsidiaries of multinational corporations. *Journal of International Business Studies*, 26(4): 729–53.

Bjorkman, I., Barner-Rasmussen, W. and Li, L. 2004. Managing knowledge transfer in multinational corporations: The impact of headquarters control mechanisms. *Journal of International Business Studies*, 35(5): 433–55.

Black, J. A. and Boal, K. B. 1994. Strategic resources: Traits, configurations and paths to sustainable competitive advantage. *Strategic Management Journal*, 15: 131–48.

Bontis, N., Dragonetti, N. C., Jacobsen, K. and Roos, G. 1999. The knowledge toolbox: A review of the tools available to measure and manage intangible resources. *European Management Journal*, 17(4): 391–402.

Bontis, N. and Girardi, J. 2000. Teaching knowledge management and intellectual capital lessons: An empirical examination of the Tango simulation. *International Journal of Technology Management*, 20: 545–55.

Bowman, C. and Ambrosini, V. 1997. Using single respondents in strategy research. *British Journal of Management*, 8: 119–31.

Bowman, S., Duncan, J. and Weir, C. 2000. Decision-making autonomy in multinational corporation subsidiaries operating in Scotland. *European Business Review*, 12(3): 129–136.

Bresman, H., Birkinshaw, J. and Nobel, R. 1999. Knowledge transfer in international acquisitions. *Journal of International Business Studies*, 30(3): 439–62.

Brooke, M. Z. 1984. *Centralization and autonomy: A study in organization behaviour*. London: Holt Rhinehart and Winston.

Brown, J. S. and Duguid, P. 1991. Organizational learning and communities-of-practice: Toward a unified view of working, learning and innovation. *Organization Science*, 2: 40–57.

Buckley, P. J. and Casson, M. 1976. *The future of the multinational enterprise*. London: Macmillan.

Buckley, P. J. and Casson, M. 1998. Models of the multinational enterprise. *Journal of International Business Studies*, 29(1): 21–44.

Calvet, A. L. 1981. A synthesis of foreign direct investment theories and theories of the multinational firm. *Journal of International Business*, 12(Spring/Summer): 43–59.

Capar, N. and Kotabe, M. 2003. The relationship between international diversification and performance in service firms. *Journal of International Business Studies*, 34(4): 345–55.

Casson, M. 1995. *The organization of international business: Studies in the economics of trust*. Aldershot, UK: Edward Elgar.

Casson, M. 1997. *Information and organization: A new perspective on the theory of the firm*. Oxford: Clarendon.

Caves, R. E. 1971, 1996. *Multinational enterprise and economic analysis*. Cambridge UK: Cambridge University Press.

Chakravarthy, B. 1997. A new strategy framework for coping with turbulence. *Sloan Management Review*, Winter, 69–97.

Chandler, A. D. 1962. *Strategy and structure*. Cambridge, Mass.: MIT Press.

Chandler, A. D. 1964. *Giant enterprise: Ford, General Motors and the automobile industry: Sources and readings*. New York: Harcourt Brace and World.

Chandler, A. D. 1977. *The visible hand: The managerial revolution on American business*. Cambridge, Mass.: Belknap Press.

Chandler, A. D. 1990. *Scale and scope: The dynamics of industrial capitalism*. Cambridge, Mass.: Belknap Press.

Chandler, A. D. 1991. Corporate strategy and structure: Some current considerations. *Society* (March/April): 35–8.

Chang, E. and Taylor, M. S. 1999. Control in multinational corporations (MNCs): The case of Korean manufacturing subsidiaries. *Journal of Management*, 25(4): 541–65.

Chiesa, V. 1999. Technology development control styles in multinational corporations: A case study. *Journal of Engineering and Technology Management*, 16(2): 191–206.

Chiesa, V. and Barbeschi, M. 1994. Technology strategy in competence based competition. In G. Hamel and A. Heene (eds), *Competence Based Competition*: 293–314. Chichester, England: John Wiley.

Coase, R. A. 1937. The nature of the firm. *Economica (new series)*, 4: 386–405.

Coff, R. W. 2003a. Bidding wars over R&D-intensive firms: Knowledge, opportunism, and the market for corporate control. *Academy of Management Journal*, 46(1): 74–85.

Coff, R. W. 2003b. The emergent knowledge-based theory of competitive advantage: An evolutionary approach to integrating economics and management. *Managerial and Decision Economics*, 24: 245–51.

Cohen, W. M. and Levinthal, D. A. 1990. Absorptive capacity: A new perspective on learning and innovation. *Administrative Science Quarterly*, 35(1): 128–52.

Collis, D. J and Montgomery, C. A 1995. Competing on resources: Strategy in the 1990's. *Harvard Business Review*, 73(July–August): 118–28.

Coman, A. 2000. IPVM: IT support of concurrent product development teams. *International Journal of Technology Management*, 20(3/4): 388–404.

Combs, J. G. and Ketchen, D. J. 1999. Explaining interfirm cooperation and performance: Towards a reconciliation of predictions from the resource-based view and organizational economics. *Strategic Management Journal*, 20: 867–88.

Conner, K. R. 1991. A historical comparison of resource-based theory and five schools of thought within industrial organization economics: Do we have a new theory of the firm? *Journal of Management*, 17(1): 121–54.

Conner, K. R. and Prahalad, C. K. 1996. A resource-based theory of the firm: Knowledge versus opportunism. *Organization Science*, 7(5): 477–501.

Cool, K. and Schendel, D. 1987. Strategic group formation and performance the case of the pharmaceutical industry, 1963–1988. *Management Science*, 33(9): 1102–24.

Cray, D. 1984. Control and coordination in multinational corporations. *Journal of International Business Studies*, 15(Fall): 85–98.

Cross, R. and Baird, L. 2000. Technology is not enough: Improving performance by building organizational memory. *Sloan Management Review*, 41 (Spring): 69–78.

Crough, G. J., Wheelwright, T. and Wilshire, T. (eds). 1980. *Australia and world capitalism*. Ringwood, Vic.: Penguin.

Crough, G. J. 1982. Foreign ownership and control of Australian industries and resources: A data compendium: 42. Sydney: Transnational Corporations Research Project, University of Sydney.

Cullen, J. B. 1999. *Multinational management: A strategic approach*. Cincinnati, Ohio: South Western College.

Daft, R. and Weick, K. 1984. Towards a model of organizations as interpretive systems. *Academy of Management Review*, 9(2): 284–95.

Davenport, T. H., De Long, D. W. and Beers, M. C. 1998. Successful knowledge management projects. *Sloan Management Review*, 39(2): 43–57.

Davenport, T. H. and Prusak, L. 1998. *Working knowledge: How organizations manage what they know*. Boston, Mass.: Harvard Business School Press.

David, P. A. 1994. Why are institutions the 'carriers of history'?: Path dependence and the evolution of conventions, organizations and institutions. *Structural Change and Economic Dynamics*, 5(2): 205–20.

D'Cruz, J. R. 1986. Strategic management of subsidiaries. In H. Etemad and L. S. Dulude (eds), *Managing the multinational subsidiary: Responses to environmental changes and to host nation R&D policies*: 75–89. London: Croom Helm.

Dedoussis, V. 1995. Simply a question of cultural barriers? The search for new perspectives in the transfer of Japanese management practices. *Journal of Management Studies*, 32(6): 731–45.

Denison, D. R. and Mishra, A. K. 1995. Towards a theory of organizational culture and effectiveness. *Organization Science*, 6(2): 204–33.

Dennis, A. R., Quek, F. and Pootheri, S. K. 1996. Using the Internet to implement support for distributed decision-making. In F. Humphreys and L. Bannon and A. McCosh and F. Migliarese and J. Pomeroi (eds), *Implementing systems for supporting management decisions: Concepts, methods, and experiences*: 139–159. London: Chapman and Hall.

Dierickx, I. and Cool, K. 1989. Asset stock accumulation and sustainability of competitive advantage. *Management science*, 35: 1504–11.

DIST. 1998. Multinationals, trade and investment: The ingredients for globalisation and growth. Canberra: Industry Analysis Branch, Department of Industry, Science and Tourism.

Donaldson, L. 1995. *American anti-management theories of organization: A critique of paradigm proliferation*. Cambridge, UK: Cambridge University Press.

Dosi, G., Teece, D. J. and Winter, S. 1992. Toward a theory of corporate coherence: Preliminary remarks. In G. Dosi and R. Giannetti and P. A. Toninelli (eds), *Technology and enterprise in a historical perspective*: 185–211. Oxford: Clarendon Press.

Doty, D. H. and Glick, W. H. 1994. Typologies as a unique form of theory building: Toward improved understanding and modeling. *Academy of Management Review*, 19(2): 230–51.

Downing, C. E. and Clark, A. S. 1999. Groupware in practice. *Information Systems Management*, 16(2): 25–31.

Doz, Y. and Prahalad, C. K. 1993. Managing DMNCs. In S. Ghoshal and D. E. Westney (eds), *Organization Theory and the Multinational Corporation*: 1–50: St Martin's Press.

Dretske, F. I. 1981. *Knowledge and the flow of information*. Cambridge, Mass.: MIT Press.

Drucker, P. F. 1999. Knowledge-worker productivity: The biggest challenge. *California Management Review*, 41(2): 79–94.

Drysdale, P. and Farrell, R. 1999. Japanese multinationals in Australia: Employment policies and industrial relations: 86. Geneva: International Labour Office.

Duhaime, I. M. and Baird, I. S. 1987. Divestment decision-making: the role of business unit size. *Journal of Management*, 13(3): 483–498.

Dunning, J. H. 1980. Toward an eclectic theory of international production. *Journal of International Business Studies*, 11(1): 9–31.

Dunning, J. H. 1986. Decision making structures in US and Japanese manufacturing affiliates in the UK: some similarities and contrasts. Geneva: Multinational Enterprises Programme, ILO.

Dunning, J. H. 1988. *Explaining international production*. London: Unwin Hyman.

Dunning, J. H. 1993. *Multinational enterprises and the global economy*. Wokingham: Addison-Wesley.

Dunning, J. H. and Rugman, A. M. 1985. The influence of Hymer's dissertation on the theory of foreign direct investment. *American Economic Review*, 75(2): 228–32.

Dunteman, G. H. 1994. Principal components analysis. In M. S. Lewis-Beck (ed.), *Factor analysis and related techniques*: 157–246. Singapore: Sage/Toppan.

Dwyer, P. and Dawley, H. 1995. The passing of 'the Shell man': An era ends as Royal Dutch/Shell vows to centralize power, *Business Week Online International Edition*, Nov 27, p. 48.

Dzinkowski, R. 2000. The value of intellectual capital. *Journal of Business Strategy*, 21(4): 3–4.

Edgington, D. W. 1988. *Japanese business down-under: Patterns of Japanese investment in Australia 1957–1985*. Sydney: Transnational Corporations Research Project, University of Sydney.

Edwards, R., Ahmad, A. and Moss, S. 2002. Subsidiary autonomy: The case of multinational subsidiaries in Malaysia, *Journal of International Business Studies*, 33(1): 183–91.

Edstrom, A. and Galbraith, J. R. 1977. Transfer of managers as a coordination and control strategy in multinational organizations. *Administrative Science Quarterly*, 22: 248–63.

Egelhoff, W. G. 1982. Strategy and structure in multinational corporations: An information processing approach. *Administrative Science Quarterly*, 27: 435–58.

Egelhoff, W. G. 1984. Patterns of control in U. S., UK, and European multinational corporations. *Journal of International Business Studies* (Fall): 73–83.

Egelhoff, W. C. 1988. Strategy and structure in multinational corporations: A revision of the Stopford and Wells model. *Strategic Management Journal*, 9: 1–14.

Eisenhardt, K. M. 1985. Control: Organizational and economic approaches. *Management Science*, 32: 134–49.

Eisenhardt, K. M. 1989. Agency theory: An assessment and review. *Academy of Management Review*, 14(1): 57–74.

Enright, G. 1997. Discussion database: What is groupware? *Info World Canada*, 22(6): 3,6.

Enright, M. J. 2000 Regional clusters and multinational enterprises: Independence, dependence, or interdependence? *International Studies of Management and Organization* 30(2): 114–38.

Everitt, B. S. 1980. *Cluster analysis* (2nd ed.). New York: Halsted.

Everitt, B. S. and Dunn, G. 1983. *Advanced methods of data exploration and modelling*. London: Heinemann.

Feinberg, S. E. and Gupta, A. K. 2004. Knowledge spillovers and the assignment of R&D responsibilities to foreign subsidiaries. *Strategic Management Journal*, 25(8–9): 823–45.

Fenwick, M. S., De Cieri, H. L. and Welch, D. E. 1999. Cultural and bureaucratic control in MNEs: The role of expatriate performance management. *Management International Review*, 39: 107–24.

Ferner, A. 2000. The underpinnings of 'bureaucratic' control systems: HRM in European multinationals. *Journal of Management Studies*, 37(4): 521–39.

Ferner, A., Edwards, P. and Sisson, K. 1995. Coming unstuck? In search of the 'corporate glue' in an international professional services firm. *Human Resource Management (1986–1998)*, 34(3): 343–61.

Fiol, C. M. and Lyles, M. A. 1985. Organizational learning. *Academy of Management Review*, 10(4): 803–13.

Forsgren, M. 2002. The concept of learning in the Uppsala internationalization process model: A critical review. *International Business Review*, 11: 257–77.

Forsgren, M. and Pederson, T. 1998. Centres of excellence in multinational corporations: The case of Denmark. In J. Birkinshaw and N. Hood (eds) *Multinational corporate evolution and subsidiary development*: 141–61. Houndsmills, Basingstoke: Macmillan.

Foss, N. J. and Knudsen, T. 2003. The resource-based tangle: Towards a sustainable explanation of competitive advantage. *Managerial and Decision Economics*, 24: 291–307.

Foss, N. J. and Pederson, T. 2004. Organizing knowledge processes in multinational corporations: An introduction. *Journal of International Business Studies*, 35(5): 340–9.

Fox, L. 1981. *Multinationals take over Australia*. Sydney: Alternative Publishing Cooperative Ltd.

Fruin, W. M. 1997. *Knowledge works: Managing intellectual capital at Toshiba*. New York: Oxford University Press.

Galbraith, J. R. and Kazanjian, R. K. 1986. *Strategy implementation: Structures, systems and processes* (2nd ed.). St Paul: West.

Garcia, R., Calantone, R. and Levine, R. 2003 The role of knowledge in resource allocation to exploration versus exploitation in technologically oriented organizations. *Decision Sciences*, 34(2): 323–49.

Garnier, G. H. 1982. Context and decision-making autonomy in the foreign affiliates of US multinational corporations. *Academy of Management Journal*, 25(4): 893–908.

Gates, S. R. and Egelhoff, W. G. 1986. Centralization in headquarters-subsidiary relationships. *Journal of International Business Studies*, 17(2): 71–92.

Ghoshal, S. 1984. Headquarters-subsidiary relations in MNCs: A review of the literature. Harvard Business School (cited in Martinez and Jarillo, 1991).

Ghoshal, S. and Bartlett, C. A. 1988. Creation, adoption and diffusion of innovations by subsidiaries of multinational corporations. *Journal of International Business Studies*, 11(3): 365–88.

Ghoshal, S. and Bartlett, C. A. 1997. *The individualized corporation: A fundamentally new approach to management.* New York: Harper Business.

Ghoshal, S., Korine, H. and Szulanski, G. 1994. Interunit communication in multinational corporations. *Management Science*, 40(1): 96–1110.

Ghoshal, S. and Nohria, N. 1989. Internal differentiation within multinational corporations. *Strategic Management Journal*, 10: 323–37.

Ghoshal, S. and Westney, D. E. (eds). 1993. *Organization theory and the multinational corporation.* New York: St Martin's Press.

Gordon, M. E. and Milne, G. R. 1999. Selecting the dimensions that define strategic groups: A novel market-driven approach. *Journal of Managerial Issues*, 11(2): 213–33.

Gorsuch, R. L. 1983. *Factor analysis* (2nd ed.). Hilldale, N. J.: Lawrence Erlbaum.

Govindarajan,V. and Fisher, J. 1990. Strategy, control systems, and resource sharing: Effects upon business-unit performance. *Academy of Management Review*, 33(2): 259–85.

Grant, R. M. 1991 The resource based theory of competitive advantage. *California Management Review*, 33(3), 114–35.

Grant, R. M. 1996 Toward a knowledge-based theory of the firm. *Strategic Management Journal* 17(Special issue): 109–122.

Greif, I. (ed.). 1988. *Computer-supported cooperative work: A book of readings.* San Mateo, California: Morgan Kaufmann.

Grinyer, P. H. and Yasai-Ardekani, M. 1980. Dimensions of organizational structure: A critical replication. *Academy of Management Journal*, 23(3): 405–21.

Grinyer, P. H. and Yasai-Ardekani, M. 1981. Some problems with measurement of macro-organizational structure. *Organization Studies*, 2(3): 287–96.

Grover, V. and Davenport, T. H. 2001 General perspectives on knowledge management: Fostering a research agenda. *Journal of Management Information Systems*, 18(1): 5–21.

Gupta, A. K. and Govindarajan, V. 1991. Knowledge flows and the structure of control within multinational corporations. *Academy of Management Review*, 16(4): 768–92.

Gupta, A. K. and Govindarajan, V. 1994. Organizing for knowledge flows within MNCs. *International Business Review*, 43 (4): 443–57.

Gupta, A. and Govindarajan, V. 2000. Knowledge flows within multinational corporations. *Strategic Management Journal*, 21: 473–96.

Gupta, A. K., Govindarajan, V. and Malhotra, A. 1999. Feedback-seeking behavior within multinational corporations. *Strategic Management Journal* 20(3): 205–22.

Hair, J. F., Anderson R. E. and Tatham, R. L. 1992. *Multivariate data analysis with readings.* Upper Saddle River, NJ: Prentice-Hall.

Hair, J. F., Anderson R. E. and Tatham, R. L. 2002. *Multivariate data analysis with readings*, 6th ed. Upper Saddle River, NJ: Prentice-Hall.

Hall, R. 1993 A framework linking intangible resources and capabilities to sustainable competitive advantage. *Strategic Management Journal*, 14, 607–18.

Hamel, G. 1991. Competition for competence in inter-partner learning with international strategic alliances. *Strategic Management Journal*, 12(1): 83–103.

Hamel, G. and Heene, A. 1994. *Competence based competition*. Chichester, UK: John Wiley.

Hamel, G. and Prahalad, C. K. 1994. *Competing for the future: Breakthrough strategies for seizing control of your industry and creating the markets of tomorrow*. Boston, Mass: Harvard Business School Press.

Hamilton III, R. D. and Kashlak, R. J. 1999. National influences on multinational corporation control system selection. *Management International Review*, 39(2): 167–89.

Hansen, M. T. and Lovas, B. 2004. How do multinational companies leverage technological competencies? Moving from single to interdependent explanations. *Strategic Management Journal*, 25(8–9): 801–22.

Harrigan, K. 1985. An application of clustering for strategic group analysis. *Strategic Management Journal*, 6(1): 55–73.

Harzing, A.-W. 1999. *Managing the multinationals: An international study of control mechanisms*. Cheltenham, UK: Edward Elgar.

Harzing, A.-W. 2002. Acquisition vs greenfield investments: International strategy and management of entry modes. *Strategic Management Journal*, 23: 211–27.

Hedlund, G. 1981. Autonomy of subsidiaries and formalization of headquarters-subsidiary relationships in Swedish MNCs. In L. Otterbeck (ed.), *The management of headquarters-subsidiary relationships in multinational corporations*: 25–78. Aldershot: Gower.

Hedlund, G. 1984. Organization in-between: the evolution of the mother-daughter structure of managing foreign subsidiaries in Swedish MNCs. *Journal of International Business Studies*, 15(Fall): 109–23.

Hedlund, G. 1986. The hypermodern MNC – a heterarchy? *Human Resource Management*, 25(1): 9–35.

Heide, J. 2001. Transaction cost research in marketing: Questions and opportunities. Paper presented to the Department of Management, University of Melbourne, 21 August.

Helfat, C. E. and Eisenhardt, K. M. 2004. Inter-temporal economies of scope, organizational modularity, and the dynamics of diversification. *Strategic Management Journal*, 25: 1271–32.

Helleloid, D. and Simonin, B. 1994 Organisational learning and a firm's core competence. In G. Hamel and A. Heene (eds). *Competence Based Competition*: 213–39. Chichester: John Wiley.

Hennart, J.-F. 1982. *A theory of multinational enterprise*. Ann Arbor, Michigan: University of Michigan Press.

Hennart, J.-F. 1991. Control in multinational firms: The role of price and hierarchy. *Management International Review*, 31(Special Issue): 71–96.

Hennart, J.-F. 1993. Control in multinational firms: The role of price and hierarchy. In S. Ghoshal and D. E. Westney (eds), *Organization theory and the multinational corporation*: 157–81. New York: St. Martin's Press.

Hennart, J.-F. and Larimo, J. 1998. The impact of culture on the strategy of multinational enterprises: Does national origin affect ownership decisions? *Journal of International Business Studies*, 29(3): 515–38.

Hennart, J.-F. and Park, Y-R. 1994. Location, governance, and strategic determinants of Japanese manufacturing investment in the United States. *Strategic Management Journal*, 15: 419–36.

Hewett, K., Roth, M. S. and Roth, K. 2003. Conditions influencing headquarters and foreign subsidiary roles in marketing activities and their effects on performance. *Journal of International Business Studies*, 34(6): 567–85.

Hiltz, S. R. and Turoff, M. 1978. *The network nation: Human communication via the computer*. Reading, MA: Addison-Wesley.

Hoffman, R. C. 1994. Generic strategies for subsidiaries of multinational corporations. *Journal of Managerial Issues*, VI(1): 69–87.

Hofstede, G. 1984. *Culture's consequences: International differences in work-related values*. London: Sage.

Hood, N. and Young, S. 1979. *The economics of multinational enterprise*. London: Longman.

Horng, C. 1993. Cultural differences, trust and their relationships to business strategy and control. *Advances in International Comparative Management*, 8: 175–9.

Hult, G. T. 2003 An integration of thoughts on knowledge management. *Decision Sciences*, 34(2): 189–95.

Hunt, S. D. 2000 *A general theory of competition: Resources, competencies, productivity, economic growth*. Thousands Oaks, CA: Sage.

Hunt, S. D and Morgan, R. M 1996 The resource-advantage theory of competition: Dynamics, path dependencies and evolutionary dimensions. *Journal of Marketing*, 60(October), 107–14.

Hurley, R. F and Hult, G. T 1998 Innovation, market orientation and organizational learning: An integration and empirical examination. *Journal of Marketing*, 62(July): 42–54.

Hutchinson, D. and Nicholas, S. J. 1994. Japanese multinationals in Australian manufacturing : facts and perceptions of foreign direct investment and technology transfer: 19. Parkville, Victoria: University of Melbourne.

Hutcheson, G. D. and Sofroniou, N. 1999. *The multivariate social scientist: Introductory statistics using generalized linear models*. London: Sage.

Hymer, S. H. 1976. *The international operations of national firms: A study of direct investment*. Cambridge, Mass.: MIT Press.

Hymer, S. H. 1990. The large multinational corporation: An analysis of some motives for the international integration of business. In M. Casson (ed.), *Multinational corporations*: 3–31. Aldershot: Edward Elgar.

Itami, H. and Roehl, T. W. 1987 *Mobilizing invisible assets*. Cambridge, MA: Harvard Uni Press.

Jaeger, A. M. and Baliga, B. R. 1985. Control systems and strategic adaptation: Lessons from the Japanese experience. *Strategic Management Journal*, 6: 115–34.

Janz, B. D. and Prasarnphanich, P. 2003 Understanding the antecedents of effective knowledge management: The importance of a knowledge-centered culture. *Decision Sciences*, 34(2): 351–84.

Jarillo, J. C. and Martinez, J. I. 1990. Different roles for subsidiaries: The case of multinational corporations in Spain. *Strategic Management Journal*, 11(7): 501–12.

Jaworski, B. and Kohli, A. K. 1993. Market orientation: Antecedents and consequences, *Journal of Marketing*, 57(3), 53–70.

Jenner, S. R. 1982. Analyzing cultural stereotypes in multinational business: United States and Australia. *Journal of Management Studies*, 19(3): 307–25.

Jensen, M. C. and Meckling, W. H. 1976. Theory of the firm: Managerial behavior, agency costs and ownership structure. *Journal of Financial Economics*, 3: 305–60.

Jermier, J. M., Slocum, J. W., Fry, L. W. and Gaines, J. 1991. Organizational subcultures in a soft bureaucracy: Resistance behind the myth and facade of an official culture. *Organization Science*, 2(2): 170–94.

Johanson, J. and Vahlne, J.-E. 1977 The internationalization process of the firm – a model of knowledge development and increasing foreign market commitments. *Journal of International Business Studies* 8: 23–32.

Johanson, J. and Vahlne, J.-E. 1990. The mechanisms of internationalization. *International Marketing Review,* 7 (4): 11–24.

Johnson, H. G. 1970. The efficiency and welfare implications of the international corporation. In C. P. Kindleberger (ed.), *The international corporation*: 35–56. Cambridge, Massachusetts: MIT Press.

Johnston, S. 2000. International business, international management and subsidiary roles in the MNC. In R. Edwards, C. Nyland and M. Coulthard (eds), *Readings in international business: An Asia-Pacific perspective*: 213–33. Maryborough, Victoria: Prentice Hall.

Katz, R. and Allen, T. J. 1982. Investigating the Not Invented Here (NIH) syndrome: A look at the performance, tenure and communication patterns of 50 R&D project groups. *R&D Management*, 12: 7–19.

Kearns, G. S and Lederer, A. L. 2003 A resource-based view of strategic IT alignment: How knowledge sharing creates competitive advantage. *Decision Sciences*, 34(1): 1–29.

Ketchen, D. J., Thomas, J. B., and Snow, C. C. 1993. Organizational configurations and performance: A comparison. *Academy of Management Journal*, 36(6): 1278–313.

Kim, C. and Mauborgne, R. A. 1988. Becoming an effective global competitor. *Journal of Business Strategy*, 9(1): 33–7

Kim, C. and Mauborgne, R. A. 1991. Implementing global strategies: The role of procedural justice. *Strategic Management Journal*, 12: 125–43.

Kim, C. and Mauborgne, R. A. 1993a. Procedural justice, attitudes and subsidiary top management compliance with multinationals' corporate strategic decisions. *Academy of Management Journal*, 36(3): 502–26.

Kim, C. and Mauborgne, R. A. 1993b. Effectively conceiving and executing multinationals' worldwide strategy. *Journal of International Business Studies*, 24(3): 493–511.

Kim, C. and Mauborgne, R. 1998. Procedural justice, strategic decision-making and the knowledge economy. *Strategic Management Journal*, 19: 323–38.

Kim, H., Hoskisson, R. E. and Wan, W. P. 2004. Power dependence, diversification strategy, and performance in keiretsu member firms. *Strategic Management Journal*, 25: 613–36.

Kim, J.-O. and Mueller, C. W. 1994. Factor analysis: Statistical methods and practical issues. In M. S. Lewis-Beck (ed.), *Factor analysis and related techniques*: 75–156. Singapore: Sage/Toppan.

Kim, Y. 2002. Different subsidiary roles and international human resource: An exploratory study of Australian subsidiaries in Asia. *Journal of Asia-Pacific Business*, 4(4): 39.

Kindleberger, C. P. 1969. *American business abroad*. New Haven, Conn.: Yale University Press.

King, A. W. and Zeithami C. P. 2003. Measuring organizational knowledge: A conceptual and methodological framework. *Strategic Management Journal*, 24(8): 763–72.

Kobrin, S. J. 1988. Expatriate reduction and strategic control in American multinational corporations. *Human Resource Management*, 27(1): 63–75.

Kobrin, S. J. 1991. An empirical analysis of the determinants of global integration. *Strategic Management Journal*, 12(1): 17–31.

Kogut, B. 1983. Foreign direct investment as a sequential process. In C. Kindleberger and D. Andretsch (eds), *The multinational corporation in the 1980s*: 38–56. Cambridge, Mass.: MIT Press.

Kogut, B. and Zander, U. 1992. Knowledge of the firm, combinative capabilities and the replication of technology. *Organization Science*, 3(3): 383–97.

Kogut, B. and Zander, U. 1993. Knowledge of the firm and the evolutionary theory of the multinational corporation. *Journal of International Business Studies*, 24(4): 625–40.

Kogut, B. and Zander, U. 1995. Knowledge, market failure and the multinational enterprise: A reply. *Journal of International Business Studies*, 26: 417–26.

Kogut, B. and Zander, U. 1996. What firms do? Coordination, identity and learning. *Organization Science*, 7(5): 502–18.

Kuhn, T. E. 1970. *The structure of scientific revolutions* (2nd ed.). Chicago: University of Chicago Press.

Leonard-Barton, D. 1992. Core capabilities and core rigidities: A paradox in managing new product development. *Strategic Management Journal*, 13(Summer Special Issue): 111–25.

Levitt, B. and March, J. G. 1988. Organizational learning. *Annual Review of Sociology*, 14: 319–40.

Li, S. X. and Greenwood, R. 2004. The effect of within-industry diversification on firm performance: synergy creation, multi-market contact and market structuration. *Strategic Management Journal*, 25(2): 1131–53.

Licklider, J. C. R. and Taylor, R. W. 1968. The computer as a communication device. *Science and Technology* (April): 21–31.

Lipshitz, R. 2000. Chic, mystique and misconception: Argyris and Schon and the rhetoric of organizational learning. *Journal of Applied Behavioral Science*, 36(4): 456–73.

Lorr, M. 1983. *Cluster analysis for social scientists*. San Francisco: Jossey-Bass.

MacDonald, G. 1994. Multinational enterprises in Australia: A preliminary overview of the effects on employment. Geneva: International Labour Office.

Mahoney, J. T. 2001. A resource-based theory of sustainable rents. *Journal of Management* 27(6): 651–660.

Mangione, T. W. 1995. *Mail surveys: Improving the quality*. Thousand Oaks, California: Sage.

March, J. G. and Simon, H. A. 1958. *Organizations*. New York: Wiley.

Marginson, D. E. W. 2002. Management control systems and their effect on strategy formation at middle management levels: Evidence from a UK organization. *Strategic Management Journal*, 23: 1019–31

Marshall, A. 1965. *Principles of economics*. London: Macmillan.

Marti, J. M. V. 2000. ICBS Intellectual capital benchmarking systems. *International Journal of Technology Management*, 20: 799–818.

Martin, W. J. 2000. Approaches to the measurement of the impact of knowledge management programmes. *Journal of Information Science*, 26(1): 21–7.

Martinez, J. I. and Jarillo, J. C. 1989. The evolution of research on coordination mechanisms in multinational corporations. *Journal of International Business Studies* 20(Fall): 489–514.

Martinez, J. I. and Jarillo, J. C. 1991. Coordination demands of international strategies. *Journal of International Business Studies* 22(Fall): 429–44.

Maurer, T. J. and Pierce, H. R. 1998. A comparison of Likert scale and traditional measures of self-efficacy. *Journal of Applied Psychology*, 83(2): 324–29.

McManus, J. C. 1972. The theory of the international firm. In G. Paquet (ed.), *The multinational firm and the nation state*: 66–93. Don Mills, Ontario: Collier-Macmillan.

Mehra, A. 1996. Resource and market based determinants of performance in the US banking industry. *Strategic Management Journal*, 17: 307–22.

Merrett, D., Nicholas, S., Purcell, W., Whitwell, G. and Kimberly, S. 1996. Management and control of multinational enterprises in Australia.: University of Melbourne.

Merrett, D., Nicholas, S. J. and Purcell, W. 1999. *Why do MNCs employ expatriate managers? Conjecture and evidence from Japanese MNCs in Australia*. Paper presented at the Australia and New Zealand International Business Academy, Sydney, Australia.

Miller, D. 1996. A preliminary typology of organizational learning: Synthesizing the literature. *Journal of Management*, 22(3): 485–505.

Miller, D. J. 2004. Firms' technological resources and the performance effects of diversification: a longitudinal study. *Strategic Management Journal*, 25(11): 1097–1119.

Moorehead, A., Steele, M., Alexander, M., Stephen, K. and Duffin, L. 1997. *Changes at work: The 1995 Australian workplace industrial relations survey*. South Melbourne: Longman.

Moorman, C. and Miner, A. S. 1997. The impact of organizational memory on new product performance and creativity. *Journal of Marketing Research*, 34(1): 91–106.

Moorman, C. and Miner, A. S. 1998. Organizational improvisation and organizational memory. *Academy of Management Review*, 23(4): 698–723.

Moran, P. and Ghoshal, S. 1996. Theories of economic organization: The case for realism and balance. *Academy of Management Review*, 21(1): 58–72.

Morgan, N. A., Zou, S., Vorhies, D. W. and Katsikeas, C. S. 2003. Experiential and informational knowledge, architectural marketing capabilities, and the adaptive performance of export ventures: A cross-national study. *Decision Sciences*, 34(2): 287–321.

Muammer, O. 1999. The use of Internet-based groupware in new product forecasting. *Journal of the Market Research Society*, 41(4): 425–38.

Muralidharan, R. and Hamilton III, R. D. 1999. Aligning multinational control systems. *Long Range Planning*, 32(3): 352–61.

Nahapiet, J. and Ghoshal, S. 1998. Social capital, intellectual capital and the organizational advantage. *Academy of Management Review*, 23(2): 242–66.

Negandhi, A. R. and Baliga, R. 1981a. Internal functioning of American, German and Japanese multinational corporations. In L. Otterbeck (ed.), *The management of headquarters-subsidiary relationships in multinational corporations*: 107–20. Aldershot: Gower.

Negandhi, A. R. and Baliga, B. R. 1981b. *Tables are turning: German and Japanese multinational companies in the United States*. Cambridge, Mass.: Oelgeschlager, Gunn and Hain.

Negandhi, A. R. and Welge, M. K. 1984. *Beyond Theory Z: Global rationalization strategies of American, German and Japanese multinational corporations*. Greenwich, Conn.: JAI Press.

Negandhi, A. R. and Serapio, M. G. 1991. Management strategies and policies of Japanese multinational companies: A re-examination. *Management Japan*, 24(1): 25–32.

Nelson, R. R. and Winter, S. G. 1982. *An evolutionary theory of economic change*. Cambridge, Massachusetts: Harvard University Press.

Neter, J., Wasserman W. and Kutner, M. H. 1985. *Applied linear statistical models: Regression, analysis of variance, and experimental design*, Homewood, IL. Richard Irwin, Inc.

Nicholas, S. J., Merrett, D., Whitwell, G., Purcell, W. and Kimberley, S. 1996. Japanese FDI in Australia in 1990s: Manufacturing, financial services and tourism: 24. Canberra: Australia-Japan Research Centre, ANU.

Nicholas, S. J. and Purcell, W. 1998. Do Japanese buyers learn? : A longitudinal study of Japanese MNE's subcontracting with Australian suppliers: 22. Parkville, Victoria: Australian Centre for International Business.

Nicholas, S. J., Gray, S. J., Purcell, W. and Zimmerman, J. 1999. Re-investing in Australia : How important are incentives and tax policy?: 12. Parkville, Victoria: Australian Centre for International Business.

Nielsen, B. B. and Ciabuschi F. 2003. Siemens ShareNet: Knowledge management in practice. *Business Strategy Review*, 14(2): 33–40

Nobel, R. and Birkinshaw, J. 1998. Innovation in multinational corporations: Control and communication patterns in international R&D operations. *Strategic Management Journal*, 19: 479–96.

Nohria, N. and Ghoshal, S. 1994. Differentiated fit and shared values: Alternatives for managing headquarters-subsidiary relations. *Strategic Management Journal*, 15: 491–502.

Nohria, N. and Ghoshal, S. 1997. *The differentiated network: Organizing multinational corporations for value creation*. San Francisco: Jossey-Bass.

Nonaka, I. 1991. The knowledge-creating company. *Harvard Business Review*, 69(November-December): 96–104.

Nonaka, I. 1994. A dynamic theory of organizational knowledge creation. *Organization Science*, 5(1): 14–37.

Nonaka, I. and Konno, N. 1998. The concept of 'ba': Building a foundation for knowledge creation. *California Management Review*, 40(3): 40–54.

Nonaka, I. and Reinmoeller, P. 2002. Knowledge creation and utilization: Promoting dynamic systems of creative routines. In M. A. Hitt, R. Amit, C. E.

Lucier and R. D. Nixon (eds) *Creating value: Winners in the new business environment*: 104–28. Oxford: Blackwell.

Nonaka, I. and Takeuchi, H. 1995. *The knowledge-creating company: How Japanese companies create the dynamics of innovation*. New York: Oxford University Press.

Nunamaker, J. F., Dennis, A. R., Valacich, J. S., Vogel, D. R. and George, J. 1991. Electronic meeting systems to support group work. *Communications of the ACM*, 34(7): 40–61.

Nunnally, J. C. 1978. *Psychometric theory*, 2nd ed., New York: McGraw-Hill.

Nygaard, A. and Dahlstrom, R. 2002. Role stress and effectiveness in horizontal alliances, *Journal of Marketing*, 66 (2), 61–82.

O'Donnell, S. W. 2000. Managing foreign subsidiaries: Agents of headquarters or an independent network. *Strategic Management Journal*, 21: 525–48.

OECD 2002. OECD science, technology and industry outlook 2002. Chapter 7 – Industrial globalisation and restructuring: 203–27.

Ommundsen, R. and Larsen, K. S. 1997. Attitudes towards illegal aliens: The reliability and validity of a Likert-type scale. *Journal of Social Psychology*, 137(5): 665–7.

Orlikowski, W. J. and Hofman, J. D. 1997. An improvisational model for change management: The case of groupware technologies. *Sloan Management Review* (Winter): 11–21.

Osborne, D. J., Stubbart, C. I., and Ramaprasad, A. 2001. Strategic groups and competitive enactment: A study of dynamic relationships between mental models and performance. *Strategic Management Journal*, 22(5): 435–54.

Otterbeck, L. 1981. Introduction and Review. In L. Otterbeck (ed.), *The management of headquarters-subsidiary relationships in multinational corporations*: 1–10. Aldershot: Gower.

Ouchi, W. G. 1977. The relationship between organizational structure and organizational control. *Administrative Science Quarterly*, 22(March): 95–112.

Ouchi, W. G. 1979. A conceptual framework for the design of organizational control mechanisms. *Management Science*, 25(9): 833–48.

Ouchi, W. G. and Jaeger, A. M. 1978. Type Z organization: Stability in the midst of mobility. *Academy of Management Review*, 3(2): 305–14

Park, C. 2003. Prior performance characteristics of related and unrelated acquirers. *Strategic Management Journal*, 24(5): 471–80.

Parry, T. G. 1974. Technology and the size of the multinational corporation subsidiary – evidence from the Australian manufacturing sector. *Journal of Industrial Economics*, 23(2): 125–34.

Parry, T. G. 1988. The multinational enterprise and restrictive conditions. *Journal of Industrial Economics*, 36(3): 359–65.

Peccei, R. and Warner, M. 1976. Decision-making in a multinational firm. *Journal of General Management*, 4(1): 66–71.

Penrose, E. 1959. *The theory of the growth of the firm*. Oxford, England: Blackwell.

Perlmutter, H. V. 1965. L'enterprise internationale – trois conceptions. *Revue Economique et Sociale*, 23: 151–65.

Perlmutter, H. V. 1969. The tortuous evolution of the multinational corporation. *Columbia Journal of World Business*, 4: 9–18.

Peteraf, M. A. 1993. The cornerstones of competitive advantage: A resource-based view. *Strategic Management Journal*, 14: 179–91.

Peterson, R. B., Napier, N. K. and Shul-Shim, W. 2000. Expatriate management: A comparison of MNCs across four parent countries. *Thunderbird International Business Review* 42(2): 145–66.

Picard, J. 1977. Factors of variance in multinational marketing control. In L.-G. Mattsson and F. Widersheim-Paul (eds), *Recent research on the internationalization of business*: 220–32. Uppsala: University of Stockholm.

Picard, J., Boddewyn, J. J. and Grosse, R. 1998. Centralization and autonomy in international marketing decision-making: A longitudinal study (1973–1993). *Journal of Global Marketing*, 12(2): 5–24.

Polanyi, M. 1967. *The tacit dimension*. London: Routledge and Kegan Paul.

Poppo, L. and Zenger, T. 1998. Testing alternative theories of the firm: Transaction cost, knowledge-based, and measurement explanations for make-or-buy decisions in information services. *Strategic Management Journal*, 19(9): 853–77.

Porter, M. E. 1980. *Competitive strategy: Techniques for analysing industries and companies*. The Free Press: NY.

Porter, M. E. 1985. *Competitive advantage: Creating and sustaining superior performance*. New York: Free Press.

Porter, M. E. 1987. From competitive advantage to corporate strategy. *Harvard Business Review*, 65(3): 43–59.

Poynter, T. A. and Rugman, A. M. 1982. World product mandates: How will multinationals respond? *Ivey Business Quarterly* 47(3): 54–61.

Prahalad, C. K. and Doz, Y. L. 1981a. An approach to strategic control in MNCs. *Sloan Management Review*, 22(Summer): 5–13.

Prahalad, C. K. and Doz, Y. L. 1981b. Strategic control – the dilemma in headquarters-subsidiary relationship. In L. Otterbeck (ed.), *The management of headquarters-subsidiary relationships in multinational corporations*: 187–204. Aldershot: Gower.

Prahalad, C. K. and Doz, Y. L. 1987. *The multinational mission: Balancing local demands and global vision*. New York: Free Press.

Pucik, V. and Katz, J. H. 1986. Information, control and human resource management in multinational firms. *Human Resource Management*, 25(1): 121–32.

Punj, D. and Stewart, D. W. 1983. Cluster analysis in marketing research: Review and suggestions for application. *Journal of Marketing Research*, 20: 134–48.

Purcell, W., Nicholas, S. J., Merrett, D. and Whitwell, G. 1998. The transfer of human resource and management practice by Japanese multinationals to Australia: Does industry, size and experience matter? 17. Parkville, Victoria: Australian Centre for International Business.

Quinn, J. B. 1992. *Intelligent enterprise*. New York: Free Press.

Ramarapu, N. K., Simkin, M. G. and Raisinghani, M. 1999. The analysis and study of the impact of technology on groups: A conceptual framework. *International Journal of Information Management*, 19(2): 157–72.

Ramsay, H. 1986. Transnational corporations in Australia: Issues for industrial democracy: 79. Canberra: Department of Employment and Industrial Relations.

Rasmussen, J. L. 1989. Analysis of Likert scale data: A reinterpretation of Gregoire and Driver. *Psychological Bulletin*, 105(1): 167–70.

Ratnayake, R. 1993. Factors affecting inter-industry variation of foreign ownership of manufacturing industry. *Applied Economics*, 25(5): 653–9.

Renwick, N. 1988. Australia and the multinationals: 139. Canberra: Department of International Relations, Australian National University.

Rindfleisch, A. and Heide, J. B. 1997. Transaction cost analysis: past, present and future. *Journal of Marketing*, 61(October): 30–54.

Robins, J. A. and Wiersema, M. F. 2003. The measurement of corporate portfolio strategy: Analysis of he content validity of related diversification indexes. *Strategic Management Journal*, 24(1): 39–59.

Ross, A. 1992. The silly world of circle babble. *Canadian Business*, 65(12): 112.

Roth, K. and Morrison, A. J. 1992. Implementing global strategy: Characteristics of global subsidiary mandates. *Journal of International Business Studies*, 23(4): 715–35.

Roth, K. and Nigh, D. 1992. The effectiveness of headquarters-subsidiary relationships: The role of coordination, control and conflict. *Journal of International Business Studies* 25(4): 277–301.

Roth, K. and O'Donnell, S. W. 1996. Foreign subsidiary compensation strategy: An agency theory perspective. *Academy of Management Journal*, 39(3): 678–703.

Rugman, A. M. 1981. *Inside the multinationals: The economics of internal markets*. New York: Columbia University Press.

Rugman, A. M. and Bennett, J. 1982. Technology transfer and world product mandating in Canada. *Columbia Journal of World Business*, 17(4): 58–62.

Rugman, A. M. 1996. *The theory of multinational enterprises: The selected scientific papers of Alan M. Rugman*. Cheltenham UK: Edward Elgar.

Rumelt, R. P. 1974. *Strategy, structure and economic performance*. Cambridge, Mass.: Harvard University Press.

Ryan, A. M., Chan, D., Ployhart, R. E. and Slade, L. A. 1999. Employee attitude surveys in a multinational organization: Considering language and culture in assessing measurement equivalence. Personnel Psychology, 52(1): 37–58.

Sabherwal, R. and Becerra-Fernandez, I. 2003. An empirical study of the effect of knowledge management processes at individual, group and organizational levels. *Decision Sciences,* 34(2): 225–60.

Sanchez, R., Heene, A. and Thomas, H. (eds) 1996. *Dynamics of competence-based competition: Theory and practice in the new strategic management*. Oxford, UK: Pergamon.

Schmid, S. and Schung, A. 2003. The development of critical capabilities in foreign subsidiaries: Disentangling the role of the subsidiary's business network. *International Business Review*, 12(6): 755–82

Scott, W. R. 1998. *Organizations: rational, natural, and open systems*, 4th ed. Upper Saddle River, N. J.: Prentice Hall.

Senge, P. M. 1990. *The fifth discipline: The art and practice of the learning organization*. New York: Doubleday Century Business.

Senge, P. M., Roberts, C., Ross, R. B., Smith, B. J. and Kleiner, A. 1994. *The fifth discipline fieldbook: Strategies and tools for building a learning organization*. New York: Doubleday Currency.

Shaw, V. T. 2001. The marketing strategies of French and German companies in the UK. *International Marketing Review*, 18(6): 611–32.

Shirani, A. I., Tafti, M. H. A. and Affisco, J. F. 1999. Task and technology fit: A comparison of two technologies for synchronous and asynchronous group communication. *Information and Management*, 36(3): 139–50.

Simoes, V. C., Biscaya, R. and Nevadao, P. 2000. Subsidiary decision-making autonomy: Competences, integration and local responsiveness. Paper presented at 26th Annual EIBA Conference, Maastricht.

Simon, H. A. 1957. *Administrative behavior: A study of decision-making processes in administrative organization* (2nd ed.). New York: Macmillan.

Simon, H. A. 1976. *Administrative behavior: A study of decision-making processes in administrative organization* (3rd ed.). New York: Free Press.

Simon, H. A. 1991. Bounded rationality and organizational learning. *Organization Science*, 2: 125–34.

Simons, R. 1995. *Levers of control*. Boston MA: Harvard Business School Press.

Simons, R. 1999. *Performance measurement and control systems for implementing strategy*. Englewood Cliffs, NJ: Prentice-Hall.

Skinner, W. 1968. *American industry in developing economies*. New York: John Wiley.

Skully, M. T. 1976. Australia and the multinational. Paper presented at the future of the multinational corporation conference, Sydney.

Sohn, J. H. D. 1994. Social knowledge as a control system. *Journal of International Business Studies*, 25(Second Quarter): 295–324.

Spencer, J. 2003. Firms' knowledge-sharing strategies in the global innovation system: Empirical evidence from the flat panel display industry. *Strategic Management Journal* 24(3): 217–37.

Spender, J.-C. 1996. Making knowledge the basis of a dynamic theory of the firm. *Strategic Management Journal*, 17(1): 45–62.

Stewart, T. A. 1997. *Intellectual capital: The new wealth of organizations*. New York: Doubleday.

Stonham, P. 1992. Christopher Bartlett on transnationals. *European Management Journal* 10(3): 271–6.

Stopford, J. and Wells, L. T. 1968. *Managing the multinational enterprise*. New York: Basic Books.

Stopford, J. M. and Wells, L. T. 1972. *Strategy and structure of the multinational enterprise*. New York: Basic Books.

Storck, J. and Hill, P. A. 2000. Knowledge diffusion through 'strategic communities'. *Sloan Management Review*, 41(Winter): 63–74.

Sveiby, K. E. 1997. *The new organizational wealth: Managing and measuring knowledge-based assets*. San Francisco: Berrett-Koehler.

Szulanski, G. 1996. Exploring internal stickiness: Impediments to the transfer of best practice within the firm. *Strategic Management Journal*, 17(Winter): 27–43.

Tabor, S. W., Pryor, A. N. and Gutierrez, C. F. 1997. Improving corporate communications with intranets. *Information Strategy*, 14(1): 7–12.

Taggart, J. H. 1996. Evolution of multinational strategy: Evidence from Scottish manufacturing subsidiaries. *Journal of Marketing Management*, 12: 533–49.

Taggart, J. H. 1997a. Autonomy and procedural justice: A framework for evaluating subsidiary strategy. *Journal of International Business Studies*, 28(1): 51–76.

Taggart, J. H. 1997b. An evaluation of the integration-responsiveness framework: MNC manufacturing subsidiaries in the UK. *Management International Review*, 37(4): 295–318.

Taggart, J. H. and Hood, N. 1999. Determinants of autonomy in multinational corporation subsidiaries. *European Management Journal*, 17(2): 226–36

Tan, B. C. Y., Wei, K.-K., and Lee-Partridge, J.-E. 1999. Effects of facilitation and leadership on meeting outcomes in a group support system environment. *European Journal of Information Systems*, 8(4): 233–46.

Tannenbaum, A. S. 1966. *Social psychology of the work organisation.* Belmont, Calif.: Wadsworth.

Teece, D. J. 1983. Multinational enterprise, internal governance and industrial organization. *American Economic Review*, 75(May): 233–8.

Teece, D. J. (ed.). 1987. *The competitive challenge: Strategies for industrial innovation and renewal.* Cambridge, Mass.: Ballinger.

Teece, D. J. 1998. Capturing value from knowledge assets: The new economy, markets for know-how and intangible assets. *California Management Review*, 40(3): 55–79.

Teece, D. J., Rumelt, R., Dosi, G. and Winter, S. 1994. Understanding corporate coherence: Theory and evidence. *Journal of Economic Behavior and Organization*, 23: 1–30.

Teece, D. J., Pisano, G. and Shuen, A. 1997. Dynamic capabilities and strategic management. *Strategic Management Journal*, 18(7): 509–33.

Teo, S. and Rodwell, J. 1998. MNCs in Australia: Striking the right balance in employee relations practice: 17. Lindfield, NSW: School of Management, University of Technology, Sydney.

Thomas, D. A. H. 1974. Error rates in multiple comparisons among means – results of a simulation exercise. *Journal of the Royal Statistical Society of Canada*, 23: 284–94.

Thompson, J. D. 1967. *Organizations in action: Social science bases of administrative theory.* New York: McGraw-Hill.

Thompson, A. A. and Strickland, A. J. 1992. *Strategy formulation and implementation.* Homewood, Ill.: Irwin.

Tihanyi, L., Ellstrand, A. E., Daily, C. M. and Dalton, D. 2000. Composition of the top management team and firm international diversification. *Journal of Management*, 26(6): 1157–1177.

Tippins, M. J. and Sohi, R. S. 2003. IT competency and firm performance: Is organizational learning a missing link? *Strategic Management Journal*, 24(8): 745–61.

Tomita, T. 1991. The inter-organisational transferability of Japanese style management. In M. Trevor (ed.), *International business and the management of change*: 121–46. Aldershot: Avebury.

Tsai, W. 2001. Knowledge transfer in interorganizational networks: Effects of network position and absorptive capacity on business unit innovation and performance. *Academy of Management Journal*, 44(5): 996–1004.

Tsai, W. and Ghoshal, S. 1998. Social capital and value creation: The role of intrafirm networks. *Academy of Management Journal*, 41: 464–76.

UNCTAD 2000. World flows exceed US$1.1 trillion in 2000. UNCTAD press release, December 7.

Urban, G. L., Carter, T., Gaskin, S. and Mucha, Z. 1986. Market share rewards to pioneering brands: An empirical analysis and strategic implications. *Management Science*, 32(6): 645–59.

Uzzi, B. and Gillespie, J. J. 2002. Knowledge spillover in corporate financing networks: Embeddedness and the firm's debt performance. *Strategic Management Journal*, 23(7): 595–618.

Vernon, R. 1966. International investment and international trade in the product cycle. *Quarterly Journal of Economics*, 80(2): 190–207.

Vernon, R. 1971. *Sovereignty at bay: The multinational spread of US enterprises.* London: Longman.

Von Krogh, G., Ichijo, K. and Nonaka, I. 2000. *Enabling knowledge creation: How to unlock the mystery of tacit knowledge and release the power of innovation.* New York: Oxford University Press.

Walsh, J. P. and Ungson, G. R. 1991. Organizational memory. *Academy of Management Review*, 16(1): 57–91.

Weber, M. 1947. *The theory of social and economic organization.* New York: Free Press.

Weick, K. E. 1979. *The social psychology of organizing.* Reading, Mass.: Addison-Wesley.

Weick, K. E. and Roberts, K. H. 1993. Collective mind in organizations: Heedful interrelating on flight decks. *Administrative Science Quarterly*, 38(3): 357–81.

Welge, M. K. 1981. The effective design of headquarters-subsidiary relationships in German MNCs. In L. Otterbeck (ed.), *The management of headquarters-subsidiary relationships in multinational corporations*: 79–106. Aldershot: Gower.

Wernerfelt, B. 1984. A resource based view of the firm. *Strategic Management Journal*, 5: 171–80.

Wheeler, B. C., Dennis, A. R., and Press, L. I. 1999. Groupware comes to the Internet: Charting a new world. *Database for Advances in Information Systems*, 34(3,4): 8–21.

White, R. E. and Poynter, T. A. 1984. Strategies for foreign-owned subsidiaries in Canada. *Ivey Business Quarterly*, 49(2): 59–69.

Wijnhoven, F. 1999. Development scenarios for organizational memory information systems. *Journal of Management Information Systems*, 16(1): 121–46.

Williamson, O. E. 1975. *Markets and hierarchies.* New York: Free Press.

Williamson, O. E. 1985. *The economic institutions of capitalism: Firms, markets, relational contracting.* New York: Free Press.

Williamson, O. E. 1996. *The mechanisms of governance.* New York: Oxford University Press.

Williamson, O. E. 1999. Strategy research: Governance and competence perspectives. *Strategic Management Journal*, 20: 1087–108.

Winer, B. J. 1971. *Statistical principles in experimental design* (2nd ed.). New York: McGraw-Hill.

Winter, S. 1987. Knowledge and competence as strategic assets. In D. J. Teece (ed.), *The competitive challenge: Strategy for industrial innovation and renewal*: 159–84. New York: Harper and Row.

Wong, B. K. and Lee, J.-S. 1998. Lotus Notes: An exploratory study of its organizational implications. *International Journal of Management*, 15(4): 469–75.

Wright, T. P. 1936. Factors affecting the cost of airplanes. *Journal of Aeronautical Sciences*, 3(February): 122–8.

Young, S., Hood, N. and Hamill, J. 1985. Decision making in foreign owned multinational subsidiaries in the United Kingdom. Geneva: Multinational Enterprises Programme, ILO.

Young, S., Hood, N., and Dunlop, S. 1988. Global strategies, multinational subsidiary roles and economic impact in Scotland. *Regional Studies*, 22(6): 487–97.

Young, S. and Tavares, A. T. 2004 Centralization and autonomy: Back to the future. *International Business Review* 13: 215–37.

Zack, M. H. 1998. Managing codified knowledge. *Sloan Management Review* (Summer): 45–58.

Zack, M. H. 1999a. Developing a knowledge strategy. *California Management Review*, 41(3): 125–45.

Zack, M. H. (ed.). 1999b. *Knowledge and strategy*. Boston, Mass.: Butterworth-Heineman.

Zander, U. and Kogut, B. 1995. Knowledge and the speed of the transfer and imitation of organizational capabilities: An empirical test. *Organization Science*, 6(1): 76–90.

Index